This book is drawn from Robert Prechter's media interviews (1977-95), selected excerpts from *The Elliott Wave Theorist*, and other sources. With a contrary yet common-sense approach to markets and a straightforward and entertaining style, Prechter tells us what modern investors go out of their way to ignore: the market is layered with complexity. An added bonus is that much of his commentary on the markets, investing, and social events is timeless in nature. In displaying the full bounty of the Wave Principle, Bob paints a compelling and highly readable portrait of both the structure and the irony behind the social activities of man.

"In the biggest imaginable picture," says Prechter, "the trend is always up, according to the Wave Principle. Mankind is on an upward path, with corrections along the way as he moves through history." Beyond this heartening message of ultimate progress, the Elliott Wave Principle's true value is the way in which it accounts for those "corrections along the way." In doing so better than any other tool yet available, it has accomplished a compelling record of forecasting success. Bob has extended this success to forecasting changes in the culture at large, which he covers in the final chapter. Join me on an enjoyable journey through *Prechter's Perspective*.

Peter Kendall, Editor

PRECHTER'S

PERSPECTIVE

by

Robert R. Prechter, Jr.

Edited by
Peter Kendall

Published by
New Classics Library

PRECHTER'S PERSPECTIVE

Copyright © 1996 by
Robert R. Prechter, Jr.

Edited by
Peter Kendall

Printed in the United States of America

First Edition: March 1996
Second Printing: June 1996

For information, address the publishers:
New Classics Library
Post Office Box 1618
Gainesville, Georgia 30503
USA

ISBN: 0-932750-40-0

Library of Congress Catalog Card Number: 95-72498

Contents

Page

4 **Acknowledgments**

5 **Foreword**

1. Explanations
9 **Prechter Meets Elliott**
34 How Markets Behave
65 Fibonacci Rules

2. Applications
96 **Money Making Rules for the Investor**
123 Putting Elliott Wave to Work in the Markets
133 Diversification and Other Myths
157 Technical vs. Conventional Approaches

3. Implications
178 **Society and the Grand Supercycle**
184 The Economy
195 The Cultural Realm
225 Politics, Inclusionism and War
254 A Giant Leap Forward

266 **Sources**

Acknowledgments

This "interviews" book has been in the making since the earliest days of New Classics Library. Quotations from various publications were originally assembled by Stephanie White, who also handled proofreading, and Sally Webb, who with Karen Latvala prepared the manuscript for printing. Leigh Tipton prepared the charts and graphs.

Our thanks are also owed to the many financial journalists who took the time to look past the immediate prospects for the markets and recognized that the Elliott Wave Principle itself warranted a deeper look.

Foreword

If you do not rest on the good foundation of nature, you will labour with little honour and less profit.

—Leonardo Da Vinci

Robert Prechter has said many times that the outstanding characteristic of the Wave Principle is the perspective it brings. In the broadest sense of the word, perspective is a mental view or prospect where all the relevant data is assimilated into a meaningful relationship. Thus the title of this book.

The dictionary also tells us that perspective is "a definitive technique." The same holds for the Wave Principle. Applying the Wave Principle is similar to the artistic technique of perspective because the analyst uses mathematical and visual relationships in a manner that Prechter tells us is a craft based upon science that is best applied by one with an artistic mind. The classical definition of art that reigned over the work of Leonardo Da Vinci and his contemporaries is, as Umberto Eco has explained, a practice in which art is one with craftsmanship. Originally, art reflected the opposite of the superficial. It pertained to activities that give man the ability to realize possibilities inherent in nature. Art was knowledge of the rules for making things. The rules were given, objective. "It was a capacity for making something, and thus, a *virtus operativa*, a power of the practical intellect." The Elliott Wave Principle exists as a result and a tool of this power.

To illustrate a three-dimensional world on a two-dimensional surface, Da Vinci incorporated methods that came to be known as projective geometry. Similarly, the main thrust of Prechter's work over the last 20 years has been to articulate the tremendous extent to which the financial markets apply to the three-dimensional world of our everyday lives. Da Vinci and the Renaissance painters brought natural images to canvas. Prechter introduced depth to a flat investment world.

As Bob explains in the following pages, there are two aspects to the Wave Principle's construction that are set deeply in the dictates of natural law. First, there is Elliott's discovery that the patterns in the market repeat themselves at different degrees of trend. Long since Elliott made this discovery in the 1930s, chaos theorists have confirmed the existence of fractals throughout the natural realm. The deeper we dig, the more "amazing coincidences" we find. Another trait that sets the Wave Principle on a higher plane of analysis is Elliott's discovery that the number of waves he observed across degrees of trend comprised the Fibonacci sequence. This numerical sequence was presented to the western world by Leonardo Fibonacci in the *Liber Abaci* (1202) or *Book of the Abacus*.

Mathematical historians are sometimes baffled by the long "dull" passages that make up large segments of Fibonacci's book. They cannot understand why the great mathematician who actually introduced Arabic numerals to Europe and was three hundred years ahead of his time wasted so much parchment on currency conversions. "The *Liber Abaci* is not a rewarding book for the modern reader...it stresses problems in commercial transactions, using a complicated system of fractions in computing exchanges of currency," complains one. Undoubtedly, this portion of his book is the "power of the practical intellect" at work. Fibonacci's deep interest in exchange shows that he and Elliott were driven by the same passion for practical application.

We know Fibonacci was anything but bored by his pursuit because he says on page 1 of the *Liber Abaci*, "Knowledge of the art very soon pleased me above all else." He refers to his craft as the "school of accounting." Elliott was an accountant as well, one who also took great pride in his work and viewed it as a higher calling. In a 1924 article, he wrote bemusedly of finding that others were not similarly enthralled. "When I introduced myself to one young lady and opened the subject of accounting, she said that the very word 'accounting' made her sick at her stomach." He then explained, "Now, I do not like accounting, but *I do like the work I am doing.*" What to Elliott was the work? As he noted in the same article, "The question is whether you are making money, and if not, WHY. In order to know why, you must know where the difficulty lies."

While practicality is widespread in Western culture, for many, difficulty with the Wave Principle lies in seeing the beauty it offers, or perhaps, in accepting it. It is a beauty so sublime that it is concealed beneath a veneer of high practicality and hard work. We know, however, that it is worth the effort because we owe its very discovery and passage down through the last half century to an underlying appreciation of the Wave Principle's aesthetic. In 1978, when Frost and Prechter were striking up their partnership to co-author *Elliott Wave Principle*, Frost put it this way in a letter to Prechter: "Truth stands so tall in a garden, the galaxies, mathematics and so many other facets of life that it is somewhat of a revelation to find it in such mundane parts of life as the stock market...Besides, it is a great way to make money."

Bob's thoughts on the matter appear in the final paragraph of this book. Here he reveals the secret behind his long fascination with Elliott. Readers don't have to read through to the last word on the subject to realize, however, that Prechter's not in it just for the money. Yet, like Elliott, Frost and Fibonacci, he wholeheartedly embraces the practical value of his studies.

From my own experience in editing this text, I think the Wave Principle brings pleasure because it prompts discovery. Indeed, in compiling these quotations and pursuing historical perspective for this foreword, I made a couple of small discoveries myself. For instance, I "met" Jakob Bernoulli, the 17th century mathematician who is the father of probability analysis. In Section 2, Bob says that "the practical application of the Wave Principle is an exercise in ranking probabilities." Bernoulli, a champion and master of the "practical intellect," was also the first Western observer to recognize the importance of the Fibonacci ratio in nature. By the end of his life, historians say he was very nearly obsessed with its amazing properties. On his tombstone, Bernoulli placed this inscription alongside an etching of the Fibonacci spiral: "The same transformed I shall rise again." Bob notes herein that it is not usually the Fibonacci numbers per se that the Elliott Wave analyst makes use of; it's the ratio between the numbers: .618. So, centuries after Bernoulli first recognized its vital importance, Elliott realized that it was one of the essential aspects of the Wave Principle. By observing that aggregate stock prices reflect proportions found throughout nature, he put more distance between his method and all other tools of financial analysis.

One more enlightening discovery was finding out that Bernoulli and his brother, Johann, discovered a mathematical relationship that foreshadowed the discovery of the fractal geometry of nature. Jakob penned this verse documenting how they felt at what may have been the dawn of our current understanding, in words as poetic as they are prescient:

So the soul of immensity dwells in minutia
And in narrowest limits no limits inhere
What joy to discern the minute in infinity
The vast to perceive in the small what divinity!

— Peter Kendall
December 1995

Prechter Meets Elliott

You graduated in 1971 with a degree in psychology from Yale University. How did you get from there to technical market analysis?

Well, at first I thought it was more of a leap than a transition. I had been peripherally interested in markets for a long time starting in high school and continuing in college, mostly because my father was a student of finance and the markets. He was a stock market investor and subscribed to market letters back in the '50s and '60s, which was less common back then. He had a small library on the stock market, and a few of the books were on technical analysis. I would say that is where my interest began. I majored in psychology, but didn't want to be a psychologist, so thought for awhile that I had wasted my education. Shortly after I decided to make markets a career, I realized that mass psychology is what they're all about. So my training was very useful in the field I finally chose. It wasn't such a leap, after all.

Why didn't you study economics in school?

My freshman year economics prof was a Marxist. I couldn't imagine wasting my time with that kind of mindset. We studied the standard textbook all year, and the idea that the economy was some kind of machine where physics formulas worked was anathema to my understanding of microeconomics. Are we dealing with people or machines? I just thought the whole approach was bogus. The economics I know I learned myself, from great books and studying markets.

You have said that you came into the markets *tabula rasa*, as a blank slate. What do you mean by that?

Just that I didn't learn a lot of theories before going head-to-head with the real thing. I didn't major in economics or finance. A lot of theories of market behavior that I think are fallacious were started by someone who dreamed up a concept and then tried to force stock market movements into it. If you come to the markets with that kind of bias, you have to unlearn a lot of stuff. My discovery of what Elliott had postulated came after my initial interest in technical analysis, which was generated from an interest in what made markets tick and ultimately how one went about making money in the market.

You found the methods to which you were predisposed, but you didn't make a beeline for Wall Street. You took a few years off to be a drummer in a rock and roll band, but your days in the music industry were numbered when you started carrying stock charts to your engagements. What was it that finally pulled you into the markets?

Quintupling my money in 16 months in South African gold stocks in the early 1970s on my father's advice. In 1972, I purchased shares of West Rand and Orange Free State and sold out with a 400% gain. Even after that, the long term gold rise still had over five years left in it. So despite a limited experience with investments, I figured one thing out early: that was a bull market. Needless to say, to this day, I haven't bettered that rate of gain in unleveraged investments. But at the time, it got my attention.

You had the bug from that point forward?

Yes. Then I started doing a little bit of trading for myself, and I think anybody who wants to do market timing is forced to turn to studying market behavior, because otherwise, you'll go bankrupt. You might go bankrupt anyway, but at least it will not be assured. Once I started studying technical methods, I investigated every one out there.

Along the way, there was naturally some exposure to the other side of stock market study, fundamental analysis. What do you see as the essential difference between technical and fundamental approaches?

Fundamental analysts use data generated outside the market to come to their conclusions. Fundamentalists assess events and situations apart from market behavior, considering them the cause of market movements. They forecast where markets are likely to go in response to those background events or conditions that they feel are significant. For example, they will study the managers of a corporation and the trend of its earnings to decide whether the company's stock is worth buying. In a macro sense, they will study the political environment, interest rates, the trade deficit and all kinds of outside factors and then will try to predict — I would use the word "guess" — where the market is going.

Since you chose to base your market analysis almost entirely on technical considerations, you've obviously become very comfortable with them. What was it about being a technician that drew you in?

The technician looks at the data generated by the market itself, the construction of patterns within the market, the psychology of the players in the market, the speed and breadth of price change, and so on. He studies past patterns of market behavior and decides from that data which way the market is likely to go next.

You mentioned psychology. How do you *measure* psychology?

We can determine, for example, how many people are short and how many shares are held short. We can calculate the volume of put buying vs. call buying, which are bets on a decline versus an advance. We poll money managers and ask, "Do you think the market is going up or down?" to determine aggregate sentiment. We study reports of the long and short commitments of various types of speculators, both the typically sophisticated and the typically unsophisticated. The latter more easily succumb to fear and hope.

Hope is a bad thing?

Hope is a four-letter word in the world of investment. Only a cold reading of the pertinent factors can keep you on track for more time than you're off.

What other aspects are there to technical analysis?

The speed and breadth of price movement is observed through what are called momentum indicators. Is the market rising with the same internal strength or declining with the same power as it was before? Momentum also considers leadership — that is, which group of stocks are doing best in an uptrend or falling fastest in a downtrend. We study the breadth of the market — how many stocks or subgroups are rising vs. falling as compared to recent history. All of these have implications with regard to where the market is likely to go next because the market has styles of behavior in this regard.

So history repeats?

I would not say that, no. The tenor of history is patterned, which is a different formulation. Thus, the tapestry of past market behavior often provides valuable information with respect to the most likely direction and extent of future price movement.

Can a novice come in and employ some basic tools and expect to have success?

A friend of mine likes to say that "a kid with a ruler" can sometimes outwit the computers, so restricting yourself to using easily recognizable chart patterns is not too bad an idea. I realized early that with just a ten-day moving average of the net advances and declines, I could make money in the stock market. However, by definition, market turns are not "easily recognizable" to the majority. So, while simple technical analysis will make money, using a comprehensive pattern recognition approach gets the most out of technical analysis and has the added benefit of opening your eyes to a good deal of truth about human nature.

Is there a basic secret to market behavior?

The single most important insight is the fact that markets act paradoxically from what novices typically expect.

Why are investor expectations so important?

The principle of investor expectations is one of the most important and least understood of all technical market concepts. To form a bullish opinion on gold, for instance, it is not enough to know that the inflation rate is rising. What is important is how much it is rising relative to what people expected to see. If it is anything equal to or less than what they expected, the price of gold will not rise, since those expectations would already be built into the price. Measuring investor expectations is difficult business, but it's business worth conducting. Ignoring that factor can result in an incorrect conclusion and a costly decision.

An interesting example, outside our field, of the importance of expectations was this headline: "[U.S. Olympic] Hockey Team Completes Collapse With a 3-3 Tie." It's from the 1984 winter Olympics. The actual chain of events was that the team lost its first two games, then tied the third. In other words, the tie was their best result yet. What's more, the team was not supposed to win any medal in the first place! *Sports Illustrated* had already rated Russia, Czechoslovakia, Sweden and West Germany as the best teams. So what, in reality, "collapsed?" Simply the fans' expectations, unrealistically based upon the "miracle" performance of the 1980 Olympic hockey team, a completely different group of players who won against terrible odds, but odds that were probably less than those for the 1984 team. The news writers and commentators pummeled a team that didn't deserve it with outpourings of despair, all because their own expectations had been unrealistically high. To relate this to a market, when in the 1980s inflation failed to provide another "miracle" performance, i.e., an unexpected rate of rise such as occurred in the last major cycle, investor expectations were dashed and the price of gold fell, *even though the money supply continued to be inflated every year since 1980.*

On the other hand, just because you mention "investor expectations" doesn't mean you've said anything sensible. Read this headline, then look below and to the right at the date it appeared:

Heating-Oil Plunges As Warmer Weather Is Seen for Northeast

— *April 26, 1984*

Doesn't late April normally coincide with the approach of "warmer weather?" I doubt that its arrival was a big jolt to investor expectations. And people wonder how another good but far more complicated concept like the Wave Principle can be misapplied!

For the most part, people don't take the relatively simple first step of measuring a system or indicator against random chance. Most see an indicator or system work once, and believe in it until one time it doesn't work.

Yes. That's the fallacy of expected perfection in a field where success can only be measured by percentages of perfection, like a batting average.

Did you investigate any technical approaches that didn't work?

Sure. There are some widely followed theories on Wall Street that I've delved into quite deeply and decided are complete fantasies. It was only the Wave Principle that really stopped me cold and said take a deeper look.

What was it about Elliott that captured your attention?

I had seen some mentions of the Wave Principle in a few market newsletters and a couple of obscure books, and I decided that either this was someone's elaborate fantasy or it was an amazing discovery. I wanted to reject it from what evidence I could find or include it as part of my growing arsenal of technical analytical methods.

How long did it take you to develop your "eye" for discerning these waves?

About 30 minutes — when I plotted my first hourly chart covering a few months. Apparently, there is such a thing as an eye for patterns. One person told me he had trouble finding the fives and threes. The key is to keep a chart. Most people have no trouble seeing the Principle at work.

You accepted it just like that?

When you begin to see the five-wave impulses and the three-wave corrections unfold over and over, it does not take long for you to say either "I see, but I refuse to believe it," or "This is obviously what's happening; let's see how far it continues." It took about a year and a half of applying it until I knew that Elliott was absolutely right. I'm pretty hard-headed, and it takes substantial reason for me to accept a new idea. By that time, I decided I had seen what amounted to proof. I then said to myself, "This is unbelievable. How come no one is commenting on this? The market is pulling back to points he said it should pull back to in the patterns. It is rising up to levels he said it should, in ways he said it should."

What was it that convinced you?

The Wave Principle proves itself when you merely keep a chart. Once I did that, I recognized what was going on rather quickly. The wave patterns are repetitive and at times, over protracted periods, they are easily discernible.

Is it possible that you were simply projecting the patterns you read about in Elliott's work onto the market?

No. For instance, I have used cycles for many years as well, and in that field, I am more of the opinion that some projection is required for the theory to maintain itself. Certainly fundamental analysts project their biases and unfounded conclusions into the market without realizing it and without checking historical correlations that would dissuade them from the effort. I didn't waste any time doing that because I recognized the invalidity of the process from the outset. Elliott is a different story. I observed and forecasted the market in light of the theory, and the results convinced me.

Sounds like you gave it a road test and liked the way it handled.

My first forecast on the market based on only minimal knowledge of the Elliott Wave Principle came to pass. Then I began to make more forecasts and decisions based on it.

They were all good calls?

Some were right and some were wrong, but the more I memorized the patterns and guidelines and became accomplished, the better things got.

Tell us about your first Elliott Wave prediction.

This was fun. One day, after learning the simplest aspect of the Elliott Wave Principle, that a "five" is followed by a correction, I was talking to my broker, who happened to be at Merrill Lynch, as most beginning investors' brokers are. I said, "Over the next few weeks, the Dow Jones Industrial Average is going to move to a new high, while the Dow Transports will not confirm." I was basically being a wise guy, but my broker said, "Well, O.K., we'll keep an eye on it."

About a month later, in July 1975, my broker called one morning to say that I was going to lose that bet I made. I said, "What bet?" "You know," he said, "about the Transports and the Industrials. The Industrials have been going higher and higher for the past few weeks to post new highs, just like you said, but the Transports are finally catching up, and today they're just points away from making a new high." So with mock confidence, I said, "Call me back at the close."

Just before 3 o'clock, he called back and said, "*How did you know?* The market is falling apart! And the Transports didn't make a new high!" In fact, the market began a rather large correction that very day. The only reason I made that forecast originally was that the Transportation Index had already completed five waves up, a typical Elliott Wave pattern, while the Industrials had not. So the Industrials completed their five waves, while the Transports failed to make a new high in their "B" wave.

A bit later I tried several other forecasts with my limited knowledge, but they did not work out so neatly. For instance, "B" waves sometimes do make new highs, under certain circumstances. So, I decided that either the theory was invalid or there was more to the concept than had been revealed in the bits and pieces I had read. And that's what turned out to be the case.

In those days, there were no comprehensive books on the subject. In fact, among the few Elliott Wave practitioners, there wasn't even agreement as to exactly what Elliott Wave was. Where did you turn for the true description?

A friend at Merrill Lynch gave me a barely readable photocopy of Bolton's 1960 book on Elliott. Hamilton Bolton wrote the *Bank Credit Analyst*. He pioneered the studies of bank credit and its relationship to stock prices. He also was the one man who kept Elliott's theories alive from Elliott's death in 1947 until 1967 when Bolton himself died. However, his book still wasn't the original source. So I tracked down R.N. Elliott's original books. They weren't even in the Library of Congress. But I finally dug around in the New York Public Library and found a catalog card listing of a copy on microfilm and had photocopies made. In studying them, I was amazed to find that there was a wealth of information that had been lost to Wall Street. Elliott had actually formulated, in a few short years, a complete and all-encompassing theory of stock market behavior.

Why was the Wave Principle so obscure at the time you rediscovered it?

Well, applying it is a fairly complex task. Few people continued to use it after his death, probably for that reason. A lot of people describe Bolton as a genius. You don't have to be a genius to apply it, but you can't be lazy, that's for sure.

Was Elliott's original work your main source of instruction, or did you have to search out other people who understood the mechanics of it?

I learned entirely from Elliott's original work. In fact, I found that most practitioners of the time were screwing it up by trying to take shortcuts or from lacking the full explanation. No one since Elliott has added anything to his observations of pattern mechanics, except for one that I believe I identified in the early 1980s. But it's so minor as to hardly be worth mentioning. None of the literature following Elliott's death has added anything to the principle's mechanics. So even though I did seek out everything written about the Wave Principle, there wasn't anything to learn other than what was in Elliott's work in the first place. However, I believe I have advanced the *implications* of the Wave Principle substantially. [See Section 3 — Ed.]

One of the happy circumstances in searching out these sources was my meeting with A.J. Frost. Frost had been an associate of Bolton's, and I got to know him when the Market Technicians Association asked me to get him to speak for their annual conference. I didn't know him, but because I was writing Elliott Wave reports for Merrill Lynch, they figured I had an "in." Everything worked out, and we met in May 1977. It was at that time we agreed to write a book together, which was certainly a good thing for me.

Your rediscovery of the Elliott Wave Principle is, at the very least, a historically significant stock market event. The theory has since become widely followed by analysts the world over. *Elliott Wave Principle* by Frost and Prechter, the product of this archeological dig, is in its seventh edition and has been translated into seven different languages. The method has also attracted notoriety for allowing its most prominent practitioners to predict every historically important turn since its discovery. In your opinion, *Elliott Wave Principle* was a definitive restatement of an immutable natural law. Did you realize what you were onto at the time?

I realized I had found something that dwarfed every other approach I had seen in terms of importance because it was all-encompassing, not only giving you the broad perspective on what markets do but also allowing you to analyze down to the smallest detail. Having a strong handle on the one or two high-probability outcomes over the next day, week or year is extremely comforting. Without that anchor and perspective, I wouldn't be involved in this business. Even more important, though, is its implications about human behavior, human progress, and perhaps even the progress of life forms and life itself through time. That is another subject, but it's what has kept me fascinated.

Your interest in markets and technical analysis took you to Merrill Lynch in 1975, where you worked as a technical analyst. In 1979, you started *The Elliott Wave Theorist*. It's been published continuously since then, initially from New York and more recently from near the shores of Lake Lanier in Gainesville, Georgia. Did your Elliott Wave outlook for the markets influence your choice of location?

Yes, I did have the coming economic debacle in mind. We have a spot on Lake Lanier where I will at least be able to catch fish for dinner if circumstances leave me high and dry some-day.

In the 1980s, you gained a measure of renown on Wall Street and eventually Main Street by making a number of accurate long term calls — first catching the tops in gold and silver in 1980 and then the bottom in stocks in 1982. By 1985, your letter was on its way to becoming the premier investment "must read" on the Street — as more than just a market letter. Your commentary extends to a wide range of topics, many of which are beyond the scope of money and markets. How did you accomplish that?

After I had published for five years, word-of-mouth interest was pretty strong. I was interested in getting some notice so that I could get to a wider audience. The way I did it was to enter the U.S. Trading Championship in 1984 in the options trading division. And I poured myself into it. The account was up 444% at the end of the four-month period. At the time, it was the highest score in the history of the contest. That got some attention from the media, and they said "This guy must be for real," and that started, I suppose, what you would call some national attention.

So a lot of people jumped on board?

Frankly, out of all the people who have ever been exposed to the message, probably 2% or 3% ever took it to heart, but that's a large number of people. They stayed interested not just because the Wave Principle has been pretty successful, but because it is so darn fascinating. You are even reading the paper in a completely different light. You are not saying "What does this article *say*?", but "What does it *imply*?"

The wonderful thing is the people who write joyous letters and say, "This is wonderful. It has changed my life, not just financially, but the way I look at everything, my understanding of what's going on in world events, social events and even when I go out and buy a different kind of tie. Or why I like certain kinds of music." That's been the great satisfaction of it. All I can ever do is present the evidence. If someone picks it up and wants to use it, great! The people who don't are the ones who create the trends from which Elliott Wave Principle users profit. If you don't have a bunch of people willing to buy when the dividend yield on stocks is 2% and the trend's been up for 60 years, you're not going to make money, because those are the people who bring values to an extreme. If you don't have someone who is willing to sell at the bottom of a bear market because they just heard some more bad news, you would not have cheap stocks to buy.

How is the monthly newsletter typically produced?

To produce EWT takes Dave Allman and myself six days. We start on Saturday. I write the entire text from then through Wednesday while Dave labels charts, checks data, arranges clippings and makes Fibonacci calculations. We do the final touches on Thursday, usually ending about midnight. On Friday, it's printed and mailed. I've just started a new trend, though, and now have a couple more guys helping me out.

Who are your subscribers?

From the indications I've gotten, the people who subscribe to my letter are generally people who've been around the markets for a while — money managers, traders and students of the market. In some cases, they have subscribed to 15 other market letters first. They are looking for something that satisfies them after going through the ones that are very basic — the ones that say, "Well, we're bullish because we think interest rates are coming down." They want to get into more detail about how the market works.

Those are the kinds of people I get, and I think a reflection of that is that even when I have been wrong in a market, I have a pretty high renewal rate. When you have a number of general public-type subscribers, as soon as you make an error — which everyone does — they cancel in droves and don't come back. They are searching for unerring perfection, and they go from advisor to advisor, hoping to find what does not exist. But my people have been around enough to know that somebody batting .700 is someone they want to listen to.

Do you expect subscribers to do exactly as you say?

Most take my input, add input from one or two other people, and ultimately make up their own minds. That's all I really want to provide: an adjunct to someone's thinking. All I do is take Elliott's observations and, using those patterns and guidelines, I rank the probabilities of the likely paths of the markets. It's just a matter of memorizing the patterns and their implications and having the discipline to apply them without letting your emotions or extraneous information cloud your judgment. And I'm not perfect at avoiding those pitfalls, either. Every now and then I get stubborn, and it's counterproductive.

For a lot of the investors who are familiar with Robert Prechter, the story begins and ends in the 1980s. Throughout the first part of the 1980s, you predicted that the great bull market would be followed by a stock market crash, but you were nonetheless surprised by the events of October 19, 1987. Is that right?

Near term, yes. No one, including me, forecast that big of a drop. Near the top early that month, I was looking for about 300 points down, which according to Mansfield Chart Service was about 700 points more than most advisors, who were then calling for 3000 by year end.

So you were still on the side of the correctly bearish minority. Was that a plus?

Oh, yes. In fact, the crash of 1987 gave us our biggest subscription month ever in November 1987 because I got a lot of publicity for the "sell" recommendation of October 5. After holding "long" for over three years from the 1984 low, it was on the front page in capital letters just before the Dow fell 900 points. That caused the biggest flood of subscriptions I ever had.

But it was what happened next that compromised your guru status?

Yeah, it wiped it out. After the crash, I didn't say to buy stocks back again. We rode the best wave of the bull market and kept all the profits, and 1988 was one of my best trading years ever. But that was followed by a poor 1989, a good 1990, and then a lousy 1991-1992.

What happened in the other markets that you follow?

We shorted the Nikkei well. We made 100% in silver mining stocks in 1993. We were short for the entire bond collapse of 1994 and covered at the low. But the stock market had been making the heroes, and my time was up. My first task is to make sure you don't lose money, and I felt that the stock market held too much risk to tell people to get back in. We've made money in other markets since then, but it was just in the wrong markets for the guru image to be maintained.

Where did you go in 1989? You weren't in the papers anymore. It seems like you went into hibernation or something.

After the crash of 1987, investors soon split into two camps. One camp said, "I'll never own stocks again the rest of my life," and the other camp said, "I'll give all my money to a professional to manage through mutual funds, and I won't have to think about it anymore." So the newsletter industry went into a steep decline because either way, people weren't timing the market or picking their own stocks. They didn't even want to hear about it. After about a year, I decided the public was no longer the place to focus my emphasis. There was no use beating the bushes if there was no one in them. So I took a sabbatical in terms of media interfacing. I decided that the right place to focus was on the institutional money managers and currency traders. First, professionals understand that market analysis is a task involving probability. Obviously no practitioner can be perfect. The question is, who is among the best? I know I can satisfy that criterion. Second, I know they will need good technical analysis when the stock and bond markets turn down. When their fundamental analysts and economists fail them, they will need our work. So I have spent five years laying the ground-work for that coming change, and we're ready for it.

You also handed off the day-to-day management of the company, Elliott Wave International.

Yes, to concentrate on building the long range vision of the business, write books and do analysis. Now I am producing books that I have had in my head for fifteen years.

Over the years, the media seemed to dwell upon the fact that you don't work out of an urban setting. I guess it was an obvious story line because your woodsy location was so far from Wall Street. But by the time the media crescendo reached a peak in October 1987, your two-story home on the outskirts of Atlanta was a "cabin in the woods," according to one foreign press account. Just to set the record straight, you live and work much of the time in an office building in a large, relatively well-populated recreational area about 60 miles from Atlanta.

That's right, and I love this environment. It's an advantage in my opinion to be away from the storm of mass psychology that exists in the financial centers. I have purposely distanced myself from New York to avoid the overload of superfluous information that you are exposed to there. I am an observer of crowd behavior. I think it is extremely difficult to shield yourself from the crowd's influence when you are part of it. In New York, people are always rushing around and panicking because prices are lower or higher for the moment. People are bursting in and out your door every two minutes to holler about some company or some movement in the market. Pretty soon you are so caught up in the whirlwind that it's difficult to focus on the larger picture and calmly do your work.

The same thing applies to quote machines, which are tools of an addiction, like gambling tables. A gesturing hand comes out and it draws you into the short-term maelstrom. I only have the stock market TV station on in the office, and I keep the sound off most of the time.

But you're still paying pretty close attention. Is it true that you didn't take a vacation for something like 20 years?

Yeah. I was afraid the very week I took off something important might happen in the market, and I would miss it. In fact, that happened in 1981, the week we moved to Georgia. I had seen a little movement in the market that indicated a change in outlook. But my computer and my mailing list were packed in the trailer, and there was no way to get the word out. So I took some flak for missing a market decline. On another occasion, I was around watching the market like a hawk, and made a good call that a dear friend of mine, who was neck-and-neck with me in the rankings at the time, missed because he was on vacation. That little thing made a big difference. In the marketing sense, there is a huge gulf between being #1 and #2.

It seems like a delicate balance between paying close attention and keeping your mind from being drawn into the mob. How do you keep from getting dragged into the emotion you're supposed to describe?

Sometimes I still fail at it, although the instances have become fewer over the years. The best antidote is a cold reading of the patterns and indicators. When they do not provide a clear message, the emotional pressure rises. The same thing happens when you have too much money at stake, which is always a prescription for disaster.

What happens when circumstances keep you away?

Back when I traveled a lot, I always tried to arrange to fly when the market was closed. Or if I had to fly when it was open, I would check the market before I left and then immediately after touchdown.

But, rather than leave the impression that the market can all of a sudden change its message, it's pretty rare for that to happen. The market is a *process*. That's why I don't need to put out a letter every week. Once a month is plenty. Novices in the market analysis game can quickly become frustrated because they feel they must know exactly where the market is going every minute. While I personally have to deal with that problem daily because it's my business, for most people it's unnecessary. The market usually gives many warnings before it changes direction.

But there are periods of uncertainty when each day might resolve the picture.

Yes. And in that case, the only thing that's necessary is keeping up your charts. No matter how difficult the pattern is to read sometimes, it always resolves satisfactorily into a classic pattern. As each day or hour is plotted, one after another, as you ponder the probabilities without satisfaction, there will come a point, as in a revelation, when the picture suddenly falls into place, and you can say, "Aha!" In my experience, it has never failed to happen. While a good Elliottician will rarely be completely surprised, the resolution to your train of thought may occasionally be one that you did not expect to find. Either way, it's always a pleasure when you arrive.

What is the greatest reward you derive from your daily work?

Watching the market operate. It is phenomenal how precisely it moves, how cleanly it advances and declines in channels and well-defined triangle patterns with boundaries, how well it reflects mathematical relationships over and over again. What it says is that human beings in the aggregate are acting a little bit as if they're conducting a concert. It's very, very precise, not just a random walk from day to day. Things are very orderly, even the panics. It's quite beautiful to watch.

What are your goals going forward?

If I have a goal as yet unrealized, it is to have R.N. Elliott receive the worldwide recognition he deserves for his pioneering work. He discovered what I think is the greatest breakthrough in sociology ever. The Wave Principle is on par with the discovery of some of the first laws of the physical sciences. I think the social sciences have been operating in a dark age ever since they began. They are in a position similar to where the physical sciences were 400 years ago, just before some of the great discoveries and advances were made.

Interest in Elliott runs deeper on Wall Street than it ever has, but he's still a long way from the history books. If he ever makes it, what will it be for?

In my opinion, all of history flows from the truth that men have a nature, that this nature produces patterns of interaction, and that these patterns of interaction produce results. Elliott broke major ground in the field of sociology when he showed that behavioral patterns inherent in human interaction shape financial events. I would add that they shape *all* collective events and trends. I'm sure that given time and attention, the Wave Principle will ultimately save sociology from the realm of meandering speculation and place it firmly in the sphere of science. Anything that's *true* and this profound ultimately wins.

Why then does Elliott remain virtually unknown outside of a relatively small circle of rogue stock market analysts?

Elliott was 50 years ahead of his time, for one thing. History is replete with examples of innovators and discoverers, men years or even centuries before their time, whose ideas reached so far ahead of their contemporaries' that they were ignored by the professional establishment of their day. While Elliott was not ignored, he most certainly was not afforded the recognition he deserved. But that will change. In fact, it already *is* changing.

He left behind no estate and few followers. His work is admired far more now than it ever was when he was alive, a fate more like that of a great artist than a great financier. You really had to dig to find out something about him.

In the end, I had good help from three other people, too, who found out some great stuff.

You were eventually able to uncover a rather extensive biography, which appears in *R. N. Elliott's Masterworks*. What was his life like?

Elliott was a fascinating guy. In 1925, he was selected by the U.S. State Department to rearrange the financial affairs of Nicaragua. That's when the U.S. basically ran that country. Previously, he had become well-known as a corporate organizer. He wrote magazine articles. He wrote books. He traveled much of the world. Basically, he was an innovative accountant who would go into one company after another and reorganize its entire financial base, putting it on sound ground.

Why was he the particular person who discovered the Wave Principle?

Precisely why, no one can know. But his accounting profession certainly made him suited to discover the Wave Principle. In fact, he billed himself as an "expert organizer." Over his entire working life, he took various details, time after time, and examined them to come up with an overall corporate plan. In other words, he took detail and turned it into a whole. And that is what led to his discovery — he took millions of bits of data on price action and came up with a comprehensive theory on what it was all about.

* * * * * * * * * * * * * *

From R.N. Elliott's Masterworks
"A Biography of R.N. Elliott"

While serving with the Central American railway system in his last corporate executive position, R.N. Elliott wrote a comprehensive book entitled *Tea Room and Cafeteria Management*. The first favorable reviews appeared in *The New York Herald-Tribune* and *The New York Times Book Review*, which commented "Mr. Elliott writes with authority upon all these matters because of his wide and varied business experience and observation." Ads referred to Elliott as "an expert organizer," an ability which was later manifest in his exposition of the Wave Principle. In the book, Elliott referred to business cycles as "the ebb and flow of circumstance," a phrase that uses the liquid metaphor he later called "waves."

* * * * * * * * * * * * * *

Is there anyone around who knew him in the late 1930s and early 1940s when he was on Wall Street?

I've talked with three people who had met him personally.

What was Elliott like as a person?

They all described him as being rather professorial. He liked to expound. He was rather impatient, particularly with people who disagreed with him. Apparently, late in his life, he was uninterested in anything other than the discovery that he had made. That makes him sound overly focused, but I think anyone who discovers anything as vitally new and important as he did would probably feel the same way about his discovery. He was obviously likable, as before his discovery, he had made friends in high places and wrote for a magazine.

Elliott was not a Wall Street person. In the latter days of his accounting career, when he was in his 50s, he was employed in South America as an accountant for several major railroads. What brought him back to the U.S.?

Elliott's lifestyle had been adventurous for decades, but time and chance caught up with him. He contracted anemia in South America. In 1927, Elliott returned to Los Angeles to adopt a more settled lifestyle after 36 years of intense work, travel and hotel living. But instead of recovering, he relapsed. Several times over the next five years he came close to death. His photograph in *Financial World* magazine a decade later shows that the relentless affliction had taken its toll, leaving Elliott much thinner than in earlier years.

If Elliott was a stock market investor at the time, he probably endured a lot of financial pain like everyone else.

It is possible, although there are no records, that he kept his money in the U.S. stock market, which was considered safe for widows and orphans in 1928. All I can surmise is that following the 1929-32 crash, Elliott was virtually broke, either from investments or from the expense of his illness. Although he was physically debilitated, he was mentally alert. A guy who had traveled as much as he had was not content to stare at the walls. He got interested in markets. After all, it was one of the most dramatic scenes of the day, not only in the late 1920s, but into the early 1930s. He began following some market letters and soon decided to dedicate the remainder of his life to discovering whether there was any way to predict movements in the stock market.

Then in May 1934, two months after his final brush with death, his observations began coming together into a general set of principles that applied to all degrees of price change in the stock averages. Today's scientific term for this part of Elliott's observation about markets is that they are "fractal." He described these component parts and how they linked together. So the former "expert organizer" of businesses had uncovered the organizational principles behind the movement of markets.

His stock market data must have covered a limited time span — about a century?

Not even. The data available to him was from 1857 until 1938, when his first book was published. He died in 1948. But the patterns he saw in that span of time had implications about the future and the past for decades in both directions.

What was he looking for in the data? Did he have a model or theory about price behavior that he was trying to establish or deny when he first observed his waves?

Elliott had no basic premises, just a mind that was open to the idea that the market might be patterned, which he undoubtedly adopted from the then relatively new Dow Theory, which was a set of very few and far more general observations about market behavior. Though the Dow Theorists formed only very rough concepts, they broke ground, tremendous ground, in merely coming up with their observations that market behavior was non-random, and tied to investor psychology. That was probably the germ of the idea that kicked off Elliott's research. He read Robert Rhea's 1932 book, *Dow Theory*, and became one of the first subscribers to Rhea's stock market service, *Dow Theory Comment*. Other than that, the Wave Principle was developed entirely empirically, without any preconceived formulations.

What was his procedure?

He did what every good researcher must do. First, he recorded the data that reality provided. He looked at the movements on chart paper and said, "Can I find forms that occur over and over again?" His answer was "Yes." He found that they occurred on hourly moves, on daily moves, weekly, yearly. He even took moves that were decades long and noticed they were following the same form. Likewise, the specific market did not matter. It could be the stock market, the gold price, interest rates or any other market. Then he organized the data, which was his talent. He began recognizing recurrences in the data, so it became clear that there were indeed repetitive patterns, which he ultimately organized into concepts. It was years later that these concepts jelled into his grand theory.

What exactly is Dow Theory and how does it relate to the Wave Principle?

The Dow Theory was developed by Charles Dow in the late 1800s. One of the tenets of Dow Theory is that, in general, a primary bull market runs in three upward phases. In the initial phase there is a lot of disbelief, and the markets are at very depressed levels. The middle phase is a kind of recognition phase when people begin to realize that the fundamentals are improving, and the markets are rising in harmony with them. And the final stage is when the euphoria and the gambling come in.

Elliott discovered that this basic formula of three-steps up, separated by two intervening corrections, was applicable not just to a primary bull market, but to any degree of advance. He also observed that corrections take a different path: a three-wave shape or variation thereof. Then he observed that these cycles were not independent of each other, but part of the market's larger tapestry, which in turn developed according to these principles.

Obviously, Elliott was the first to put his observation to the acid test. What happened when he applied what he saw in past markets to real time stock market activity?

As he later put it, he felt "something like the inventor who is trying to become proficient as an operator of a machine of his own design." As he got more proficient and corrected errors in his initial formulation, he made more and more accurate forecasts.

* * * * * * * * * * * * * *

From R.N. Elliott's Masterworks
"A Biography of R.N. Elliott"

Collins had put off the numerous correspondents who continually offered him systems for beating the market by asking them to forecast the market. Any truly worthwhile system would stand out when applied in current time. Not surprisingly, the vast majority of these systems proved to be dismal failures. Elliott's principle, however, was another story.

The Dow Jones average had been declining throughout early 1935, and Elliott had pinpointed hourly turns by telegram with a fair degree of accuracy. In the second week of February, the Dow Jones Rail Average, as Elliott had predicted broke below its 1934 low of 33.19. Advisors were turning negative and memories of the 1929-32 crash were rekindled as bearish pronouncements about the future course of the economy proliferated. The Dow Industrials had fallen about 11% and were approaching the 96 level, while the rails had fallen 50% from their 1933 peak to the 27 level.

On March 13, 1935, just after the close of trading, with the Dow Jones averages finishing near the lows for the day, Elliott sent this famous telegram to Collins: "NOTWITHSTANDING BEARISH (DOW) IMPLICATIONS ALL AVERAGES ARE MAKING FINAL BOTTOM."

Collins read the telegram on the morning of the next day, the day of the closing low for the Dow Industrial that year. The day prior to the telegram, March 12, marked the 1935 closing low for the Dow Jones Rails. The 13-month corrective wave was over, and the market immediately turned to the upside.

* * * * * * * * * * * * * *

It is through Collins that we know about the genesis of the theory. He more or less sponsored Elliott's introduction to Wall Street and helped him think through various aspects of becoming professional. In fact, he was the ghostwriter of a good deal of Elliott's first important work, *The Wave Principle*, which came out in 1938. Did Collins make any contribution to the theory itself?

Yes. The catalyst that tied the Principle to grander natural forces was Collins' discovery that the number of waves in Elliott's observed patterns reflected the Fibonacci sequence perfectly, with no repetitions and no omissions. Collins wrote Elliott during the development of the theory and said in essence, "You ought to read this book by Jay Hambidge on Fibonacci ratios and spirals because I noticed that when you count the waves through lower and lower degrees of trend, you find the Fibonacci sequence." That sent Elliott off on the track to his grand conclusion. It is comforting to know that he did not *start* with the Fibonacci sequence or a theory based on it and then force nature to it. Nature showed its law, and these two men observed it.

We'll talk about Fibonacci some more later, but is it really that crucial to the theory?

It is not crucial to the what, but it is crucial to the why. Elliott first observed the Wave Principle operate. Then he took the next step and asked, "*Why* does it exist?" He concluded that there must be some progression that human beings go through as they move overall from a state of deep pessimism to extreme optimism and back again, because they continue to trace out these patterns. His eventual conclusion was that it was a natural law of human behavior, that human beings were part of the natural world, and just like trees and wolves and lemmings and anything else you can name, they have certain ways of acting. It shows up in the charts vividly, making it clear that mass psychology is structured. The unifying conclusion, that mankind's progress follows a law of nature exhibited by countless forms of life, is a profound and reasonable explanation that fits the facts.

Were other analysts working with Elliott, or along the same lines as Elliott, at the time he published his theory?

No. Since I have all of Elliott's early correspondence with Charles Collins, I know he had no collaborators. And there is no evidence any other analyst was working on any concept of the sort, except to a far lesser degree the Dow Theorists who preceded him. Neither did Elliott ever mention any other theory. In pouring over the research from that time, I don't find anyone else's research to be remotely similar prior to Elliott's first publication date. His achievement was a leap in understanding, to put it modestly.

* * * * * * * * * * * * * *

From the Foreword to Elliott Wave Principle
by Charles J. Collins

Human nature does not change, nor does its pattern. Four men in our generation have built their reputations in the economic field on this truth: Arthur Pigou, Charles H. Dow, Bernard Baruch and Ralph Nelson Elliott.

Pigou, the English economist, reduced it to the human equation. The upward and downward swings in business, Pigou said, are caused by excesses of optimism followed by excesses of pessimism. An excess in one direction breeds an excess in the other and so on, diastole and systole in never ending succession.

Charles H. Dow, one of America's most profound students of stock market movements, noted a certain repetition in the market's continuing gyrations. Out of this seeming confusion, Dow observed that the market was not like a balloon plunging aimlessly hither and thither in the wind but moved through orderly sequence. Dow enunciated two principles that stood the test of time. His first was that the market in its primary uptrend was characterized by three upward swings. Dow's second principle was that at some point in every market swing, whether up or down, there would be a reverse movement canceling three-eighths or more of such swing.

Baruch, a multi-millionaire through stock market operation and adviser to American presidents, hit the nail on the head in just a few words. "What actually registers in the stock market's fluctuations are not events themselves, but the human reactions to the events. In short, how millions of individual men and women feel these happenings may affect their future. Above all else, the stock market is people. It is people trying to read the future."

Now we come to Ralph N. Elliott, who at the time he evolved his theory had probably never heard of Pigou. Elliott had been working down in Mexico but due to a physical malady – I think he said it was anemia – had graduated to a rocking chair on a front porch in California. With time on his hands, as he endeavored to throw off his difficulty, Elliott turned to a study of the stock market as reflected by the history and movement of the Dow Jones averages. Elliott, in developing his theory through observation, study and thought, incorporated what Dow had discovered but went well beyond Dow's theory in comprehensiveness and exactitude. Both men had sensed the involutions of the human equation that dominated market movements, but Dow painted with broad strokes of the brush and Elliott in detail.

* * * * * * * * * * * * * *

Was Elliott a trader?

There is no evidence that he traded. Nor should he have. He was already 65 years old by the time he began to research the stock market. By the time he had fully developed the theory and moved to Wall Street, he was nearly 70. The idea of making $10 million couldn't have appealed to him that much. I think it was much more important to him, at that time in his life, to be remembered in history as someone who made a great discovery.

Was most of his analysis directed toward the stock market?

Yes. He took a look at some commodity markets and economic data and made some occasional comments, but for the most part, his focus was the stock market. In fact, I think it was fortunate, because his entire idea that mankind as a whole is traveling along a natural growth pattern is particularly reflected by the stock market. The stock market is essentially a record of the valuation of mankind's productive capacity, which has been in a growth spiral since caveman days.

Why do you say the stock market is a "record" of human progress?

What is the stock market? It is an arena in which people are valuing their fellows' progress every minute it is open. It is a wonderful coincidence that people are so interested in money, because it means that for quite a long time, human beings have kept intricate records of their valuation of productive enterprise. It's the one area of social mood where we have intricate data. You can plot it and see the fractal patterns. The market is not a perfect reflection of overall social mood, but it is a good one.

Implying what?

Since the prices on the New York Stock Exchange are a sensitive valuation of man's productive capacity, and by extension, his emotional, psychological and spiritual feelings of well-being, the fluctuations in those prices are a direct and sensitive record of changes in mankind's feeling of self-worth, which weaves itself into an overall pattern of progress and regress.

You say the best representation of that pattern is the Dow Jones Industrial Average. Why is an average of 30 somewhat randomly chosen stocks so reliable in exhibiting over and over again these phenomena of construction?

I think that part of the answer to the Dow's precision lies in the concept of biofeedback. The Dow Industrial Average is the most widely followed market index in the world. It not only *reflects* the pulse of investors, it *affects* the pulse of investors. Not only do our investment decisions force the Dow to go in a certain direction, but the direction of the Dow often causes us to make those very investment decisions. There is a complex emotional involvement there of which we're quite aware but which we don't fully understand. How else can we explain the fact, for instance, that even though 3M was substituted for Anaconda in the Dow in 1976, the 1976-78 decline still managed to fall exactly to the level which retraced a Fibonacci ratio .618 of the 1974-76 advance?

But the academics say the relationship is not there. The view on campus is that the market is a random walk with an upward bias.

Yes, but that view is rapidly being discredited. I have kept a file on Random Walk for years with plans to refute it. That's no longer necessary. Mathematically speaking, it is much more implausible to argue that the patterns reflected by the market are random or coincidence than it is to accept what is happening: that changes in mass emotions, as reflected by the stock market and most especially the Dow Jones Industrial Average, have a certain form to them. If you accept the Wave Principle, then you must further accept that to a phenomenal extent, the DJIA appears to know exactly where it is, exactly where it has been, and exactly where it is going.

* * * * * * * * * * * * * * *

Elliott Wave Principle

If, through a microscope, we were to observe a tiny droplet of water, its individuality might be quite evident in terms of size, color, shape, density, salinity, bacteria count, etc., but when that droplet is part of a wave in the ocean, it becomes swept along with the force of the waves and the tides, despite its individuality. With over twenty million "droplets" owning stocks listed on the New York Stock Exchange, is it any wonder that the market averages are one of the greatest manifestations of mass psychology in the world?

* * * * * * * * * * * * * * *

How Markets Behave

What does the fact that the stock market is patterned *mean*?

My addition to the theory is that the stock market is a direct reflection of mass psychological change, which in turn shapes events. If you study the patterns produced by the averages, you must conclude that mankind goes through natural and rhythmic sociological changes. In other words, such changes are not reactions to events, as is popularly assumed, but are natural and occur ahead of related events, which are the results. This is a profound conclusion, and contrary to what everyone has always believed about history. It's going to take a whole book some day to develop and present this idea fully.

That sounds like determinism.

It's almost incomprehensible to consider that there could be a mathematical expression which explains mass human behavior. That is the most fascinating aspect of the Wave Principle. People are a long way from accepting it as a possibility in the social sciences. However, this is not determinism. As individuals, we can unquestionably exert free will. But the style of behavior of the crowd is entirely different from that of an individual. It is based upon unconscious mental processes, not reason, and that is why most people do not understand them, do not accept the possibility, and go on participating in it day after day, year after year!

I'm not sure I see. Is human psychological response the Wave Principle's causal agent?

Not exactly. My opinion is more radical than that. Market psychology is not responsive. It is not the result of events outside the market. Collective psychology is impulsive, self-generating, self-sustaining and self-reversing. The dynamics of social psychology operate by the same dynamics over and over again, regardless of different attendant historical or cultural specifics. Events that make history are the result of the mass mental states that take time to develop. This is the only possible explanation for the constancy of structure and consistency of pattern that markets reveal.

The fact that markets follow the Wave Principle, as opposed to some other law, provides the added insight that social mood, and its result, history, follow the same law of pattern found throughout nature in other processes of growth and decay. That is what makes the subject more engaging than, say, the put/call ratio.

You said "markets" and not just "the market." Do you apply it to a lot of different trading arenas?

Yes. And while this is another of the properties that make the Wave Principle attractive, it can also hurt the reputation of the theory if it is applied where it doesn't belong.

Such as?

The Wave Principle works best with markets that are the most heavily influenced by mass psychology. An individual stock

may have a lot of reasons for going up or down according to the
various investors involved. When you're discussing the entire
market, or an average of blue-chip stocks, the bottom line —
after all the individual decisions about whether to buy or sell
stock A, B or C — is the answer to the question, "As a whole,
are people putting money into or taking money out of the stock
market?" The answer to that question depends upon their collective emotional state.

Gold in particular follows the Wave Principle impeccably.
Gold is a wonderful reflector of the Wave Principle because unlike, say, pork bellies, it is traded by people around the globe,
so the prime mover is the psychology of human beings at the
most shared and basic level. It is a barometer of how everybody
in the world who invests in precious metals and watches currencies and politics and everything else feels about the future.
Gold is traded on *confidence* in the future, in which case it is
usually trending sideways or down, or *anxiety* about the future, in which case it's usually trending up. Gold is probably
the purest distillation of mass psychology there is. I think that's
one reason the wave structure has been so perfect. If you trade
gold or silver, think about using Elliott. It will keep you on track
much of the time.

I thought gold went up and down with inflation.

Not exactly. It does reflect a psychological orientation to
rates of inflation as they relate to investor expectations, which
is quite a different thing.

But there is some connection?

Sure, but understand what it is. Gold's price relative to
currencies certainly reflects the inflationary and deflationary
forces in the various states' money supplies, which is made up
mostly of promissory notes called bonds, notes, bills and currency. But, now, most people respond that this observation
proves that markets are mechanical responses, which is utterly false. After all, *inflation and deflation are at root primarily
psychological phenomena as well.* They derive mostly from the
expansion and contraction of credit, and the other side of the
transaction, debt, which is based upon the waxing and waning
of aggregate confidence in the financial future. So it still comes
back to social psychology, which is the driving force behind
change in the rates of debt accumulation and dissolution, and

thus of inflation and deflation. For that reason, interest rates reflect the Wave Principle as well as gold.

Can't a big fundamental change shake psychology and therefore interest rates or the gold market?

The gold price is not a function of fundamentals, but of market dynamics. No sudden event can change those dynamics. Social events are the result of forces that take time to build. The market is not blind to them. It is part and parcel of them.

I just can't shake the idea that inflation caused gold to go up. Or maybe I should say a rising rate of inflation.

Go ahead and say that, if it makes you believe you understand the phenomenon. Then say that disinflation made it stop. Now ask, *what caused the changes in the rate of inflation?* Maybe you will answer, "The government created too much credit, and then cut back." Fine, *why did it create too much credit and then cut back?* Keep going, and you keep arriving right back where you started; the question remains the same. What *caused* it? The train of causality is infinite until it ends at one point, which is that *people,* acting in concert, created the phenomenon. If people caused it, then study the behavior of people to answer the original question without taking any intermediate steps. What's actually happening becomes even more compelling when you notice that the market's trends often precede changes in the supposed cause.

* * * * * * * * * * * * * *

The Atlanta Journal / The Atlanta Constitution
March 5, 1989

The Wave Principle reveals that social psychology is patterned, and to a great degree predictable. The nature of man has within it the seeds, the desire and the requirement of and for change. It's the way people are.

* * * * * * * * * * * * * *

I think I get it now, so let's switch gears. You have made dramatic forecasts in gold, for instance. But a lot of analysts have looked at the production and demand for gold and reasoned that it would be very

difficult for gold to get above $390 or below $250 based on its economic value alone.

I have two responses. First, I do not think you can compute the economic value of gold very well. A lot of people do it based on what it costs to bring it out of the ground, which is irrelevant, or on what industry is willing to pay today, which doesn't reflect what they will pay tomorrow. Prices are a current market mechanism. There is no such thing as so-called intrinsic value. Value is what people are willing to pay for something at a particular moment in time, and that's all.

How about interest rates, where we have the tremendous effect of and control by the Federal Reserve Board?

When I first started following interest rates, I figured, "I'm not going to see wave structures in here, because to a great degree, they are manipulated." I started in 1979, and that was two years into Jimmy Carter's administration. Chaos reigned in the bond market, and upon examination, it was unbelievable how closely the price of money was following typical Elliott Wave structures. When the anchor of gold was kicked away by Nixon in the early 1970s, the bond market became a boiling pit of mass psychology. It has been a mixing bowl of confidence, anxiety, hope and fear, shifting back and forth as the players try to guess what the government will do and the government tries to guess what the voters want. That is a terrific background for clear Elliott Wave patterns. As for the Fed, today the bond market is bigger than the Fed. The Fed cannot do whatever it wants anymore. If it acts, the market will make a judgment, and depending upon the psychology of bond investors, they can support, neutralize and reverse whatever the Fed attempts to do to affect the money supply. The market is in charge, and the Fed knows it. Why do you think the Chairman keeps going on TV to explain what he's doing? He doesn't want bondholders to panic. Most of the time, though, the Fed doesn't *act*. It *reacts* to what the market has already signaled. Watch closely and you can see it. The idea that these people are masterminds pulling the strings is ridiculous.

O.K., so the Wave Principle is applicable to the stock averages, precious metals, and interest rates.

And currencies, many commodities, and even to hot stocks that reveal powerful psychological forces at work.

Does it also apply to economic trends, such as those in money supply, federal deficits, trade imbalances and the inflation rate?

Yes, but to a lesser degree, because these trends are less direct reflections of the social psychology at work. They *result* from that psychology. Still, they are not *that* far removed, so they often show Wave Principle patterns.

It works on orange juice, too. But only to a "lesser degree." How come?

The Wave Principle cannot forecast freezes in Florida. It will reflect the psychology of the players *about* such an event, but it cannot anticipate the event itself.

* * * * * * * * * * * * * *

What is the Elliott Wave Principle?

Over the years, the Wave Principle has been described in a lot of different ways by journalists and financial writers. Here is a short representation of how the basic idea has been expressed by a host of publications since 1977:

Financial World
October 15, 1977

Market watchers have long felt intuitively that price changes were wavelike. But until 1938, nobody had formulated these intuitions into a cohesive principle that made counting feasible. In that year, Ralph N. Elliott, a retired accountant, published a monograph that established an entirely new way of looking at the stock market. He not only detected systems of waves in price charts of the DJI but discovered ways of counting them and measuring them that proved to have significant predictive value.

Financial World
September 15, 1979

The Elliott Wave is a statistician's delight — though for others, following its swoops and wiggles can be daunting. Basically, Elliotticians predict the Dow on the theory that mass psychology reacts to and feeds on itself in a swelling pattern known as the Fibonacci ratio.

The (New York) *Daily News*

May 25, 1981

Prechter closely follows such indicators as trading volume on the Big board, advance-decline figures, activities of corporate insiders and advisory service sentiment. But the backbone is the Elliott Wave principle. A brainchild of the late R.N. Elliott, it's based on the theory —developed from massive research—that all bull markets are based on five up-and-down moves; in other words, up, down, up, down, up. The most important and vigorous of these—the one, says Prechter, "where just about everyone makes money"— is the third stage.

Barron's

February 28, 1983

Elliott's axiom was that there is form and pattern in human action no less than there is in physics. In the market there is a regular pattern of building up and tearing down. In a bull market, for instance, there are five waves, three up and two down. Waves one, three and five are up, and two and four are down. Two and four "correct" one and three. Just why there are five, said Elliott, "is one of the secrets of nature."

Financial Planning

October 1984

In Prechter's words, "Elliott told himself, 'I'd better figure out what makes this thing tick.'" With an accountant's quiet, methodical zeal, Elliott began watching the market — keeping daily, hourly, and even half-hourly charts of price movements. Only after several years of intense study did he begin to draw conclusions about the patterns he observed. What he found formed the basis of his Elliott Wave Theory, which posits that price movements are the results of mass investor psychology that swings from pessimism to optimism and back in a natural sequence, creating specific, and predictable, patterns.

Wealth

Winter 1985

[The Elliott Wave Principle] is not a cycle theory, for it is not based on the assumption that history repeats itself in a cyclical pattern over and over again, without progressing. On the contrary, Elliott's Wave Principle is a spiral theory, based on his belief in growth through time on a path that is ever upward, with corrections along the way.

Business Week

March 24, 1986

The Elliott Wave theory is based on a simple idea: investor psychology — not earnings, interest rates or OPEC — is the driving force behind the stock market. This mass psychology swings from pessimism to optimism in a more or less rhythmic fashion, much like such natural phenomena as the tides. Elliott's work describes the structure of market waves in great detail.

Newsweek

January 17, 1987

How does Prechter know so much? He sees it in the waves, that's how. If it sounds a little weird, take note: Prechter is one of the most accurate market forecasters in America. And he does it using waves — Elliott Waves, Prechter is the foremost practitioner of Elliott wave theory, an arcane method of stock market analysis originated by Depression-era accountant R.N. Elliott. Prechter has used the theory to predict every major ebb and flow of the stock market since 1982. Just who is Robert Prechter — and what is his secret formula? Prechter's theory maintains that predictable waves of investor psychology — not interest rates, earnings or oil prices — are the driving force behind stock market cycles. It further holds that such patterns repeat themselves in a complicated numerical sequence first discovered by 13th century mathematician Leonardo Fibonacci. While many analysts find the theory mystical, to say the least, Prechter defends its logic. "It simply says that human beings have a nature and they follow that nature," he says. "People do not act randomly."

The Wall Street Journal

March 18, 1987

The idea behind the Elliott Principle is that stock prices are a barometer of the national mood and that the mood moves in predictable waves between optimism and pessimism. The waves, which are based on stock market data, unfold in specific sequences. For example, the wave in a bull market rally will go up, down, up, down and up, followed by a correction in which waves will go down, up, down. Each wave contains smaller series of waves so that, for example, between January and July of 1984, the market was in a second wave on one scale and a fifth wave on another. A single large wave can last as long as several centuries; one that occurs within other waves can last as short a time as an hour.

The Economist
April 18, 1987

Elliott wave theory teaches that the market moves in a predictable pattern. Such is his confidence in the tenets of Mr. Elliott that Mr. Prechter had been waiting for the bull market of the 1980s ever since 1975. That was when he recognized the market would soon be entering, in Elliott Wave-speak, the "fifth wave" of a bullish five wave trend that began in 1932. In Elliott's theory, each upward move is characterized by three up waves and two down (and each downward move by two down and one up). The final fifth up-wave cycle from 1932 began in August 1982.

The Atlanta Journal / The Atlanta Constitution
March 5, 1989

The wave principle reveals that social psychology is patterned and to a great degree predictable. More simply put, its key tenet holds that people, being part of nature react [collectively] according to mathematically precise natural laws, the same ones that make it possible for scientists using geometric equations to calculate the rate of growth of plants and animals. The stock market acts according to these laws because it is a creation of man.

Barron's
May 8, 1989

"Market trends," [Prechter] explains, "are determined by a naturally developing pattern of human [mass] psychology, which in turn is governed by precise mathematical laws. World events are useless as a forecasting tool because they are an ultimate result of the dynamic, and not a cause." Prechter firmly believes that the extent and intensity of the coming blight, which he says will descend sometime before the middle of the next century, depends entirely on the severity of the bear market. Prechter, much like Willa Cather, whom he quotes in his latest opus (*A Turn of the Tidal Wave*), believes there are only two or three human stories, and they continually repeat themselves as if they had never occurred.

Citicorp Futures
November 1995

CFC: Mr. Prechter, in your original book, *The Elliott Wave Principle* you described how "crowd behavior trends and reverses in recognizable patterns." Can you elaborate a little more on what you believe the source of these constant patterns may be?

RP: Sure. People have often accepted the evidence that markets unfold in patterns, but no one has suggested a mechanism for them. It is my opinion that the desire among many individuals to belong to and be accepted by the group, as well as letting others think for them in intellectually difficult fields, make their unconscious minds dominate their conscious minds in emotionally charged social settings. When the market panics, for instance, investors are not panicking individually in isolation but in response to the panic of others. The same is true of their buying, but that is a slower process and therefore less obvious. Now, when the unconscious mind dominates, it does not do so randomly (as that would mean no thought at all), but in patterns peculiar to it. Those patterns show up in price movement.

* * * * * * * * * * * * * *

What is the Wave Principle?

The Wave Principle is, first and foremost, a detailed description of how markets behave. Now, there's probably more that is not in that sentence than is in that sentence. For instance, a detailed description of how markets behave does not refer to what outside events are occurring, such as in the fields of economics, politics, or social trends. It's strictly a study of how human beings behave collectively in the trading arena.

What specifically did Elliott discover?

Elliott's most important discovery was that the patterns that develop in the stock market occur at all degrees of trend. The larger patterns are made up of components that are themselves composed of smaller ones. The same patterns on a smaller scale combine to create any one of those patterns on a larger scale. The larger pattern will combine with several others of the same degree to create an even larger pattern and so on. He described in detail exactly what those patterns look like. He identified 13 of them. Only recently has data been available for general stock prices back to the late 1700s, and the patterns are there as well.

How did he label the "degrees" of trend?

Elliott began by naming a particular structure with an arbitrary label, Primary degree, a term borrowed from Dow Theory. The next larger degree he called Cycle, and the next larger Supercycle. The lower degrees he named Intermediate, Minor, and so on. We therefore have a way to refer to the degrees of trend that we are talking about.

What was the biggest degree trend he talked about?

Grand Supercycle, which he guessed dated back to the founding of the United States. Since then, more detailed stock market data has confirmed that he was right. That's not the biggest degree, though, as all waves are components of larger ones.

You once referred to the Wave Principle as the "purest form of technical analysis." Why?

For a hundred years, investors have noticed that events external to the market often seem to have no effect on the market's progress. With the knowledge that the market continuously unfolds in waves that are related to each other through form and ratio, we can see why there is little connection. The market has a life of its own. It is mass psychology that is registering. Changes in feelings show up directly as price changes in the barometer known as the DJIA. The Wave Principle is a catalog of the ways that the crowd goes from the extreme point of pessimism at the bottom to the extreme point of optimism at the top. It is a description of the steps human beings go through when they are part of the investment crowd, to change their psychological orientation from bullish to bearish. That description fits the movement of any market, as long as human beings are involved, rather than Martians, who may have a differently operating unconscious mind. Since people don't change much, the path they follow in moving from extreme pessimism to extreme optimism and back again tends to be the same over and over and over, regardless of news and extraneous events.

What is the basic path?

Very simply, Elliott recognized that movement in the direction of the one larger trend subdivides into five waves. Movement against the trend subdivides into a three-wave pattern or some variation involving several three-wave patterns. In rising markets, true bull markets, the subdivisions occur in five waves up, an up-down-up-down-up sequence. Bear markets tend to occur in three wave sequences, down-up-down. Each one of those movements has a shape and a personality. As long as you can recognize the shapes that are occurring, you have a handle on what might happen next.

But the five-wave form does occur on the downside.

Yes, but only as a component of a larger three-wave pattern. The essence of the Wave Principle is that the moves in the direction of the one larger trend are five-wave structures, while moves against the one larger trend are three-wave structures. From that, you can tell what the underlying trend is and invest accordingly.

You just go on Elliott's description alone. Does that mean you must act without knowing what's causing the pattern?

On the contrary, I know what is causing the patterns: human nature as it relates to a person interacting with his fellows. When you ask what outside force is "causing" the patterns, you are asking the wrong question, so you are already on the wrong path. Elliott's description of how markets behave forces you to a conclusion about cause and effect in social events. All of the causes most people assume to be operative are not, such as the latest political speeches or the latest numbers on the economy. They are simply results of the patterns of mass human psychology.

Is Elliott's a mechanical system?

Not really. What we're dealing with here is the behavior of people. If the tools you work with measure something other than the behavior of people, you'll be removed from the reality of what's going on. One of the biggest failures, in terms of approaching the stock market, is to assume that the market is mechanical in the sense that outside action causes market reaction, such as the idea that the market "responds" to Fed policy or the trade balance or political decisions. Others have tried to reduce it to a sum of periodic sine waves, but always find that it cannot be done, because the market is not a time-repetitive machine in its essence.

From the standpoint of theory, market behavior is tied to a mathematical law, but it is just not the same type of law found in the physical sciences. From the standpoint of practical application, the Wave Principle is tracking a living system, which is allowed variation in its forms, in fact, infinite variation, but limited by an essential form. Whereas a rigid system with numbers, strict mechanical numbers, never works.

Doesn't infinite variation imply that anything goes?

Not at all. Trees vary infinitely, but they all look like trees, don't they? And you can tell them apart from clouds, which also vary infinitely, and buildings as well. In fact, despite infinite variability, they are amazingly similar. The same is true of market patterns.

* * * * * * * * * * * * * *

Elliott Wave Principle

The Wave Principle reveals that the market reflects more the properties of a spiral than a circle, more the properties of nature than a machine.

* * * * * * * * * * * * * *

Does knowing Elliott guarantee profits?

Only the most trained and experienced market participants can act contrarily to their natural tendencies. I have yet to meet a man who invested or traded with a completely rational program based on reasonable probabilities without allowing his greed, his fear, his extraneous opinions or his irrelevant judgments to interfere. It is man's emotional side, particularly his social dependency, that makes him think the way his fellows do, and when he does that, he loses money in the markets. At least using Elliott, you have a basis that makes winning possible.

Most people are more interested in how it works than why it works. Is there any one thing people need to remember to make it work for them?

The key to Elliott Wave patterns is that the market goes three steps forward for every two steps back. If you do not get scared by the two steps back, and if you are not euphorically confident after the third step forward, you're light-years ahead of the pack. Even then, I would add that it is one easy thing to recognize that the Wave Principle governs stock prices, while it is quite another to predict the next wave, and still another to profit from the exercise. There is no substitute for experience, so that you can learn what you feel and when you feel it, with respect to market behavior.

Jack Frost has described the Wave Principle as something that has to be *seen* to be believed. What does he mean by that?

The principle is complicated to express in words. With the Wave Principle, you are dealing with a phenomenon that reveals itself visually. Try describing the concept and variations of "tree" in detail to someone who's never seen one and you'll see that it can be a complex task. Saying, "Look! There's one," is a lot easier. The human brain is very good at recognizing a pattern visually. If a computer must be programmed to recognize shapes in the sky, it would be difficult to teach it the difference between a cloud and bird and an airplane. Once you have that programmed, of course, a blimp floats by and the computer is in trouble. The human brain works differently, however, and is extremely efficient at pattern recognition. If you draw out the Principle, it is much more quickly grasped. Then when you compare actual market pictures with the model, you can accept the truth more readily. It is at the *perceptual* level that it is best presented, then, not the conceptual.

Can you really teach it?

Sure. Video is an excellent approach, for instance. A lot of people have learned how to apply it that way. Some have trouble at first, but then say "Once I saw your video tape, I understood it all."

What are the Wave Principle's key strengths?

Frost liked to say, "Its most striking characteristics are its generality and its accuracy." Its generality gives market perspective most of the time, and its accuracy in pointing out changes in direction is almost unbelievable at times.

Why does the Wave Principle work so well?

Because it is 100% technical. No armchair theorizing from economics and politics is required.

What are its biggest shortcomings?

There is one main weakness, and this accounts for just about all the problems. There are eleven different patterns for corrections. When a correction starts, it is impossible to tell in advance which pattern has begun, so you do not know how it is going to unfold. Therefore, the best that you can do is apply some of Elliott's observations as guidelines in making an intelligent guess as to what it is.

Another problem is that corrections can do what Elliott called "double" or "triple" — that is, repeat several times. Triple corrections are the largest formations possible, so at least there is a limit. These repetitions can be frustrating because they can last decades. For example, we had a 16-year sideways correction in the Dow Jones Industrial Average from 1966 to 1982. A.J. Frost and I thought it was over in 1974, and the market was ready for another bull wave. To be sure, most stocks rose from that point forward, but the Dow went sideways for another eight years in a doubling of the time element, which caused some frustrations before the next bull wave finally began on August 12, 1982.

It sounds like a chess game. The number of possibilities, and therefore the probabilities of success, vary at certain junctures.

Chess provides an excellent analogy. The market can do whatever it wants, except that it will always do it in an Elliott Wave structure. Similarly, your opponent can move chess pieces wherever he wants, except that he must follow basic rules. On the other side of the board, you still have a lot of hard thinking to do despite your absolute knowledge that pieces must move according to those rules.

Are there situations where the Wave Principle does not hold true?

No, it always holds true. But of course, it is one thing to say the markets will follow the Wave Principle and another thing entirely to forecast the future based on that knowledge. It is always a question of probabilities. Once you have hands-on experience with it, once you understand all the rules and guidelines, it is a lot like becoming Sherlock Holmes. There are many possible outcomes, but guidelines force you along certain paths of thinking. You finally reach a point where the evidence becomes overwhelming for a certain conclusion.

Have you ever had a case where you thought the probability of a certain outcome was high, say 90%, but the market went otherwise from your expectation? What did you do then?

Of course it happens. But you should never be wrong for long relative to the degree that you are trying to assess. One of the terrific things about the approach is that it's price that tips you off. With other approaches, price can go a long way before the reason behind your opinion changes, if it ever does. No matter how difficult the pattern is to read sometimes, it always resolves satisfactorily into a classic pattern.

Can you illustrate how knowledge of "wave structure" comes into play when trading?

For instance, the bottom of the fourth wave, which is a pullback, cannot overlap the peak of the first rally. If it does, then it's not a fourth wave. The fourth wave is still ahead of you, and the third wave is subdividing. Knowing this tenet can keep you out of a lot of trouble that an armchair wave counter would encounter. Another very basic tenet is that wave three is never the shortest. It is usually the longest. Wave three is the recognition stage when most people get aboard.

* * * * * * * * * * * * * *

R.N. Elliott

(in a letter to Charles Collins)

February 19, 1935

Waves do not make errors, but my version may be defective.

* * * * * * * * * * * * * *

But if there is always a correct pattern, and it is only a matter of seeing it, why aren't accuracy levels higher than the 40%, 50%, 60% or even the 80% ratios of hits to misses?

First, just because R.N. Elliott discerned that the market follows rules as in a chess game doesn't mean you can predict the market's next move. All you can give are probabilities. But the psychological difficulties are at least an equal impediment. Hamilton Bolton once said that the hardest thing he had to learn when using Elliott was to believe what he saw. Despite all I know, I have fallen prey to that problem more than once. The fact that even perfect analysis only results in the best probabil-

ity provides the uncertainty that feeds the psychological un-
ease. As Frost is fond of saying, "The market always leaves its
options open." So when you combine human weakness with a
game of probability, the result is many errors in judgment. Nevertheless, I must stress that the ratio of success with Elliott is
better than that with other approaches, and that is the only
rational basis for judging its value. Besides, the inestimable
value of the Wave Principle is not so much that it provides a
high percentage of correct "calls" on the market, but that it
always gives the investor a sense of perspective.

**Is it possible that the system merely takes into account every possible
pattern and thus allows the practitioner to force things into a
satisfactory wave count retrospectively — but not prospectively?**

No, for two reasons. First, if that were true, then there would
be no record of success such as the Wave Principle has over the
decades. There are numerological approaches to the market,
ones based on fantasy that may as well be dealing with a random walk, and they produce worthless results, as they should.
As Paul Montgomery likes to say, a good test of a theory is
whether it can predict. Second, there are many non-Elliott patterns that the market *could* trace out if it were a random walk;
but it has never done it. I have never seen a market unfold in
other than an Elliott Wave pattern.

**That's the way it often worked throughout your career. I recall another
time that you were incorrectly bearish on bonds for a number of months
and shorted them continually on your Hotline, but ended up actually
making a point and a half of profit.**

Yeah, I was proud of that. The near term patterns kept telling me exactly where to sell short. When the market pulled back,
I placed the stops properly. All of them were hit, but some were
below entry points, so we made money. Well, actually we probably broke even after commissions. But that's better than losing
the fifteen points that an unhedged bear would have done.

**But there has been one big exception. You have shorted the stock
indexes for a few years and lost money at it. Why is that?**

If I could answer that question, maybe I would never lose
money again! There are two reasons. First, the market has provided subnormal corrections ever since 1987. Twice I was ready

to cover at a profit and buy if only the market had corrected a bit further, but it didn't. Probably the overriding reason, though, has been the degree of the coming trend change. Calling the top of a one-year trend within ten trading days would be a great call. Calling the top of a 200-year uptrend within ten years is an equally good call, and I think I'll be able to do that. So I'm on the wrong side for a relatively short period, though it is a long time in terms of people's market experience. I know the biggest bear market in nearly 300 years is coming, and I'm confident that whatever we've lost over the past few years will be recovered in a matter of months when the trend changes.

* * * * * * * * * * * * * *

The Elliott Wave Theorist
January 28, 1994

Making money in markets is normally difficult. Making money in the past three years in stocks has been easy, but only if you believe that making money in markets is easy. Those who think making money is easy will not sell before the market turns down, and their profits will be wiped out in a matter of weeks. Those who are positioned to catch the trend change will make more money in one year than the longs will have made in five.

* * * * * * * * * * * * * *

Have you ever had a sure thing — a case where the market absolutely had to go up or down?

All Elliott can do is order the probabilities, and they are never 100%. But there have definitely been times when my own mind *felt* that the probability was 100%. I get so excited I can barely contain myself when that happens. I'm usually right then, but not always!

Keep in mind that while one can never say that a certain event must happen, there are times when one can say that a particular market event is impossible. There's always an alternate count, but there are certain things that can't happen under Elliott. And that is a very useful fact.

The calls you made on stocks, bonds and gold helped you to establish yourself as a media presence in the 1980s. But one response to the record is to say that the Wave Principle is not behind your success. Some say it is gut feel or instinct, rather than the method. In other

words, it's not the theory, it's the theorist. You've always insisted that it is the Wave Principle. How can you be sure it's giving you the edge and not the other way around?

Gut feel and instinct will get you clobbered in the market. The market *is* the collective gut, which means you have to be counter-instinctual to beat it. The only way to do that is with a method that takes that reality into account.

Looking in more detail at an Elliott Wave, what is the progression that takes place over the course of an "impulse," which is Elliott's term for the classic five-wave pattern?

If you watch any of these wave structures, whether over the last 40 weeks, 40 years or 40 minutes, you see the same progression recurring. After a market reaches its low, so-called strong hands — people who have been around a long time, do some buying. Psychology has passed its low point. News remains scary because it is the tangible result of the prior downtrend in psychology. That is the first wave up.

Then the second wave, the correction of the first move, takes place. The vast majority of investors are convinced that wave 1 was merely a bounce in the previous bear market and that wave 2 is the beginning of the next phase of decline. Usually, the fears that were around at the actual bottom recur at the bottom of wave 2. Again, news is very dark, but the prices are ahead of news. They do not fall to a new low.

From that base, wave 3 begins, which is the middle portion of the larger advance, and that third wave is almost always accompanied by increasingly positive news and "fundamentals." Those better fundamentals are the result of the increase in optimism, and they reinforce the psychological upturn. That is why wave 3, as Elliott noted, is most often the longest, strongest and broadest in the sequence. Every day, there is reason to be optimistic. All of those people who thought during waves 1 and 2 that the long term trend was down finally become convinced that the long-term trend is up.

That change persists all the way to the top of wave 3. Then comes wave 4, which is a correction of that long third. Most people have finally become convinced by the top of wave 3 that the long term trend is up. Wave 4 is a surprising disappointment.

From the fourth wave correction low, the market stages the final wave up. The fifth wave is generally easy to recognize because the psychology tends to be more speculative and euphoric, while at the same time, the internal strength, or momentum, of the market is not as strong as it was during wave 3. The psychology goes through its final binge in the fifth wave. That's when, figuratively speaking, the last guy puts his last nickel in, and that's the end of the sequence.

Let's examine one of these waves — the fifth wave — since, by your wave count, the Dow Jones Industrial Average has been in a fifth wave of Grand Supercycle, Supercycle *and* Cycle degree for the better part of many people's lives. What is the profile?

The market is usually quite selective and rotational in a fifth, creating a weak upward trend or even a sideways trend in the advance-decline line. You will often see huge rises in certain individual issues, while many lag significantly. Usually in fifth waves, the general speculation is concentrated most heavily in the blue chip sector. You also generally see the market attracting new players, unsophisticated players who have been watching the bull market year after year and finally became convinced that they should be involved.

That is one reason why the market, or at least large segments of the market, become extremely overvalued. It is attracting new players who have no concept of value and are just willing to buy because they think someone else will be buying from them tomorrow. In other words, it's an engine that is running on increasingly available fuel — which is more people with money — with its forward movement as it own end. The situation creates a speculative bubble, a chasing of paper value for quick profit. Often it is a craze that sinks very deeply into the society. We had this style of advance in the 1920s, for instance.

In this most recent fifth wave, mechanisms were put in place that fostered terrific speculation. There was the development of the stock index futures market and the very intricate options markets, with options on stocks, options on futures indexes, and so forth. There has been an increased media coverage as well. In fact, it's an incalculable increase. Television, for instance, didn't report on business or markets prior to the 1981 launch of Financial News Network, which is now CNBC. It has been so successful that more all-business news networks are about to be launched. It's a great major top signal.

* * * * * * * * * * * * * *

Money Maker
August/September 1986

Let's take a look at the big picture...From extreme pessimism of the depression lows of 1932, we traced out a textbook five-wave upward stock structure according to Elliott's observations, forming wave I to 1937. We have wave II, a downward correction of that first wave up, which lasted into 1942. We have wave III, a middle upward movement, ending in 1966. Then occurred a fourth wave lasting all the way into 1982, with the Dow Jones Industrial Average moving sideways for 16 years. In inflation-adjusted terms, of course, stock prices during those years were getting killed.

From August of 1982, we have been in the fifth wave. At least it has all the earmarks of a fifth wave, both on a fundamental and a technical basis.

Now that fifth wave, in turn, can also be expected to subdivide into five waves. From the extremes of pessimism in August 1982, we should reach a corresponding stage of optimism at the top. And we have indeed had a first wave up ending in January 1984 with a 500-point rally. We had that 200-point decline in July of 1984, ending phase two. We have been enjoying wave ③ ever since, as I interpret it.

And how high will wave ③ go?

There's no good way to be certain about that. The third wave is not particularly forecastable. However, the later we get into the third wave — in other words, into the fifth intermediate wave within it — the higher we go and the closer we get, the more I'll be able to say it's likely we're going to a particular level. But just from the typical shape of third waves, which tend to be quite long, I estimated at the beginning of this year we would see a minimum of 2700 and a maximum of 3200 in the third leg. And probably, we'll know more later if my prediction for this year holds up.

And after a fourth wave correction, you project that a fifth wave will take the Dow to 3,600?

That's right.

Before asking what happens next, let's clarify: In addition to the two uptrends you mentioned, are we also in a third larger trend?

Yes, we are talking about the uptrend from 1982, the uptrend from 1932 and the uptrend from the late 1700s. Each one is clearly tracing a five-wave upward structure. The largest has lasted 200 years. History shows that when any five-wave pattern is finished, there is a correspondingly severe correction, or bear market. And we are in the extremely late stages of this 200-year trend.

In effect, all three of these trends will end at the same time. Is that true?

Oh yeah. Each one is a component of another. They will all end at the same instant in time.

The Dow will hit the 3600 area and then what will happen?

We will have the largest bear market in the history of the United States.

And an attendant Depression?

The world hasn't experienced a major stock market collapse without a severe economic problem following it.

How far down will the Dow go?

Well, based on Elliott's guidelines, it should fall, I would say, at least 90%. This century has already given us one instance where this has happened. So we know this kind of drop occurs; it is merely a matter of deciding when.

* * * * * * * * * * * * * *

What is the relationship between a Kondratieff "long wave" and an Elliott Wave Supercycle?

The Elliott Wave Principle and the Kondratieff cycle are entirely different concepts. The Wave Principle is a study and recognition of behavioral patterns that are not tied to periodicity. The Kondratieff is an economic cycle of inflation and deflation that lasts approximately 54 years. The Kondratieff cycle is an interpretation of the data that says that the economy has a recognizable rhythm by which expansion and inflation generally move together until inflation becomes overwhelming and the inflationary side of the cycle peaks. There is then a recessionary period when the increase in inflation stops. Then comes what is called the "plateau" period lasting about ten years, during which time inflation is not severe and financial assets boom in value. That is followed ultimately by the "secondary" depression, a severely deflationary period during which prices fall precipitously and economic activity contracts substantially. Today, the "plateau" period is ending. In 1982, I concluded that the last Kondratieff cycle low was in 1949, not back in the 1930s, as most practitioners think, or even in 1942. 1982 to the present has been the "plateau" period, which followed the recession of 1982. The "secondary depression" is due next and should last until 2003. And that fits the outlook on the Elliott Wave Principle although they are two different approaches. I explain all this in detail in Appendix B of *Tidal Wave*.

You've never been timid about making forecasts. But for much of the bull market, you declined to go into great detail about an even larger degree of trend: the Grand Supercycle, which is now the focus of your commentary. Where does the Grand Supercycle begin and end and why the earlier unwillingness?

I didn't discuss that degree much in public because people are not willing to accept that trends and patterns can express themselves over centuries. However, Frost and I certainly made that point in our book, and that is the entire focus of my new one. To summarize, the Grand Supercycle is one degree larger trend than the Supercycle, and the Supercycle advance from 1932 to 1995 was the fifth and final phase of a two-century-long period of progress that began in the late 1700s, suggesting even more powerfully that the coming bear market is going to be one for the history books.

But now you're talking about it. Why?

I believe that we are near the cusp of the trend change. If so, then the result will be obvious in half a dozen years, and the Wave Principle will have shown its incalculable worth once again.

We'll talk about those results when we get to the implications of your work in Section 3. For now, let's figure out where the boundaries are in terms of time. How far back in history does the Elliott Wave apply?

If man's actions are patterned over five days, five weeks, five years and fifty years, they are probably patterned over 500 years and 5000 years. In applying wave analysis to historical trends and events, it is my contention that all of history can be understood from the standpoint of wave patterns, and in fact at the deepest level *only* from that standpoint. The same patterns appear to be in force back to the start of the Bronze Age.

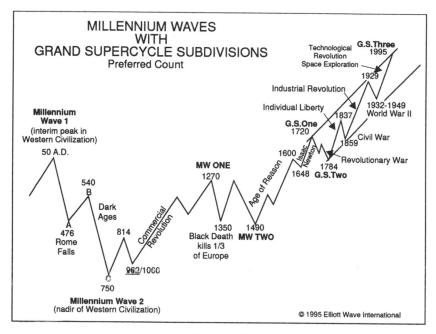

MILLENNIUM WAVES
WITH
GRAND SUPERCYCLE SUBDIVISIONS
Preferred Count

Technological G.S.Three
Revolution 1995
Space Exploration
1929
Industrial Revolution
Individual Liberty 1932-1949
World War II
1837
G.S.One
1720
Civil War
Millennium 1859
Wave 1 Revolutionary War
(interim peak in 1600 1784
Western Civilization) 1648 G.S.Two
50 A.D. MW ONE Isaac Newton
1270 Age of Reason
540
B
Dark
Ages Commercial Revolution
476 814 1350 1490
Rome Black Death MW TWO
Falls kills 1/3
of Europe
962/1000
750
Millennium Wave 2
(nadir of Western Civilization)
© 1995 Elliott Wave International

Figure 1-1

So the degrees of trend don't stop at Grand Supercycle, big as that is, do they? There's Millennium degree and Supermillennium degree beyond that. How can you possibly get data across such expansive time frames?

For the last 200 years, data available for researching investment price trends is not especially difficult to attain. But prior to that time, we have to rely on less exact statistics for perspective. In *Elliott Wave Principle*, we used a long term market price index for a simple "basket of human needs" beginning in 950 A.D. Strangely enough, this diagram, while only a very rough indication of general price trends, produced an unmistakable five-wave Elliott pattern. To get the picture of social progress, however, I have to work "backwards." That is, I have to assess the social events and make an assumption about where the waves were in their patterns that they would have produced such events. On that basis, a Millennium degree bull market began at the low or the end of the Dark Ages, in either the 700s or the 900s. We've been in a bull market of that degree ever since (see Figure 1-1).

History should show that this 1000-year advance was preceded by a long bear market which was preceded by a bull and so on ad infinitum. Of course, we have no data to capture the wave form, but does the broad outline of history actually show such a pattern?

Rome, whose cultural peak probably coincided with the peak of the previous Supermillennium wave, began to deteriorate shortly after the time of Jesus. The rot continued for a few hundred years until 476 A.D., when Rome fell to the Germans. The next three centuries were dismal. Population was stagnant. Disease ran rampant. Mass slaughters occurred. Progress and the search for knowledge became almost extinct. So that was a bear market all right, and it was of Supermillennium degree.

What happened next?

The Commercial Revolution from 962/1066 to 1270 or so was behind Millennium wave ONE, an expansion that ushered in the Middle Ages. The leveling of prices from 1270 to 1490 forms wave TWO and represents a "correction" of the progress made during the Commercial Revolution.

The next phase of rising prices began Millennium wave Three, which is extending. It has been coinciding with the great period of exploration, expansion and cultural advancement. In Grand Supercycle wave One, business expanded and prices rose during this period of creative brilliance and luxury. We may not see the likes of it again until the start of the next third wave of Millennium degree. By 1720, prices had reached a peak. The correction that followed, and ended in the late 1700s, was Grand Supercycle wave Two of an extended Millennium wave THREE. The advance from 1784 until now has been Grand Supercycle wave Three. Its center took place from 1859 to 1929, the most rapid period of material progress the world has ever known. Recall that technically speaking, third waves in the stock market have the greatest momentum, and you can see that the concept is the same at the cultural level at large degree.

Those who are skeptical of Grand Supercycles are less likely to accept the concept of Millennium and Supermillennium wave patterns. On the other hand, a lot of people have the idea that the Wave Principle should only be applied to longer term averages. Are such restrictions appropriate?

The Wave Principle is better suited to long term study than any other approach I know, but it is also perfectly well suited to assessing trends that last only hours. As long as you are following the averages, and as long as you can record those trends as the market is moving, you'll find that the same patterns of psychological change occur over and over at the smallest measurable degree as well as the largest. In fact, for one period of time, I kept a computer-generated tick by tick chart of gold trading. Even on that basis, where mass psychology is getting down to a very small measurement, the patterns persisted. It was a little more erratic, but the basic outline repeated even at that level, which means that some players in the market, those closest to it, are reflecting the smallest fluctuations in aggregate psychology.

In following in Elliott's footsteps, you moved out onto some relatively unexplored intellectual terrain. Your idea that history reflects the Wave Principle is one of them. Your identification of cultural trends as reflective of the overall mood is another. Regardless of the subfield you discuss, though, you reiterate that "mass psychology is structured," and that Elliott identified the structure. After witnessing this movement in the stock market data and its apparent constancy, both you and Elliott have concluded that collective human sociology is not random, but travels a path as if following a law of nature, like gravity or thermodynamics. If this is true, then science, the study of nature, should supply some corroborating testimony. Is there anything going on in science to support you on this?

During the past 20 years, several scientists have reintroduced the idea of the fractal geometry of nature. The recent work has been pioneered by Benoit Mandelbrot. His computer studies revealed that many processes in nature, while at first appearing chaotic, are actually very structured, but in ways most people have never considered. The component structures are not simple geometric forms like circles and squares; they may be very jagged constructs. But the components of the jagged pattern are jagged to the same degree as the larger pattern itself. If you take a stalk of broccoli as a common example, and you break off a piece near the top, the piece you break off looks exactly like a stalk of broccoli. If you break off a smaller piece from it, it also looks exactly like a stalk of broccoli — just smaller. The components take the shape of the whole. What's exciting to me is that Elliott noticed the same thing about stock market prices half a century before Mandelbrot.

* * * * * * * * * * * * * * *

Speech to the Market Technicians Association
May 1986

Benoit Mandelbrot discovered that most patterns that scientists had assumed were chaotic in nature were not. In looking at clouds, seacoasts and mountain ranges, for instance, the typical conclusion was that they were chaotic, governed by no specific geometry. Mandelbrot said that's not true. They follow a relational form that scientists hadn't thought of.

I just want to read some excerpts from an article about his ideas on the way nature develops: "He has invented a new way of describing, calculating and thinking about shapes that are irregular and fragmented, jagged and broken. They turn out to be nature's own...The interesting feature of a lightning bolt's path, for example, is not the straight line direction, but rather the distribution of its zigs and zags...A new kind of symmetry has emerged, not of left to right or front to back, but of small scale patterns to patterns on larger and larger scales — the self-similarity of a broccoli floret whose tiny bifurcations echo the branching of the stalk as a whole...Oddly...the mathematical description of them seemed to apply just as well to very different problems, from fluctuating cotton prices since the 19th century to the rising and falling of the Nile River through two millenniums...In unexpectedly orderly fashion, they have self-similarity on different scales." This description echoes Elliott's observation that stock market movements trace out five waves in the direction of the one larger trend and three waves against that trend *at all degrees, or sizes, of trend*, producing *self-similarity on different scales*...The article continues, "When you zoom in, looking closer and closer, the irregularities don't smooth out. Rather, they tend to look exactly as irregular as before. Some of Mandelbrot's fractal patterns looked indistinguishable from records of stock market prices. Economists needed to understand the heretical idea that prices don't change in a smooth, continuous flow. They can change abruptly in instantaneous jumps. Dam builders and risk insurers of all kinds need to understand that traditional notions of probability lead them to underestimate the likelihood of the rarest, most catastrophic events." Similarly, Elliott recognized that big bear markets are no different in shape from short term reactions. They're just on a larger scale and thus occur less often. They do not, however, occur less often relative to the scale of advances that precede them. A headline making market "crash," for instance, is merely a large version of what happens all the time on smaller scales.

* * * * * * * * * * * * * * *

It is important to note, however, that the personality of wave structures will vary somewhat for different markets. With respect to stocks and commodities, for instance, you've noted some critical differences. Give us an example of how a fifth wave plays differently in stocks than commodities.

When stock markets move into their fifth wave, it's on rising optimism. When commodities move into their fifth wave it's on rising *fear* — fear of inflation, fear of crop shortages, fear of deficits. That's why commodity tops look like stock market bottoms.

From an Elliott Wave perspective, there are also differences within the same market. Advances and declines, bull and bear markets, take different shapes. Is this also true of the psychology in bull and bear markets?

The problem with declines is that they can follow a lot more paths, because there are numerous corrective patterns. At the start of a bear market, all you have are hints. You have little certainty about which one of the shapes is going to take place. All you can say is it is going to be rough for a while. Bob Farrell says that a bear market goes from caution to concern to capitulation. In most patterns, that's true, but in contracting triangles, it goes the opposite way: capitulation, concern, then caution, or at least complete disregard.

Bear markets tend to bring bad news in one form or another, regardless of their shape. Triangles, for instance, are seemingly moderate sideways patterns. Yet there is almost always a scary event or point of focus in wave e, the last wave, that keeps you out of the next advance. In a large bear market, wave e of an upward triangle correction usually features a bullish event that gets you to buy just before the rug is pulled. However, the worst news — the news that turns out making the history books — usually awaits the end of a large bear market. Bull markets do it again, only the other way around. They save the best news for last. Just look at the amazing world news of the past six years: Communists giving up power, old enemies signing peace pacts, the implications of the computer revolution.

Do the different psychologies of bull and bear markets show up in other non-Elliott areas, like momentum indicators?

Oh, yes. For instance, extreme overbought conditions generally indicate further advance until the overboughts become milder. By contrast, extreme oversold conditions often accompany the price low of a decline. Fear does not need a period of dissipation as does greed.

So, a technically strengthening upward thrust in stock prices is usually closer to a bottom than a top?

Acceleration into a top is typical of commodities, but not of stocks. The stock market has always given plenty of warning from a momentum standpoint that a top was in the making. From December 1985 to March of 1986, when the bull market of the 1980s was at its epicenter, all the talk of a "blowoff" was coming from the commodity futures traders who have less experience with the stock market than with commodities. Stocks just don't blow off. If you throw a ball into the air, it has to slow down before it comes down. The market doesn't exactly follow the laws of physics, but its action does seem to reflect this one.

Even the 1929 high was accompanied by "top building," i.e., a glaring divergence in the 6-month percentage rate of change. As the great Dow Theorist Richard Russell says, "A blowoff is when the market goes up big, and you were bearish the whole rise." In other words, in the stock market, the idea is a psychological feeling more than a true description of a stock market chart formation.

Does this slow topping process serve any function?

Many manias in history have outlasted the Cassandras to the end of devastating the finances of the largest possible number of people.

The crowd is buying fantasies. That is why the professional who can measure the amount of emotional activity in a market and relate it to the degree of the wave in progress is going to make money. When fantasies get far out of line with reality, you've been presented with the opportunity to make money, whether it's on the downside or the upside.

Yet you see something more complex underlying the market that can't be discerned with standard momentum and moving average analysis, right?

Momentum is important. Investor sentiment is important. But they are not nearly so valuable alone as they are when used in conjunction with the Wave Principle, because only with a knowledge of the developing patterns can you anticipate the *degree* of an approaching trend change, and therefore the extent that momentum and sentiment indicators should reach at a particular market juncture.

So even a contrary stance can't be rewarding unless one is following the Wave Principle?

Precisely. The problem again is that contrarianism is only a one-way comment. The observation made by contrarians is that at the top of a market, there will be a substantially greater number of bulls than bears. This is a fact, but it doesn't tell you how far the pendulum can swing in one or the other direction. That is why the Wave Principle is necessary.

In real time, the Wave Principle is a lot more complicated than it sounds when you simply describe the types of waves. Dealing with corrections is particularly difficult. What makes it so much more difficult to pinpoint your position in a corrective wave than an impulse waves?

Five-stage movements are generally uniform, with very few exceptions to the rule. When prices are moving with the trend, they are moving very freely, and you get the full five-wave structure. In that case, analysis is not that much harder than it sounds on paper. But when the short term trend is fighting the intermediate term trend, it is going against the tide. Corrective processes by their very nature are fighting the larger flow of price movement. When the market is fighting the flow, it can only go so far. It never develops the five waves. In 10 years of studying the market, I've never seen an exception.

Is this also why there are several different ways that corrections can unfold?

Corrections are the point at which the outflowing river meets the incoming tide. The jumble that results is far less uniform than the river's flow or the tidal force. As a result, knowing exactly which of the corrective patterns has begun is impossible at the outset. The analyst knows that moves against the larger trend never develop into a full five waves, but he does not know precisely which non-five wave structure it will be. Nevertheless, R.N. Elliott's compilation of the list of countertrend patterns is the product of brilliance. Though there are a number of them, he described them clearly, and that is of substantial value in practical application.

Is there a simple guideline that a novice can follow to help him weather corrective Elliott Wave patterns?

Sure. During these periods in which Elliott Wave analysis is the most difficult, do nothing. It is not necessary to forecast all the time unless you are in the business, like I am. So just wait for the pattern to clear and then take action.

Some analysts get annoyed at this. They say, "That's the problem with the Wave Principle. It doesn't work in bear markets."

Well, tough break! Bear markets are what they are. If someone objects to what the market *is*, then he is arguing with nature and the reality of markets. "Less predictable" does not mean impossible, indecipherable, disorderly or random, either. You can form *some* useful opinions about corrections. The ultimate price goal of a fourth wave correction, for instance, can be forecast with more accuracy than most impulses. What's more, it is the Wave Principle that tells the analyst when to expect less predictability. So your overheard "objection" is not a problem with the Wave Principle, much less a revelation of where the Wave Principle cannot be applied. That the Wave Principle recognizes the differences in market behavior is one of its greatest strengths.

What about those who say investing with impulse waves, or in the direction of the trend, isn't that hard anyway?

Tell that to 83% of the professional money managers who underperformed the Standard & Poor's or the Dow Jones Industrial Average for three years in the heart of the bull market of the 1980s. Tell it to the 98% of money managers who got killed in the last downward impulse in 1973-1974. Tell that to the 99% of the public, who lose money in their investments over the long run. I, for one, recognize the fact that successful investing is extremely difficult. Anyone who tells you it is not is headed for a fall.

Can Elliott save you from a fall?

It can save you from a catastrophic loss. It is one of the few concepts I know that allows the investor to get out of a losing position with a small loss for an objective reason. The alternatives are to ride it out or simply get out because an arbitrary "stop" level has been reached, which nine times out of ten gets you out just before the big gains are due.

Sometimes a corrective process can take the form of what Elliott called a triangle. Are those difficult?

To the novice, they are bugaboos. But once you get used to them, they are a great blessing. Elliott discovered that there were four distinct types. They are not just movements within the shape of two converging lines. They are a specific number of moves within it and specific subdivisions within those. There are several rules about triangles, but simply finding out that you are in one can help you make a lot of forecasts about what is going to happen next. You can often recognize the end of an "E" wave and take quite a large position with a very close stop, which is paradise for a speculator.

Fibonacci Rules

Another useful aspect is the way in which the extents of the waves relate to one another within a given sequence. For instance, you used one such guideline in your first book to predict the Dow's rise to 2722. Explain how that was done.

In our 1978 book, *Elliott Wave Principle*, A. J. Frost and I maintained our conclusion that the Cycle wave IV bear market had ended in 1974, since it had met Frost's downside target to the point. We then used Elliott's guideline of "equality" to project the ultimate high. Stated simply, we said that Cycle wave V should produce the same percentage gain as Cycle wave I from 1932 to 1937. Applying the 4.716x multiple of wave I to the 1974 closing low at 577.60 projected a peak close at 2724. In the book, we rounded the expected gain to a 5x multiple, since the guideline was stated as a *tendency*, not a precise relationship. Subsequent events, however, showed an exact equality, as the 1987 closing high occurred at 2722.

But that was to the high in August 1987. Where did 3664 come from, and why have we passed it?

While it proved true that the *low price* had been seen in 1974, Cycle wave IV continued for eight years beyond 1974, finally completing a complex bear market pattern called a "double three" in August 1982. This pattern produced a critical fact that was terrifically exciting at the time: the higher price at which wave IV finally ended raised the upside target for wave V. The guideline of equality still applied, so the essential forecast was exactly the same, that wave V would equal the percentage gain of wave I from 1932 to 1937. However, the 4.716x multiple now applied to the 1982 low at 776.92, thus projecting a peak at 3664.

Well, this time the market went past your target.

Yes, and it may be because the Dow will fulfill its next most common relationship, a 1.618 Fibonacci multiple of the percentage gain of wave I, in which case wave V will gain just over 600% and rise all the way to 5444. In fact, a peak at that level would also create a .618 relationship to wave III, which would be an even more satisfying web of Fibonacci relationships. Although I'm disappointed that my first target was surpassed, I think the fact that the market made it to 3686 is quite a testimony to the value of long term forecasting using the Wave Principle.

O.K., we've gotten back to Fibonacci here. Who was Fibonacci?

Leonardo of Pisa was the son of a successful merchant named Bonacci, thus Fi for "son of" Bonacci. Fibonacci introduced the Arabic number system to the Western world and was the most famous mathematician of his time. In the 13th century, he would entertain royal courts with mathematical problems. One of those problems was the famous rabbit problem, the answer to which is the sequence that is now named after him. The Fibonacci sequence is a self-generated sequence obtained by adding two adjacent figures to obtain the next. Start at the number 1 and add the preceding number. There isn't any, so you get another 1. Add the preceding number, 1, to that 1 and you get 2; take 2 and add the preceding number, which is 1, and you get 3: take 3 and add the preceding number, which is 2, and you get 5; take 5 and add the preceding number, which is 3, and you get 8, and so on to 13, 21, 34, 55, etc. Actually, Fibonacci rediscovered the sequence and the ratio which governs it, which had been known by the Greeks and as far back as the ancient Egyptians. It has been treated as a very special thing by mathematicians and scientists that far back, and to this day.

How does this sequence relate to the market?

As Collins pointed out, Fibonacci mathematics are the main determinant of all of the constructs Elliott observed. In the stock market, the simplest description of a bear market is a straight line down, one wave. The simplest description of a bull market is a straight line up. Elliott found that bear markets most often subdivide into three waves: down, up, down. Bull markets subdivide into five: up, down, up, down, up. It takes one complete bear market and one bull market to make a cycle. At the simplest level, that is 1 rise and 1 fall, for a total of 2 waves. The bear market subdivides into 3 waves, the bull market into 5, and the total is 8. When you drop to the next subdivision, you find that a bear market has 13 waves, a bull market has 21, and the total is 34. And so on to infinity; each new number is the sum of the previous two. *That is the Fibonacci sequence.*

In addition to the revelation that stock price patterns are self-similar at different degrees of trend, Elliott made another important contribution which is critical to his theory and represents an important breakthrough in the field. He discovered the existence of, and guidelines for the application of, the Fibonacci ratio in markets. Can you explain what the Fibonacci ratio is?

As the Fibonacci sequence progresses, the ratio between adjacent numbers is always 0.618, called *phi*, which has an inverse of 1.618. I.e., .618 times 1.618 equals 1. It is the only ratio whose inverse is itself plus 1. This ratio governs all additive progressions of this type, no matter what number you begin with.

Wait a minute. Start with three instead of one.

Sure. The result is 3, 3, 6, 9, 15, 24, 39, 63, 102, and so on to infinity. What always remains constant? The Golden Ratio *between* the numbers after the first few terms. Let's hit the calculator and see. In this example, 63/102=.61765.

So, in essence, nine is a Fibonacci number, also.

While the specific numbers making up the Fibonacci sequence may be more natural in that they begin with the number 1, they are not essential to the ratio, which governs a basic law of geometric progression.

What's the significance? Why is this relationship so critical?

The fact that the ratio governs all additive sequences derived by adding a term to the previous to get the next makes it ideal mathematics for growth patterns. That is undoubtedly why it is found in growth and decay patterns and in expansion and contraction patterns throughout nature. Many things — plants, animals, spiraling galaxies, cloud formations, hurricanes — display characteristics of motion, growth, and, in some rare cases, decay in ways that reflect the workings of the Fibonacci ratio. As a result, this ratio has fascinated scientists and mathematicians for centuries.

Why should it be *this* particular ratio?

Phi, or 1.618..., governs spirals, such as those seen from the nautilus shell to galaxies. In contrast, *pi*, or 3.1416..., another irrational number, governs the geometric shape known as the circle. The circle is a *static* shape. It doesn't imply motion; it implies stasis. A spiral, on the other hand, implies expansion and contraction, *progress and regress*. The stock market, as a direct reflection of the popular valuation of mankind's productive enterprise, is a record of man's progress or regress in that regard. Like other things in nature, then, human history seems to be following a pattern that conforms to a natural law based upon the same ratio. That mankind is producing a natural growth pattern throughout history may be a grand concept, but it is hardly fantastic.

So how do you use the ratio in markets?

One example of the use of the Fibonacci ratio in the Elliott Wave Principle is to establish the target based upon common relationships among waves. Elliott pointed out one example of when an impulse was likely to display a Fibonacci relationship among its components. I have catalogued a whole lot more.

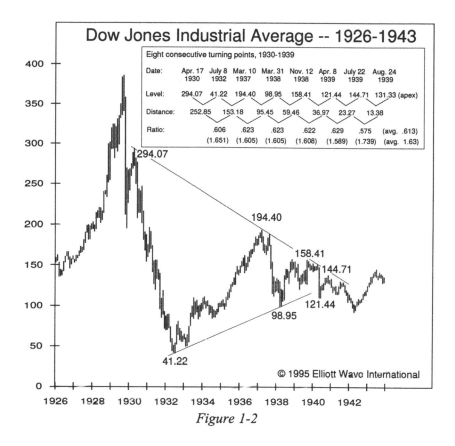

Date:	Apr. 17 1930	July 8 1932	Mar. 10 1937	Mar. 31 1938	Nov. 12 1938	Apr. 8 1939	July 22 1939	Aug. 24 1939
Level:	294.07	41.22	194.40	98.95	158.41	121.44	144.71	131.33 (apex)
Distance:	252.85	153.18	95.45	59.46	36.97	23.27	13.38	
Ratio:		.606	.623	.623	.622	.629	.575	(avg. .613)
		(1.651)	(1.605)	(1.605)	(1.608)	(1.589)	(1.739)	(avg. 1.63)

Eight consecutive turning points, 1930-1939

Dow Jones Industrial Average -- 1926-1943

© 1995 Elliott Wave International

Figure 1-2

You and a lot of other traders have made profitable use of such targets. In many cases, historic turns have conformed to Fibonacci multiples. Give us a good example.

Well, let's take a look at the 1930-1939 period in Fibonacci terms, for starters. It was one of the most amazing periods for Fibonacci mathematics in stock market history. Figure 1-2 illustrates the relationships of the price lengths of the eight, a Fibonacci number, swings. The prices quoted are closing prices. Having observed hourly readings for the past 20 years, I would be willing to bet, however, that the true turning points were likely even closer to the ideal .618 ratio. Even so, the average of the eight closing turning points is .613, less than 1% error.

As in this example, it is my opinion that it is not the numbers per se that guide the Fibonacci relationships most often,

but the ratios between them. Fibonacci numbers themselves
do not mark index turning points or determine price lengths
often enough to rely on any such expectations. Like the man
who has seen a flying saucer land in his own backyard, however, I have found that the Golden Ratio is so inarguably present
in the stock and commodity market data that its presence cannot be doubted.

It is definitely there in the price action, but what about time?

I have found that time sequences fit less reliably into precise Fibonacci mathematics than price swings. However, when
they do, they do often reflect Fibonacci numbers. The distances
between the turning points we just discussed, for instance if
we start from 1929 high (rather than 1930, when the price relationships begin), correspond to the Fibonacci sequence. The
time periods from peak to trough of these swings, in months,
give or take a few weeks, was 34, 55, 13, 8, 5, 3, and 1 month —
all Fibonacci numbers.

Does the Fibonacci ratio govern every degree all the time?

Not that I can determine. My studies show that there are
many times when one should not expect a Fibonacci relationship. Knowing when to look for one is the key to successful
application, and I have spent a lot of time standardizing my
expectations in that regard. No, old Fibonacci doesn't rule the
world. Still, I can't help thinking that if he were a trader, he
might well own the New York Stock Exchange.

* * * * * * * * * * * * * * *

Barton Biggs

Morgan Stanley Strategy Memorandum

February 1986

Over the years I have been sent a multitude of weird and
wonderful treatises on systems for forecasting the stock market
ranging from relative strength to astrology. Technical analysis does
not intrigue me, and I ignore the occult. Kondratieff waves are
about as metaphysical as I get, but for years I have been fascinated
with the Fibonacci numbers and their possible application to the
stock market in the Elliott Wave Theory.

Fibonacci found the sequence had many strange and intriguing characteristics. But most cosmic, if you divide a Fibonacci by

the next highest number, you will discover that it is precisely .618034 times as large as the number that follows. And .618034 is the magic number. The "golden proportion" of .618034 to 1 is the mathematic basis of the Parthenon, sunflowers, snail shells, Greek vases, the great spiral galaxies of outer space and playing cards. It is the most pleasing shape, whether in rectangular or spiral form, in the universe.

The golden proportion has been and is everywhere. The great Pyramid of Gizeh has an elevation to its base of 61.8%. The Greeks also were aware of the .618034 and called it the "golden mean." They based much of their art and architecture on its dynamic symmetry, "whirling squares that seemed to vibrate with intense energy." The secret was lost with the fall of Greece until Fibonacci discovered it again, and in the 17th century, Jakob Bernoulli transposed the golden rectangle into a golden spiral and linked it to nature.

Fibonacci numbers and both the golden rectangle and spiral are broadcast throughout nature. *Science Magazine* has published several scholarly articles on the subject, and my summary is that the numbers are found in everything from daisy petals and sunflower spirals (55 counterclockwise and 89 clockwise) to phyllotaxis, which is the arrangement of leaves on the stalk of a plant. The golden spiral appears in horns, claws, teeth, shells and even the web of a spider. Bacteria multiply at a Fibonacci sequence, and the examples go on and on. The human body has five extremities, five fingers and five toes, and in music the octave has 13 keys with 8 white and 5 black. The musical chord that gives the greatest satisfaction is the major sixth, and the note E vibrates at a ratio of .625 to the note C. The ear itself is a golden spiral.

There are no real good explanations of why the sequence exists. One response is that God was a mathematician; others say it is all pure coincidence and the humbug of feverish minds. Some scientists argue that the Fibonacci sequence and the golden spiral are so widespread that they must be part of some recurring growth pattern. Others speculate that it is nature's way of building quantity without sacrificing quality.

As you would expect, attempts have been made to apply Fibonacci to the stock market, most notably by R.N. Elliott in the early 1930s. The Elliott Wave theorists have been saying for sometime that the fourth Supercycle wave ran from 1966 to 1982 and that U.S. equities are now in the fifth wave of the Supercycle that will take prices to the mid-3000s on the Dow. A killer three-wave downer will follow. Maybe God is a technician.

* * * * * * * * * * * * * *

Now that we have all the working parts in place, give an example of how Elliott works in real time. How about one where it kept you right on the money? Or one of those cases where Elliott helped you stay on the right side even though your interpretation was not exactly right?

O.K., here's a good story that includes both. Gold staged a blowoff in January 1980. It was clear that an ideal Elliott scenario for the next year or two would be an A wave down to $477 because of wave structure and Fibonacci relationships, then a strong rally forming B, followed by a declining wave C down to final target of $388. $388 was a 61.8% retracement of the advance that had occurred from August 1976 to the January 1980 high. In April 6, 1980, gold declined to a low of $474, a normal first stop, and the decline was a five wave structure. That's all I had to know: Wave A was over. In EWT I said, "The first important phase of reaction is almost over and should lead to the best rally since the highs." On May 12, a month later, after prices started to build a base for awhile, I got a little more comfortable. I said, "A 61.8% retracement of the decline to just over $700 should be the maximum potential of any intermediate rally." The reason I said that was when wave A starts in five waves, it's in a formation known as a zigzag. The typical maximum retracement within zigzags is 61.8%. So, it was easy to say the maximum retracement 61.8% should bring gold to $710.

Keep in mind that in 1980, all the way through to the end of that year, finding somebody who thought gold would go under $400 was very difficult. I spoke in Montreal for Jim Blanchard in June 1980, and everyone up there speaking was bullish except yours truly. Although the audience was generously receptive, it was like talking to a brick wall in terms of changing opinions. No one wanted to hear any such thing. So at the time, I was nervous and sweating. It was my first major speech, after all. I was thinking, "Am I crazy? I'm talking about this stuff going down another 45% in value from the next rally high. There are all sorts of things to think about. I mean, Jimmy Carter's in office!" The whole bit. I stuck to my guns, of course. That is what Charles Collins did in 1966 when he called the top in the stock market. You can't buckle under the pressure. Besides, by this time, I had followed gold enough to be quite confident about it. Maybe too confident. I'll get to that in a minute.

On September 23rd, which was the exact day of the high, the rally showed a 5-3-5 structure, which is a typical wave B, subdividing a-b-c. So the wave structure said, "We are close to a top in this B wave." Gold opened up that morning with an a.m. fix in London of $720. The p.m. fix was $710. So at the close, I put out a one-page Special Report calling the top of the rally. From that day forward, gold entered a relentless bear phase, which is typical of C waves. My downside target was still $388, so on August 2, 1981, I was sure we were close to the final bottom. The wave structure looked acceptable, so I said, "$388 should be met this week. Cover all shorts and buy." Two days later, on August 4, the exact low of London gold from the Bank of Nova Scotia was $388.00. Gold started to rally. I was certain we had caught the low. In the next letter, I said to put a stop at $388 and let the profits ride. I thought gold was going much higher. But I had a stop, and its level was objectively determined. Gold had met a Fibonacci retracement, the structure was acceptable, and if gold was going to continue making higher highs in a long term bull market, it had to have turned from there.

The rally took a three wave shape and lasted only a matter of weeks. It went up, down, up and stopped. It never made a fifth. As I was watching the chart in November, gold started pulling back. It came under the high of the first wave. I said, "We don't have a five wave rally. This is not a bull market. It was just a bear market rally."

So in early January, as gold had just come under $400 again, I said, "A break of the $388 level is now extremely likely. I suggest reinstating your short position." That was strictly from wave structure. I was unhappy that my forecast didn't work out, but it was irrelevant financially. Not only did we not lose any money during that period, but we were all set up to go short again as if we had never covered in the first place. And that's what we did. So there is a description of how you can be both perfectly right and very wrong with Elliott Wave based forecasts, yet make money in the first instance and not lose money in the second.

Your story demonstrates the utility of the theory. But as theories for making money in the stock market go, you've really staked out some high ground here, with Fibonacci mathematics, fractal geometry and a mass psychological condition that guides all of history. From both the practical and intellectual standpoints, how come more people aren't aware of it and rushing to embrace it?

Well, they have, to a great degree. But the majority doesn't realize they need it. The bull market is being mistaken for good forecasting. That illusion is temporary, so we will have many more adherents in coming years.

There should be legions of people expanding upon it with related concepts.

Well, I'm doing it, so that's a start.

But there are many more on Wall Street who won't have any truck with it.

Some people reject such ideas out of hand. They grasp the idea, perhaps, but choose not to believe it. They will not expend the energy required to find out if it is true because they have decided it cannot be true.

In the old days, those who understood the theory's immense value did their best to keep it secret. Early on, I was asked several times by students of the Wave Principle to refrain from publishing any material at all on it for fear that "too many" people would start using the Wave Principle in their investment timing, thus diluting the utility of the theory. But human nature being what it is, there is no way the theory will be overused.

Will the Wave Principle win out over those people and become an accepted science?

Yes, because it's true. It has already won out over obscurity in finance. The new science of chaos will prime even more people to give it the time of day. And we shouldn't forget the *incentive* to do so. After all, the Wave Principle may be nature's way of giving us a peek at the future. Of course, that is only a peek, not the full panorama. Foretelling the future with exactitude all the time is not one of the blessings available to man, and likely never will be. But what an advantage some of us now have over everyone else in that endeavor! As in so many fields, all it takes is an edge over the competition, and you win the game.

Does your Wave Principle analysis have its own waves of popular acceptance and non-acceptance?

I find that my services do go in and out of popularity. If I've just called a big rally, people love it. When the inevitable error occurs, even if those errors average only 30% of the time, people give up on the approach. Then they miss its next string of successes, which attracts new people. Its popularity also ebbs and flows with people's perception of whether they need it. As trends mature, few people think they need guidance. As they develop, the psychological stress is high and people desire input. So it goes back and forth, just like the market. Of course, some people are knowledgeable enough to know that market forecasting is a task involving probability, like hitting in baseball. If you have a high percentage of success, you are doing the best that can be done. Batting 1.000 is not possible. Yet most new stock market fans don't get that fact, and they fire every batter who doesn't do it. Which means everyone. And they wonder what the *advisors'* problem is!

What would happen if your accuracy rate increased to 90% or 95%, resulting in a proportional increase in the number of people who accept your forecasts and act upon them. In other words, if your track record encouraged more people to follow your forecasts and stick to them, would your forecasting ability lead to its own destruction? And would the market become so influenced by your forecasts that it would behave in reaction to them?

Theoretically speaking, if everyone felt that Bob Prechter was correct, there would be no difference of opinion and therefore, by definition, no market. But the question is impractical and contradicts itself. You're asking, if I become very successful, must I therefore become unsuccessful? The converse certainly isn't true. If a forecaster is unsuccessful, it doesn't mean he must become successful, does it? Nor is the question necessarily a reflection of causality. If someone is more successful than normal, he will have a period to balance it, to return to whatever his norm is. If a baseball player bats .560 for two weeks, you can be sure he will not maintain that level.

Truly, questions like this are not uncommon, but they are primarily a reflection of the human trait of skepticism. It's a good trait in that it aids survival in many ways, but it is counterproductive in areas where success is a matter of probability. That trait is why I could be right four out of five times and still be met by skepticism. Your question proves my point. You're saying, in essence, that no matter how good my forecasting, you will believe that the whole thing could turn worthless overnight. When my forecasting is bad, you will simply walk away; you won't take the other side of the argument and say it's time to follow my advice because it is due for a period of success. So opposite actions on my part lead to the same conclusion on your part.

So skepticism is unavoidable.

Right. One thing that you and I both know is that I will never be right 100% of the time; so there will be errors. In such a case, not only do the errors generate skepticism, but the periods of success do, too, because everyone knows, consciously or otherwise, that 100% success is impossible. This is as it should be. When the market is selling off against the trend, the standard conclusion I hear is: "The Elliott outlook has failed; it doesn't work." On the other side of the coin is the standard objection in my best years that "Now Elliott has worked so perfectly, it must be attracting attention, so it can't work from here." People say, "Why should I follow you? You've been right so long, you're due for a fall." People always find a reason for not doing what I suggest doing. I never fail to hear these objections, over and over, at seminars and conferences.

The mere fact that people ask the question, "If you or Elliott Wave become too popular, won't that destroy the theory?" provides the answer to the question. As I said, it is normal human behavior to be skeptical, doubting and cautious. It's a good trait. It is one of the tools by which the species has kept itself alive for so many millennia. It's just that in the market arena, it can prevent you from making money. You have to apply caution correctly.

* * * * * * * * * * * * * *

The Elliott Wave Theorist
August 12, 1991

Long term forecasts which indicate a change in trend at the right time will always fail to achieve widespread acceptance. One reason that such forecasting is dismissed is that by nature, human beings project the future linearly, not cyclically. If you think about the consequences of this trait, you will realize that it is precisely that trait which causes the social excesses which produce the cyclicality. A good deal of study and practice (and for most, experience) is required to unlearn the natural tendency and adopt the correct orientation. The Wave Principle is a tool for anticipating trend changes and events; it doesn't merely reflect them. By definition, it cannot be popularly accepted until the forecasted trend is well past its centerpoint. When the superbullish Elliott Wave Principle was published in 1978, almost nobody bought it. Eight years later, deep into the bull market, tens of thousands of copies were being sold. Thirteen years later, except for some minor points, I wouldn't change the forecasts in Elliott Wave Principle.

* * * * * * * * * * * * * *

In your business is it success that breeds failure?

I have had years in which I've been right in the stock market 90% of the time, 1983 through 1988, for instance. And I've had years when I got everything wrong, such as 1989 through 1992. The successful period didn't cause the unsuccessful one; it merely followed it. Anyone who tries to guess when I'll be better than other times is engaging in analysis, and unless he's a better analyst than I am, he will miss profits and take losses to a greater degree than if he follows all my recommendations.

But your own experience can be instructive can it not? In the early 1980s, your following increased rapidly because you were one of the lone bulls anticipating the great rise of the 1980s. By 1986, your public image was entwined in that middle phase of the bull market. You were actually being credited and/or blamed with movements in the marketplace. Massive media coverage of your work reached a feverish peak with the crash in 1987.

Of all of the forecasts I've been right on, the one I'm most proud of is knowing when my own trend was going to peak in terms of social acceptance. In fact, on October 9, 1987 there was an article on the front page of the Money section of *USA Today*, if you ever want to dig it out. In the last paragraph, I said people are going to start focusing on my failures and errors when the trend of my image changes to down and enters its own bear market.

How did you figure that out?

I had studied pop music stars, actors, the kind of trends they were popular in, and what happened when the popularity waned. Television shows are another example. Go back and check and see how many of the family sitcoms and so forth went off the air in 1966 at the end of a bull market, as an example. So I was one of those. I was a family sitcom, I was a bull market with a certain shelf life. I may be the only beneficiary of a guru image who *knew it*.

You could predict that your star was going to go out, but you couldn't change it?

No, but I tried to alleviate the coming damage. When I did interviews during 1987, I'd say, "I want you to point out the fact that I've made errors on markets. I don't want people to get the wrong opinion and think I'm always right, because they'll risk their money and could lose it."

They never paid attention to that.

Not during the uptrend in the image. It didn't fit. One article did, as I recall. The one in *The Wall Street Journal* in March, 1987. So at least it's on the record that I said it.

Didn't their later stories objectively reflect an actual change in your performance?

I had made errors previously, and I had successes during the negative blitz. For instance, in 1988, I was among the top three timers for all three markets I cover: stocks, bonds and gold, in *Commodity Traders Consumer Report*. Despite that record, I got the worst coverage that year. Some implied that I was the worst market forecaster that ever hit the pike. I'd say, "Call the independent rating services; they'll give you the real numbers." Well, they wouldn't bother, because they were writing an article or doing a TV show for the downside of my image. If there was a change in the success rate of 35%, they made it look like 135%. It wasn't emotionally easy to accept, but intellectually I knew exactly what was going on. The key is that the media writes success stories when the trend of a person's public image is up, and when it turns down, they write failure stories. It's that simple. And no, theirs is not an objective approach.

You predicted the change. Did you do anything about it?

I sure did. When 1988 was over, I retired from all media exposure, public speaking, you name it. I knew from plotting my own professional success by way of subscriptions that I had begun a bear market. My worst forecasting years, which were 1989 through 1992, actually *followed* the media's change of focus, which shows that they were not objective and that I got out of the limelight at the right time.

And if you had stayed in?

If you are foolish enough to fight a public image in transition, you will be destroyed. Several former gurus tried to do it. All it did was make things worse for them. The media can't stand someone opposing their image of him. They will just bash you with it until you acknowledge their view or quit. So I used the time productively. I built an international business. Now my trend is up again, and it's time to emerge from the background.

So you're going back on the circuit?

No way. I don't have the stamina for that any more. But you'll see my name around.

But you're not concerned that you could become too powerful? If your forecast about the next big move works out, a lot of people could bail out and cause the kind of deep decline you been anticipating.

The "power" of advisors is a myth. Advisers have almost no power to move markets. People used to say that Joe Granville could move the market. Baloney. He was merely making great calls. The proof of that is his last major call, which he made in 1982. The market didn't do what he said it would, and supposedly he was at the height of his power. But of course, that "power" just does not exist. The impression of the combined trends of the market is the main influence on the crowd's market opinion. Markets are bigger than anybody.

A lot of other people aren't so sure. In fact, in the wake of the crash, some that are pretty knowledgeable about the market, like the internationally famous hedge fund manager George Soros, said that your views had actually pushed the market over the edge that day. And someone else may have believed in your power as well. Is it true that one of your appearances on the Financial News Network right after the crash was actually blacked out?

There is no question that I was blacked out, because it happened twice, across the entire country, on live hookups about an hour apart. On Thursday, two days after the crash ended, FNN called for my weekly commentary, as usual. I gave the whole commentary twice over the telephone, not being able to tell that a nationwide blackout was in effect. As soon as I finished talking, FNN returned on-air. They couldn't explain it, but they knew it had happened, calling back both times to re-schedule. The third time, an hour later, I was broadcast, so whoever did it must have decided I was not making alarming statements. It was my only exposure to the kind of event that makes the conspiracy theorists look as if they are onto some-thing. The only organizations with the motive and potential means to accomplish such a thing are the government and the Fed, unless you believe in the power of the Trilateral Commis-sion.

So, what if everyone all at once became more accepting, not of your opinion, perhaps, but suppose everyone agreed, "It's not always right, but the Wave Principle really is *the* answer?"

Well, let me begin my answer with a quote from a national financial magazine dated October 1977, over eighteen years ago. "Over the last few years, the Wave Principle has gathered too much of a following and, therefore, it has less value today. Al-most invariably, you can write off a technique when it gets too much of a following." How does that statement look in light of the decade that followed it? "Elliott" had one of its greatest suc-cesses ever. Like the Energizer Bunny, it keeps going and going. And I believe its next success will be its biggest ever. The Prin-ciple itself is undoubtedly on an upward spiral of acceptance: three steps forward and two steps back.

Now let's suppose that a large number of educated people accepted the Wave Principle, which is not an impossible idea for say, a thousand years from now. There would still be room for differences of opinion on the market and the future. And there are countless other factors. Even people who practice the craft don't necessarily take action when they get a signal. Un-conscious doubt and worry often foil people's action. Very few traders have the emotional strength to turn even good analysis into trading profits. So the whole line of questioning is in a theoretical realm that does not conform to reality.

The Wave Principle is intrinsically contrarian. Does it have some built-in defense against becoming the consensus?

I think so. The Wave Principle is a description of natural human behavior. This is what human beings are; this is part of their nature — how they behave. In order for markets to continue to go through these stages, a part of human nature must be to believe that such theories of mass psychology are incapable of being defended as a theory — that is, something not worth examining. They must be primed to accept bullish arguments at tops and bearish arguments at bottoms. That means they have to be ever open to bogus theories of market behavior. How else will they create the patterns that fear, greed and hope produce?

* * * * * * * * * * * * * * *

An Elliott Wave Wave

In the late 1970s and early 1980s, The Elliott Wave Theorist's *success in forecasting the gold and stock markets made the Elliott Wave Principle known to the investment world. But the media did not immediately and wholeheartedly embrace the Wave Principle. It was generally described as "esoteric" (*Barron's, *July 16, 1984) and its primary proponent was received in friendly terms, but in such a way as to put some distance between the writer and the subject matter. In December 1984, after Prechter had accurately anticipated the first wave of the bull market, but before his call for a powerful third wave was realized, this description from* Money *was typical: "The man who believes this is neither a mystic nor a quack. In fact, Robert R. Prechter Jr., 35, is a manifestly levelheaded father of two from Gainesville, Ga." Later, after the third wave hit in September 1985, the financial press had an increasingly (and as it turned out fleetingly) tolerant view of Elliott. The tone of press clippings changed dramatically. Instead of arcane, The Wave Principle was an insightful tool which had as "its most practiced diviner," (*Newsweek *February 3, 1986) "the popular guru of this bull market" (*Christian Science Monitor, *August 10, 1987). The volume of press coverage also increased exponentially as big and small papers around the world picked up wire stories hyping the notion that Prechter's Elliott Wave forecasts*

*were somehow guiding the market. Some examples of the mania for El-
liott Wave that unfolded in the mid-1980s and culminated with the crash
of 1987 follow.*

Business Week

March 24, 1986

Outlandish predictions? Perhaps, but nobody scoffs at Prechter's erudite monthly, *The Elliott Wave Theorist*. His stock market forecasts have been uncannily correct. Prechter's buy and sell signals carry a lot of clout these days because of his large following among the stock-index options and futures crowd. "Given the depth of his readership, Prechter definitely has an impact on the markets," says Paul Tudor Jones, a futures trader. "There are few pros who are not aware of his recommendations."

Newsday

June 14, 1986

The Minds That Move the Market

The seers who move financial markets and the rock and rollers who catapult to the top of the record charts often seem to share the evanescent life span of a May fly. After all, they are both creations of good press and often become the media's supper in the end.

(Robert) Prechter attained (his) growing stature because of consistently intelligent calls over the past four years on which way the market will turn.

Prechter, Georgia-born and 37 years old, is a bohemian by Wall Street standards, following a sociologically inspired investment strategy based on anticipating human responses to market highs and lows called the Elliott Wave Theory after its designer R.N. Elliott.

The Media General Financial Weekly

July 14, 1986

Wave Analyst Rings Warning Bell at Top

According to the saying, "Nobody rings a bell at market tops," but at least one analyst sounded a loud and clear alarm at the most recent top.

On Wednesday July 2, with the Dow Jones Industrial Average at a record high of 1909.03, Robert Prechter warned readers of his newsletter, *The Elliott Wave Theorist*, of an impending intermediate correction. Prechter had been consistently bullish since issuing a buy signal in July 1984, at a major intermediate market bottom. But two weeks ago, he recommended that traders take profits and stand aside.

His timing couldn't have been better. The market did an abrupt about face and plummeted from its peak.

Prechter bases his calls on the somewhat abstruse and controversial wave theory propounded by R.N. Elliott during the 1930s and '40s.

Some press reports on last week's market action cited Prechter's sell signal as a contributing factor in the market's sharp decline, but he disagrees strongly. "I think that's a myth," he said. "Had I come out on July 2 and said, 'I think the market's going to go up 50 points on Monday,' it would have crashed anyway. So I have no power to move the market whatsoever."

The New York Times
February 18, 1987

Yesterday, the market got an added push when word spread throughout Wall Street that Robert Prechter, editor of The Elliott Wave Theorist, was predicting that the Dow would advance to the 2,300 level before any correction. He made the prediction over his recorded hot-line service on Friday night.

The prediction sent futures prices moving widely ahead of the stock market, and speculators stepped in to capture the difference by selling futures and buying stocks in an arbitrage technique called program trading, setting off a buying frenzy.

The New York Times
February 19, 1987

"Enjoy the party." That succinct advice comes from Robert R. Prechter Jr., who in the past year has emerged as the market's leading guru. He believes the best is yet to come.

"Bob Prechter set out his long-term case for the bull market shortly after it began in August 1982 with the Dow at 776.92 and he has stuck to his guns," said Robert S. Robbins, a strategist with the Robinson Humphrey Co. in Atlanta. "That makes him the best-known super bull in the business."

Hollywood Squares
September 18, 1987

"Stock market analyst Robert Prechter says that as skirt heights rise, stock prices move with them. True or false?"

The Atlanta Journal / The Atlanta Constitution
October 8, 1987

Prechter Predicted Market's Tumble About a Month Ago

What did Bob Prechter say, and when did he say it?

That's the question investors were still asking Wednesday, the day after the stock market's biggest one-day point decline in history.

Forget about the prime rate being hiked, or Robert Bork's Supreme Court nomination being on the skids, or the threat of oil prices rising due to the Persian Gulf War. What investors wanted to know was what Prechter had said, if anything, to touch off the market's tumble.

Few had any idea, but rumors that he'd turned bearish cause tremors on Wall Street, and the Dow ended the day with a 91.55-point loss, its biggest one-day decline ever.

His method, and his uncannily accurate forecasts, have earned him the distinction of being ranked tops among the nation's market forecasters for several years in a row.

USA Today
October 9, 1987

A Man who Moves Markets

From his home and office in the misty foothills of north Georgia, Robert Prechter can stick out his foot, and Wall Street stumbles.

Prechter has rescued the late Ralph Nelson Elliott from obscurity and made the Long Island accountant's theory the rage of Wall Street.

Although he's now riding high, he has no illusions that will last forever. Like the stock market travels along those waves he and Ralph Nelson Elliott made famous, Prechter knows there are some dips in store... "There will come a time that people will focus on the bad calls."

The Atlanta Journal / The Atlanta Constitution
October 23, 1987

Who is Robert Prechter and What Has He Done?

At Home, Prechter Just Another Guy
Some Unaware of His Impact on Market

The outside world knows Robert Prechter as the reigning king of the stock market gurus — so influential, some say, that when he turned bearish earlier this month, so did the market.

On Thursday Robert James, editor of Timers Digest, a Florida service that tracks and rates stock market newsletter writers, called Prechter "one of the premier market timers, now and probably for all time."

Fred Harkins, who owns a gas station less than a mile from Prechter's home, said he's tired be being asked for directions to the forecaster's obscure house.

"He's a nice guy who keeps his business to himself," Harkins said. "Press people are always asking me what he's like, but I don't pay them much mind."

The New York Times
October 28, 1987

As far as Mr. Soros is concerned, the crack came two weeks ago, when Robert Prechter, the popular market forecaster who had run at the front of the herd of bulls for five years, reversed course in mid-stride and warned his clients to pull out of the market.

"I was stunned by his comments, just

as everyone else was," Mr. Soros said. Mr. Prechter had predicted for years that the Dow Jones Industrial average would crest next year at 3686. In his view, investors would pour into the stock market the same way they had into all sorts of markets periodically for thousands of years, indulging in a buying frenzy that would ignore underlying values in the belief that tomorrow would bring a bigger fool willing to pay even more than the ridiculous price of today.

"Mr. Prechter's reversal proved to be the crack that started the avalanche," Mr. Soros said yesterday.

The Elliott Wave Theorist

March 1, 1991

When I put together *The Major Works of R.N. Elliott* in 1979, at a time when the Wave Principle was virtually unknown, it was necessary to answer those few practitioners who thought that revealing "the secret" would cause it to stop working since so many would then be privy to the true hierarchy of probabilities for future market action. In response, I commented as follows:

> Readers must realize that despite the basic simplicity of the concept itself, "Elliott" is not that easy to apply if one's goal is to do it well. On the other hand, it is very easy to apply haphazardly, and most part-time practitioners do exactly that. Even if the Wave Principle became popular, there would be so many opportunistic hacks floating about their ill-considered opinions that the truth would be lost to the investment majority in the ensuing babble.

As you can see, those were the days when my language was less tempered. However, "Elliott" has become quite popular indeed, to the point that in a single *week* on television there are more "Elliott Wave" commentators than there were in any *year* up until about 1989.

* * * * * * * * * * * * * * *

How big is the pool of analysts who rely on the Wave Principle?

I think there are quite a few people who are proficient in applying Elliott to past and present markets, say perhaps 1% of all technical analysts, which is a pretty good number of people, I suppose. A lot of those are my subscribers, and they learned it through studying the *Theorist*. However, as far as the number of people proficient at applying the Wave Principle for *forecasting* market turns, which is significantly more difficult than applying it in real time, I think there are very few.

This has been the basis of some criticism. To quote one critic, "relying on arcane methods does have one advantage. Interpreting the linear squiggles is left in the hands of the major heir to Elliott's work." How do you respond to those who contend the complexity of the theory is a cover that allows you to retain the Wave Principle as your personal theory?

With regard to any supposed self-serving secrecy, not only did I co-author a book on how to apply the Wave Principle, as well as reprint Elliott's writings against protest from practitioners, but also I continually go into great, some might say excruciating, detail in each issue of *The Elliott Wave Theorist* explaining exactly what I think the market has done and will do, and why I think it. If there is any market letter that has educated potential competitors, it is mine. The reason is that the study of markets is more important to me than exclusivity, secrecy or power.

Another common approach critics take when they try to dismiss Elliott as bunk is to refer to you as a mystic or a prophet, terms which seem to indicate you don't operate with both feet on the ground.

A mystic believes in things for which there is no evidence, only desire. I do not consider myself a mystic at all. My approach is objective. The empirical basis of Elliott's discovery speaks to that fact. So do the results of the trading competition. Not once during any month since the independent rating services have been following market timers has a timer using a mystical approach such as "Gann" analysis ever placed in the top 10 rankings. Just as would be expected, they don't work!

The true mystics are those who believe, for instance, that current economic performance is a basis upon which to predict stock market prices. There is no evidence for it. They just feel comfortable with the idea, so they hold it.

So you say the challenge to validity is on the other side?

You're darn right, it is. I am no longer at the point where I have to justify the objectivity of the Wave Principle. I think the results have done that. Technical analysis is entirely rational and has proven itself. If someone goes back and looks at the record of Elliott Wave writers over the decades, he will find a track record of forecasting success that is well beyond a random result or chance. If you can do that, the ball is in the other guy's court. It's up to him to show that this is luck or something.

What's more, the only challenge to a theory is a better theory, and I haven't seen a contender yet.

You don't feel you have been effectively challenged by any fundamental approaches?

I think there's a place for fundamental analysis of individual companies, but I am firmly convinced that you can make a very rational argument showing pretty clearly that fundamental analysis applied to overall market timing is like reading the entrails of goats. In fact, I plan to present such a critique in an upcoming book. If my ideas are controversial now, just wait.

But that's not to say Elliott Wave doesn't have its shortcomings. We've already talked about the problem of corrections. Another limitation is that of time. Frequently, you can say with some accuracy where the market is going, but you seem less certain about when it will get there. The bull market that began in 1982 is a good example. It took a lot longer to get there than you thought it would, and it's gone further.

Yes, but your objection is that I didn't have a perfect handle on the extent of the bull market *before it started*, which is when no one understood the coming event except Elliott Wave guys! Its value was far greater than any disvalue. But to answer your question, I thought the bull market would last five years, eight at the outside. To date, it has lasted thirteen years. The time factor is the least predictable element in the Wave Principle. Form is unfailing — you only have 13 patterns. Price level is second most predictable, and even there, I called for equality with wave I and we are now more likely to see a 1.618 multiple. *But we will still see a phenomenon reflecting these criteria.*

* * * * * * * * * * * * * *

The (New Orleans) *Times Picayune*
November 9, 1994

"I'll tell you right up front when I've been wrong, it has been on timing," Prechter said. Prechter understands people can be wrong. He admits his advice to people after the crash of 1987 to stay out of the stock market "killed off the image of the perfect guru that the public loves so well."

The market, he said, "was a lot smarter than I was."

* * * * * * * * * * * * * *

Do you think the problem of time forecasting will be permanent?

No, someone may crack the time code some day. I have done a lot of work on time aspects of the market lately and have made some exciting observations. If the DJIA peaks on a long term basis in late 1995, one of those ideas will look very powerful. If not, well, we'll be in the same boat.

Given that time is the most difficult element to predict, how have you attempted to predict it?

There are ways within the Wave Principle to get some pretty good ideas about time, particularly late in wave development. Elliott provided all sorts of guidelines to indicate the upcoming end of a wave sequence.

I also use time cycles, which is a concept completely outside the Wave Principle. But there is no question, going over the price charts, that there is often a prolonged tendency for lows in the stock market to occur at particular regular intervals. There are usually groups of cycles operating at any one time on prices. And it's quite surprising how precise these cycles can be. In other words, if a cycle is X days long, it usually falls within one day of expectation.

But they don't repeat like clockwork, I take it. One has to analyze continuously.

Yes, and that is an unavoidable aspect of market analysis. Nevertheless, I have a pretty good handle on how to determine what the important intervals are. I can also recognize *changes* in those intervals, which is the key to avoiding losses. In fact, there have been times when certain cycles became popular and I knew they would fail. [See *Futures* article below. —Ed.] However, cycles don't reflect the essence of stock market behavior, which is strictly the realm of the Wave Principle. So, many times my cyclic forecasts have just plain flopped.

Where can prospective cycle theory students go to get started?

Two cycles books I recommend are *Cycles — The Mysterious Forces that Trigger Events* by E.R. Dewey, and *The Profit Magic of Stock Market Timing* by J.M. Hurst.

* * * * * * * * * * * * * * *

Riding a Cycle

In late 1985, the Dow Jones Industrial Average was stalling in the middle of a multi-year advance. Due to expectations of a peak in the four year cycle and other factors mentioned below, most observers were suggesting that the bull market was in for a decline. Even though it was past the third year in a historic bull market, Robert Prechter took the contrary view in declaring that 1986 was going to be another good year.

Futures

January 1986

1986 Stock Market Battle: Elliott Wave vs. Four-Year Cycle

The majority on Wall Street "knows" that 1986 is supposed to be a bear market year in stocks.

Fueling the fearsome forecasts are numerous fundamental negatives: The federal deficit is out of control; foreign loans are a disaster for banks; the majority of economists are predicting an economic recession.

On the technical side, institutions are said to lack cash reserves with which to buy stocks. The market is said to be "an old bull," running out of time by historical standards. The four-year cycle, which has been regular since 1934, is scheduled to be pointing down this year. Is there a dissenting voice in the house?

Some of the arguments can be dismissed easily. "Fundamentals," a misnomer for facts peripheral to the market but assumed to impact the market, have never had much predictive value. The age of a bull market per se is no case for a top, as the eight-year advance of the 1920s proved.

The "lack of money" argument ignores the billions of dollars in money market accounts, foreign money and new buying power generated by the Federal Reserve Board and by an expanding economy. A mere fraction of this total would be enough to propel the Dow Jones Industrial Average, along with the rest of market, to its lofty Elliott Wave target.

What about the four-year cycle, which last bottomed in 1982? First, it should be pointed out that, although cycle lows came on schedule in 1978 and 1982, the intervening price action strayed far from the normal profile. So already the cycle was giving some evidence of irregularity.

Look at how the market performed against four-year cycle expectations in 1984 and 1985. You may recall that, based upon this popular mode, the 1984 market was supposed to be up in the first half of the year and down in the second half. The actual path of prices was exactly the opposite.

On the other hand, 1985 was definitely supposed to be a down year for the stock market, according to cycle theory. In addition to being a bearish post-election year, it was scheduled to lead prices into the four-year cycle low due in 1986. However, 1985 may, in fact, end up being more profitable on the upside than 1983.

So what is happening to this widely followed cycle? R.N. Elliott provided the answer years ago. He recognized that, when one of the three main impulse waves in a five-wave sequence is extended (that is substantially longer than the others), the other two impulse waves tend toward similarity.

Because Wave III was the extended wave in the Supercycle advance from 1932 (from 1942 to 1966), A.J. Frost and I concluded in *Elliott Wave Principle* in 1978 that "Wave V should be a simpler structure with shorter cycle lengths and could provide for the sudden contraction of the popular four-year cycle."

Relying on the four-year cycle has caused investors to lose money by holding through the sharp correction of early 1984 and missing the big rise or shorting since then. In contrast, the Elliott Wave Principle provided a reliable road map for the actual course of prices during those years. In dealing with cycles, it is imperative that an analysis be discarded whenever the market deviates significantly from expectations. In other words, if it is broke, fix it. However, the investing public is doing no such thing with the four-year cycle, and their reliance on this concept may have them walking into another trap.

1986 turned out to be one of the best years of the bull market. The Dow Jones Industrials gained 23%.

* * * * * * * * * * * * * *

That sounds useful. But you say working with cycles can be frustrating at times.

I sometimes get letters demanding to know why I don't "throw the cycles out" because the Wave Principle is more accurate. Sure, they fail to provide turns at times, but you have to be flexible enough to deal with that fact. I can't figure out why anyone would want to throw away his second-best forecasting tool just because his best forecasting tool is better! Cycles are sometimes shockingly accurate, and the few times that they lead you astray are a small price to pay for the terrific advantage gained overall.

How do you establish that a specific cycle length exists?

I disagree with the common cycle methodologies and have developed an approach which so far has worked well. I start with a series of momentum oscillators, which are simply rates of change for a particular index. I use the New York Composite Index in the last X number of time units. I use shorter time periods for shorter cycles and longer time periods for longer term cycles. Once I put all of these on graphs, I observe where the deepest oversold conditions have occurred. The bottoms of the cycles create deep oversold conditions in the oscillators, and you can pinpoint them. The same is not necessarily true of prices, because sometimes cyclic forces will cause very little movement in prices but will show up in the oscillators, clear as a bell. Even if the market has made very little progress, — let's say it's gone sideways — if your oscillator has gone from an extreme reading to neutral, it could be time for a resumption of the previous trend.

That's pretty straightforward. What makes cycles so hard to deal with?

There are two things that cause cycles to be difficult. One of them is that occasionally there is a shift in one subharmonic. If you have, for instance, a 24-week cycle and it subdivides into three eight-week cycles, occasionally you find that there is a fourth eight-week cycle that you can't explain, pushing the more severe bottom out eight weeks.

The other thing, which is rarer, is a complete shift in cyclic length. One big key to good cycle work is to stay on the alert for a shift in dominance of the different length cycles. Long term subscribers will recall the shift to the 23/8/4-week complex in stocks that occurred in September 1981. Recognizing that all-important cycle change allowed EWT to forecast almost every intermediate term low in 1983 and 1984. Prior to that time, there was no clear and regular eight-week cycle. Following that crash low, all of a sudden an eight-week cycle emerged. It was just wonderful to trade. It lasted into 1986, which is a long time.

How do you know when an old cycle is going to fail or a new cycle is going to emerge?

The market starts topping and bottoming differently than what you would expect if the cycles you have identified were operating. It's that simple. Often it will give warnings before you experience any losses.

While fixed-time cycles can shorten, lengthen, and disappear at times, it never pays to *presume* a change. The probabilities of success in anticipating market trends is always greatest if you take each indicator at face value until proven false.

* * * * * * * * * * * * * *

The Elliott Wave Theorist
March, 1992

Fixed time cycles are slippery things. There is enough repetition to prove that markets adhere to cyclicality much of the time, yet enough variation to make precise prediction impossible. So what is their value? Cycles are useful in alerting the investor to the probable, and therefore in preparing him to take action if certain market events occur. It is better to buy in an oversold condition than in an overbought one and better to buy near a cycle low than elsewhere. That cycle analysis can help you recognize such points may not guarantee profits, but it substantially increases the probability of profits. If an oversold condition is in effect within two weeks of a scheduled bottom for a 23-week cycle, then it is reasonable to conclude that the probability for a rally is higher than it was before. Conversely, if the market is in an overbought condition within 12 weeks prior to that time window, then the probability for a decline is higher than it was before.

* * * * * * * * * * * * * *

Fourier analysis is used to analyze cycles, isn't it?

Yes, and the results show that cycles do not govern stock prices. I have studied dozens of Fourier-based projections, and the empirical evidence is overwhelming: the market is *not* a result of regular periodicities. Nor is it logical that Fourier analysis should work, because it applies to processes that are mechanically periodic, not those that are of an arrhythmic yet patterned nature. Examples of things analyzable by Fourier are sound and electricity. Ask yourself this: Why in the world should the dynamics of social crowd behavior necessarily follow the laws of mechanical processes? If they did, every statistician and engineer would have figured out stock price movement years ago. But every attempt at this type of analysis has failed. The only way to approach cycles is as I described earlier. Treat them as products of a living thing, and be alert for changes.

Are there any other benefits to the observation of market cycles?

I think cycle analysis is extremely useful for a number of reasons. It trains you to be patient, waiting for possible opportune times. It orients you toward buying into market lows and selling into tops. It gives you a frame of reference for making decisions. It gives you a frame of reference for changing your opinion so you won't be "wrong too long." Finally, the mere idea of cycles puts you in a frame of mind for anticipating changes in market direction, thus consistently keeping you from joining the trend following herd.

* * * * * * * * * * * * * * *

Elliott Wave Principle

While the Wave Principle has some application to individual stocks, the count for many issues is often too fuzzy to be of great practical value. In other words, Elliott will tell you if the track is fast but not which horse is going to win.

* * * * * * * * * * * * * *

You've stated that individual stocks reflect the Wave Principle too fuzzily to have great practical value. Why is the analyst less likely to have success trying to apply wave counts to a given stock?

The reason the Wave Principle is so clear in *aggregate* stock price indices is that the Wave Principle is simply a reflection of changes in mass psychology. Now, when you are dealing with an individual stock, there may be many reasons to buy or sell a particular issue of XYZ; e.g., what the competition is doing, what foreigners are doing with similar products, government policy, whether the CEO is having family problems, or whether the brain behind the company has left. There are a lot of specific and individual reasons why a single stock will be going up or down on a particular day, week or month. So, if you try to follow an individual stock, it won't necessarily trace out patterns that are perfectly reflective of the Wave Principle.

On the other hand, the market *averages* show you whether people involved in the market as a whole are putting their money in or taking it out. When they put more in, they tend to be more optimistic about the future. When they take it out, they tend to be more pessimistic.

The same thing is true of gold. It's a globally traded metal, and it's a barometer of people's fear about the future when it's rising, or their hope or complacency about the future if it is neutral or falling. There's no reason such behavior would show up in an individual stock except when that stock is the focus of public involvement. In that case, its price is heavily dictated by crowd emotion, and we are more likely to see Elliott patterns.

What the Elliott Wave can answer is not whether such and such a person is going to sell GM, but whether or not he or she is likely to put it under a mattress or turn around and buy IBM.

Yes, in other words, whether there's a net money flow into or out of the market. How investors in general feel won't necessarily determine price movements for every stock.

Obviously, though, if the averages are headed lower, a lot of individual stocks are going down.

Yes. Despite the important distinction I have just made, many stocks tend to move more or less in harmony with the general market. An old adage says that 75% of all stocks move up with the market and 90% of all stocks move down with the market.

But individual stocks do trace out their own patterns. Under what circumstances is it worthwhile to act on the wave pattern of a stock?

The best approach seems to be to avoid trying to analyze each issue on an Elliott basis unless a clear, unmistakable wave pattern unfolds before your eyes and commands attention. Decisive action is best taken only then.

Even if your count for the overall market is headed in the opposite direction?

Regardless of the wave count for the market as a whole.

So, a stock can go its own way and act individualistically. Couldn't a couple of maverick performers upset the averages and throw the long term wave count out of whack?

No. The unique circumstances surrounding each company cancel each other out, leaving as residue a mirror of the mass mind alone. Therefore, the progress of general business activity is well reflected by the Wave Principle, while each individual area of activity has its own essence, its own life expectancy, and a set of forces which may relate to it alone. After all, many companies go out of business. That's hardly an Elliott Wave, which continues progressing, is it?

I guess you could say the same thing about an individual investor vs. the group.

Absolutely. An individual's capacity to reason allows him to understand the Wave Principle, and his free will gives him the capacity to alter his own actions so as to avoid the pressures of the crowd and even take advantage of the opportunities presented. But his individual action will not change the forward momentum of the group, just as one falling stock will not change a bull market, nor a rising stock a bear.

Money Making Rules for the Investor

What qualities do you feel contributed most to your success as an investor?

When I have been successful, it was due to discipline, which usually means taking decisive action immediately when called for. When I've lost money, it is because I did not do that.

Describe that discipline.

When I first began trading, I did what many others who start out in the markets do: I developed a list of trading rules. The list was created piecemeal, with each new rule garnered from books on trading. I would typically add one following the conclusion of an unsuccessful trade. I continually asked myself, what would I do differently next time to make sure this mistake would not recur? The resulting list of do's and don'ts ultimately comprised 16 statements. About six months after the completion of my carved-in-stone list of trading rules, I balled up the paper and threw it in the trash.

I'll bite. Why?

Well, after attempting to apply the "rules," I realized that I made not merely a mistake here and there in the list, but a fundamental error in compiling the list in the first place. The error was in taking aim at the *last* trade, as if the next trading situation would present a similar situation. When rules are situation-specific, you can't apply them generally. In fact, they lead to contradictions.

Like what?

O.K., here's an example of the kind of ironies that result. One of the most popular maxims is, "You can't go broke taking a profit." The brokers invented that one, which is one reason that new traders always hear it. This trading maxim appears to make wonderful sense, but only when viewed in the context of a recent trade with a specific outcome. When you have entered a trade at a good price, watched it go your way for a while, then watched it go against you and turn into a loss, the maxim is a pronouncement of divine wisdom. What you're really saying, however, is "I should have sold when I had a small profit."

Now let's see what happens on the next trade. You enter a trade, and after just a few days of watching it go your way, you sell out, only to stare in amazement as it continues to go in the direction you had expected, racking up paper gains of several hundred percent. You ask a more experienced investor what your error was. He advises you sagely while peering over his glasses, "Remember this forever: Cut losses short; let your profits run." So you reach for your list of trading rules and write this new maxim, which means, of course, "I should not have sold when I had a small profit."

So now your trading rules #2 and #14 are in direct conflict. Is this an isolated incident? What about rule #3, which reads, "Stay cool; never let emotions rule your trading," and #8, which reads, "If a trade is obviously going against you, get out of the way before it turns into a disaster." Stripped of its fancy attire, #3 says "Don't panic," and #8 says "Go ahead and panic!" Such formulations are in the final analysis utterly useless. And believe me, this is the typical method used to generate lists of trading rules.

But there must be some steps you can advise for the average investor?

Well, my best advice to the average investor is stop being an average investor. You cannot survive as an average investor. The pros will beat the pants off of you and the markets will too, because what seems logical is exactly what will not happen. That is one of the first keys to understanding how not to lose money in markets. So step one is: stop being the average guy. Get a foundation. And the only way to do that is to start reading.

Can you just imagine deciding tomorrow, "I think I'm going to be a structural engineer, and I'm going to build a skyscraper.

I'm going to go get some wood and some bricks and get going."
You haven't read the first thing about it. You haven't studied it.
People reach the ripe old age of 60, they've worked all their lives
in a business that they know inside and out. They know a com-
petitor couldn't walk in and take over from them without
knowledge and work and study and experience. But they decide to put all their money into silver futures because they're
sure they'll go up. They don't study the craft. They don't realize
this is work. It takes effort and study. To do it right, to be a
winner, you've got to understand how it works and what's going on. If you want to take risks, become an expert. Otherwise,
put your money in areas that have as little risk as possible and
forget about investing. Before you make that decision, understand what's involved. Making money in the market requires a
good deal of education, like any craft or business. If you've got
the time, the drive and the right psychological makeup, you
can enter that elite realm of the truly successful trader or investor.

**Assuming one decides to go for it, what does it take to be a successful
investor?**

Well, let's define "successful investor" as someone who can
profit consistently through the exchange of speculative goods
for ones of higher value without himself adding value (other
than liquidity to the marketplace). Now you have to gather the
necessary tools to do it.

How did you proceed in your own search for an investment philosophy?

What I finally desired to create was a description not of
each of the trees, but of the forest. After several years of trading
I came up with — guess what?— another list! But this is not a
list of "trading rules." It's a list of requirements for successful
trading. Most worthwhile truths are simple, and this list contains only six items. In fact, most are actually subsets of the
first one.

* * * * * * * * * * * * * * *

*Commonly accepted Wall Street wisdom can provide plenty of rea-
sons to buy and sell at any given time. But over the years, Robert Prechter
was asked for investment guidelines over and above the Wave Principle.
He developed six general rules.*

The Elliott Wave Theorist
November 1986

WHAT EVERY TRADER NEEDS TO BE SUCCESSFUL

#1 **A method**. Any time you enter or exit a market, it must be for a predetermined reason that will also apply in the future.

#2 **Discipline** to follow the method. Without discipline, you really have no method in the first place.

#3 **Experience**. The School of Hard Knocks is the only school that will teach you the emotional aspects of investing, and the tuition is expensive.

#4 **Acceptance of responsibility**. Don't blame the news, "insiders," "floor traders," or "THEM" for your losses. Accept responsibility, and you will retain control of your ultimate success to the extent that the market allows.

#5 **Accommodation of losses**. The perfect trading system does not exist, so your method must deal with taking losses.

#6 **Acceptance of huge gains**. When the big winner finally comes along, you need the self-esteem and confidence in your method to take all that it promised.

* * * * * * * * * * * * * * *

What is the first requirement?

Get a method. I mean an objectively definable method — one you've thought out in its entirety, so that if someone asks how you make your decisions, you can explain it. And if he asks you again in six months, the answer will be essentially the same. It must be developed as a totality before it is implemented.

It arrives full blown?

The point is that it must be in place before you start trading. It doesn't typically "arrive" though. While a method has to reflect market reality, which is difficult enough, it also has to suit the user's psychological makeup. To that extent, it must be built.

So you build your house and then live in it.

That's a good analogy. You can redecorate; in other words, alter and improve your method from time to time. You can even move to an entirely new house. But don't move in before the roof is on or all the walls are built. And above all, don't tear down the doorway because the piano didn't fit through it. Accepting the fact that you cannot achieve a perfect trading record is prerequisite for obtaining a reliable method. People who demand it are wasting their time searching for the Holy Grail. The number of people who waste time at it is amazing, and they never get beyond this first step of obtaining a method. They spend all their time designing and rebuilding, and never move into the house.

We don't need three guesses to figure out what your method is?

Not unless you tuned into this discussion right here. In my opinion, the Wave Principle is the best way to understand the framework of a market and where prices are within that framework. Choose the degree appropriate to your trade and buy and sell according to whether the best Elliott Wave interpretation is bullish or bearish. And if the odds are too closely matched, stand aside.

There are a hundred other methods that will work if successful trading is your only goal. As I have often said, a simple ten-day moving average of the daily advances minus declines, one of the first indicators that many stock market technicians learn, can be used as a trading tool when objectively defined rules are created for its use. You don't even have to understand in detail how the market works to make money with a tool like that. All you need to know is one aspect of market behavior: that the market usually stays within certain bounds of persistence as it moves up and down.

What is the first thing you must do?

Sit down and admit, "I need reasons for making my decisions." Then spell out those reasons.

I'm not sure that would be so easy.

Like most rewards life offers, market profits aren't as easy to come by as the novice believes. Obtaining a method comes down to one thing: creating parameters for making decisions for entering and exiting markets. There are two areas involved: opinion generation and money management. Money management tools are techniques to preserve capital, things like stops, where you will tell yourself to get out of a position despite your original opinion.

While this step is the easiest to apply among the requirements for successful investing, it can be a huge hurdle if you
have not done all that reading I mentioned earlier. It is also
time consuming. Most investors don't even bother with it. So
they guarantee they will lose before their first position is taken.

How about requirement #2?

You need the discipline to follow your method. Among the
true professionals, this requirement is so widely understood
that it's almost a cliché. Nevertheless, it is such an important
cliché that it cannot be sidestepped, ignored, or excepted.

Any system with a decent track record will be profitable if
you apply it rigorously and honestly. As I indicated before, using the ten-day advance/decline oscillator with reasonable
parameters, you can make money seven times out of ten. But
very few people have the discipline to do it. Discipline is much
more difficult to obtain than method.

More often than not, a well-constructed system will work, but the investor doesn't?

Well, certainly a lot of work is required. But that's not the
only aspect of the task. Lots of workaholics fail at trading. What
you need is the guts to do what is right when it *feels* wrong.
That takes immense courage and discipline. It struck me one
day that among a handful of consistently successful professional options and futures traders of my acquaintance, three of
them are former Marines. In fact, the only advisor, as ranked by
Commodity Traders Consumer Report, consistently to beat my
Telephone Hotline record from 1983 to 1985 was a former Marine.

The few, the proud?

The few, for sure! Among my acquaintances anyway, this
is a ratio way out of proportion to the ratio of former Marines as
a percentage of the general population. This anomaly implies to
me that discipline is extremely important. At some point in their
lives, these guys volunteered to serve in an organization which
requires discipline and stamina. These are people who asked
for the opportunity to go charging through a jungle pointing a
bayonet and pitching grenades, surviving on roots and bugs
when necessary. That's an overdramatization perhaps, but you
get the point. These people knew they were "tough," and wanted
the chance to prove it. Being "tough" in this context means

having the ability to suppress a host of emotions in order to act in a manner which would cause most people to shrink back in fear.

But you don't seem like the Marine type.

No, I'm not. But years ago while attending summer school with Georgia's Governor's Honors Program, I was given a psychological test and told that one of my skewed traits was "tough-mindedness." I didn't exactly know what that meant, but after trading and forecasting the markets for fourteen years, it is clear that without that trait I would have been forced long ago to elect another profession. The pressures are enormous, and they get to everyone, including me. If you are not disciplined, forget the markets.

Can't anyone follow rules if he puts his mind to it?

A lot of people will tell you that they have that discipline, but when it comes to actually doing it, they don't. The markets aren't merely an intellectual exercise. They're an emotional one as well. By the time the emotions have eaten away at you for several weeks, it's even physical. Trading is incredibly difficult to do, and it's one reason I do not like trading.

The most important factor in the market strategy is learning to stand fast if your system tells you to do so, even when the news, your friends, and the tape are screaming at you to do the opposite. Outside forces don't really affect the market, and never have. People hear horrible things on the news — the assassination of President Kennedy is a good example — and they panic and sell. A crisis may influence where prices go that afternoon, but not overall. You have to learn to avoid that natural human reaction to what looks catastrophic or hopeful. Stick with your system; never second-guess it; always follow it.

You've made this point clear. It doesn't pay to play the news or follow your emotions. But aren't there times when traders can use the news to gauge how strong a trend is? Let's say the news is all bad and the market holds up or only goes down a little, can that be used to say that there is underlying strength in the market?

It's sometimes said that "Because the market is holding up in the face of bad news, that's bullish." That false belief once cost me a pile of money in my more naive days, and I've never forgotten it.

When was that mistake made exactly?

The 1979 stock market rally ended after holding up "beautifully" day after day for a month despite terrible news, heartening many an investor. The situation resolved with the "October massacre." When searching for characteristics of a major market low, pervasive bearish sentiment is more important than bad news per se.

The truth is that news is virtually irrelevant to explaining and forecasting market trends. I say "virtually," because there is a relationship in that much social news lags market trends. There is some forecasting utility in that fact, but only if you have a trading method that recognizes degree, such as the Wave Principle or time cycles. Then certain types of news can be a confirming indicator. In fact, some of the best analysts I know use certain types of media reports as market indicators. Paul Montgomery and Ned Davis use magazine covers, for instance. When a national general news magazine finds a trend so exciting that it makes the cover, the trend is generally one to three months from ending.

News doesn't cause any market movement?

It sometimes appears to affect the market for a few minutes, maybe up to an hour. When it moves the market in the direction you expected, it is irrelevant. If it moves it in the other direction, you can use it to your advantage by quickly increasing your position. Otherwise, news is irrelevant to trends. Sometimes it appears to fit a day's trading so perfectly that everyone "knows" what the cause of the day's move was. Other times the market does the opposite of what everyone would have expected. This unreliability proves that news is not the determinant of the trend. There is almost always enough news to make causal claims in retrospect, which is what news people do constantly. It's occasionally funny to hear a commentator say, "Well, the market is way up today, so investors must not be focusing on the dramatic shutdown of the U.S. government and the impasse between Congress and the President; they must be focusing on the PPI figures, which were unchanged from last month...." And when they can't find a reason in all the day's news for a movement in the market, then they say the move was "technical."

You've established that news and events are not behind market movement. But if you're able to predict at all, something must be

causing the market to move the way you say it does. What is that causal agent?

The psychology of human interaction is the basic fundamental. The one thing that never changes is the dynamics of social psychology. I think it was Bernard Baruch who said that the stock market was nothing but everyone's combined hopes and fears about the future. I take it one giant step further and say that the market is the direct recording of the psychology that later *creates* the future.

Does discipline mean you should stick to one or two markets?

Not in my opinion. One of the most important characteristics of a successful commodity trader is the flexibility to go into any tradable market. If he is "married" to particular markets, he may find himself forcing a trade where none exists. The flexible trader can ignore 80% of the charts that are saying nothing and concentrate on the 20% that are calling for action. On the other hand, if one's method is market-specific to some degree, then specialization can add value.

* * * * * * * * * * * * * *

Elliott Wave Principle

When the market rests, do the same.

* * * * * * * * * * * * * *

What about requirement #3?

Get experience. I can't stress that enough. I don't care how much you read or how brilliant you are, you won't find out how easy it is to lose the market game until you trade with your own real money.

If you buy a computer baseball game and become a hitting expert with the joystick while sitting quietly alone on the floor of your living room, you may conclude that you are one talented baseball player. Now let the Mean Green Giant reach in, pick you up, and place you in the batter's box at the bottom of the ninth inning in the final game of the World Series with your team behind by one run, the third base coach flashing signals one after another, a fastball heading toward your face at 90 m.p.h., and 60 beer-soaked fans in the front row screaming, "Yer a bum! Yer a bum!" Guess what? You feel different! Suddenly you can't approach the task with the same cool detachment you displayed in your living room. This new situation is real, it matters, it is physical, it is dangerous, other people are watching, and you are being bombarded with stimuli. This is what your life is like when you are actually speculating. You know it is real, you know it matters, you must physically pick up the phone and speak to place orders. You perform under the scrutiny of your broker or clients, your spouse and business acquaintances, and you must operate while thousands of conflicting messages are thrown at you from the financial media, the brokerage industry, analysts, the market itself, and your own inner demons. In short, trading real money successfully requires you to conquer a host of problems, most of which relate to your own inner strength in battling powerful forces and your emotional reaction to them.

Isn't requirement #3 just a reiteration or warning about #2?

Yes, this is a derivative rule, just as #2 is derivative of #1.

In essence, you're saying something is going to come into play to make following requirement #2 really hard.

Exactly. And to the extent that it ruins novices, it is worth listing separately. You must learn that if you get emotional over the market, you are immediately vulnerable. It is emotion that creates movement in the market. Of course, few people really want to admit that most of their decisions are emotionally based and emotionally driven rather than rationally based and rationally driven. There was a study that showed up in *USA Today* several years ago. They surveyed something like 200 average investors. They asked "How many of you read the annual reports before you bought your stocks?" I think they got a "yes" from three people. The rest did it on tips and reading the paper, which of course, is influence from other people. That's what it's all about: other people influencing your emotions and your decisions and, in turn, your decision influencing them until a trend is in force.

Once you get emotional, your objectivity decreases dramatically. Beating the market requires a transcendence of emotional involvement. That is not to say you must deny your emotions. Quite the opposite. You must yank them out of your unconscious and view them in the cold light of reason. Then you can devise ways to deal with them.

And beat them. How is this accomplished?

The first step is to try to invert your emotions. Don't use a market rise as a reason to buy and a drop as a reason to sell. Take each move as a potential opportunity to do the opposite. That way, you're more attuned to buying low and selling high, which is the opposite of what everyone else does. Eventually it will become a habit. While this change will not solve the investment problem, it deters you from making the worst mistakes.

Is it possible that the markets are evolving away from the rule of emotion? At some point, will trading be so highly computerized or so heavily hedged through derivatives trading that emotion will cease to be a significant force in the markets?

No way, ever. First, I expect most derivative stock market products to be outlawed sometime during or shortly following the next major bear market. For emotional reasons, of course. Second, and this also applies to the futures markets, a lot of computer programs have the emotional factors built in. Remember portfolio insurance? Its strategy was to sell more as the market declined, just like people in panic. Those programs participated with gusto in the 1987 crash. The same idea applies to all trading programs. To the same extent that the world of investors is divided into those who sell rallies and buy declines versus those who buy rallies and sell declines with "stop" strategies, this ratio will persist in the computer programs, which of course are designed by people. Entries and stops will all be triggered at points that the same people would presumably have chosen anyway. Even today, you can often predict "emotional" days by observing times when the market is about to break a 40-week moving average, which many computerized strategies employ as a trigger point. As new programmers try to anticipate such days by triggering action earlier or to scalp in the opposite direction, what will ultimately emerge is the same market action that would have existed otherwise.

Is there any way to ease into the experience? To take your method and discipline and put it to the test without risking your neck?

Before trading real money, satisfy yourself that your method works. Paper trading is useful for the testing of methodology. Some people advocate it as a learning tool, but it is of no value in learning about speculating with real money. Paper trading omits the emotional factor, which is precisely the obstacle that one must overcome to be successful. In fact, it can be detrimental by imbuing the novice with a false sense of security. He may know that he has successfully paper-traded the past six months, thus believing that the next six months with real money will be no different. In fact, nothing could be further from the truth.

When you start, you're better off speculating with small amounts of real money. Using large amounts of money will bankrupt you early, which, while an excellent lesson, is rather painful.

It sounds painful. Is there any way at least to *reduce* the hard knocks?

There is one shortcut to obtaining experience, and that is to find a mentor. This person does exist, but it is hard to find him. Locate someone who has proved himself over the years to be a successful trader or investor, and go visit him. Listen to him. Sit down with him, if possible, for six months. Watch what he does. More important, watch what he doesn't do. Finding a guy who knows what he is doing is the best lesson you could ever have. You will undoubtedly find that he is very friendly as well, since his runaway ego of yesteryear, which undoubtedly got him involved in the markets in the first place, has long since been humbled, matured by the experience of trading. He will usually welcome the opportunity to tell you what he knows.

Requirement #4?

Accept responsibility. There are many evasions of responsibility that automatically disqualify millions of people from the joining the ranks of successful speculators. For instance, to moan that "pools," "manipulators," "insiders," "they," "the big boys," "program trading," or the Trilateral Commission are to blame for one's losses is a common fault. Anyone who utters such a conviction is doomed before he starts. He has philosophically conceded that the market is random or "fixed." If he believes that, then there is no case to be made for trying to make money at it. Take every gain and loss as your due, and you will retain control of your ultimate success to the extent that the market will allow.

Requirement #5?

You need the mental fortitude to accept the fact that losses are part of the game. My observation, after twenty years in the business, is that most people's biggest obstacle to successful speculation is a failure even to recognize and accept this simple fact. Expecting, or hoping for, perfection is a guarantee of failure. Speculation is akin to developing a batting average in baseball. It will never be 1.000, but the higher it is, the better you are. A player hitting .300 is good. A player hitting .400 is great. But even the great player fails to hit successfully 60% of the time! He strikes out often. But he still earns a seven-figure salary because, although not perfect, he has approached the best that can be achieved. You don't have to be perfect to win in the markets, either; you "merely" have to be better than almost everybody else, and that's hard enough. The amazing thing is that people accept this idea with respect to baseball without a second thought. But they don't accept it in investing. When they lose, they immediately question their very value, or the value of their method or advisor. Even though they may have a great percentage of success overall.

* * * * * * * * * * * * * *

The Elliott Wave Theorist
January 7, 1985

Take responsibility for your own successes and failures in trading. It still makes me ill to read whining complaints. "Some game!" says one writer. "The big players bet on a sure thing and all the other investors are left to hold the bag." "A sure thing?" Give me a break. The market is very tough, but it isn't rigged. Don't sing the "loser's lament." Learn the craft, and you'll use all the market's noise to your advantage.

* * * * * * * * * * * * * *

Are there specific techniques you use for coping with losses?

The coping part should come before the loss. If you take a position large enough to inflict serious financial damage upon yourself, you are a loser going out of the gate. You should determine an appropriate amount of risk in advance. It is important to be honest with yourself. Most people cope with losses by lying to others and sometimes even to themselves. If you can't be honest, you're probably not handling losses well.

Is this where money management comes in — handling the losing trades?

Yes. Practically speaking, you must include an objective money management system when formulating your trading method in the first place. There are many ways to do it. Some methods use stops. If stops are impractical, such as with options, you may decide to risk only small amounts of total capital at a time. After all is said and done, learning to take and handle losses will be your greatest triumph.

* * * * * * * * * * * * * *

The Elliott Wave Theorist
May 31, 1983

Specific forecasts plus a batting average of 70%, along with some sensible money management, are all you need to ride the Wall Street wave like a California surfer. The occasional wipe-out is the price you pay in striving to be a master of the sport.

* * * * * * * * * * * * * *

What about accepting gains, requirement #6? This doesn't sound like a problem. Besides, you've got a nice round Fibonacci number of rules without it.

You've got a point! And when I advocate having the mental fortitude to accept huge gains, the comment usually gets a hearty laugh. Which merely goes to show how little most people have determined it actually to be a problem. But to win the game, you have to understand why you are in it. I have seen this problem stymie lifelong traders, guys who have gained or lost one point for a living for so long that they cannot make the big money when it comes, even when they say they know what is happening. The big moves in markets only come once or twice a year. Those are the ones that will pay you for all the work, fear, sweat and aggravation of the previous 11 months or even 11 years. Don't miss them for reasons other than those required by your objectively defined method. Stay with a position during those rare times when it is hugely successful. Most people can't do it. Even though their method is telling them don't sell yet, they can't stand it. If they get double their usual profit, they get out, and they're thankful.

O.K., so once again, this is a derivative of requirement #1. But what's wrong with a 100% return?

What's wrong with it is that it may not make up for all your 15% losses. Let me give you an example of what can happen when you focus on how much money you're making instead of how it is you make it. Let's say for a full year, you trade futures contracts, making $1000 here, losing $1500 there, making $3000 here and losing $2000 there. Once again, you enter a trade because your method told you to do so. Within a week, you're up $4000. Your friend/partner/acquaintance/broker/advisor calls you and, looking out only for your welfare, tells you to take your profit. You have guts, though, and you wait. The following week, your position is up $8000, the best gain you have ever experienced. "Get out!" says your friend. You sweat, still hoping for further gains. The next Monday, your contract opens limit against you. Your friend calls and says, "I told you so. You got greedy. But hey, you're still way up on the trade. Get out tomorrow." The next day, on the opening, you exit the trade, taking a $5000 profit. It's your biggest profit of the year, and you click your heels, smiling gratefully, proud of yourself. Then, day after day for the next six months, you watch the market continue to go in the direction of your original trade. You try to find another entry point and continue to miss. At the end of six months, your method finally, quietly, calmly says, "Get out." You check the figures and realize that your initial entry, if held, would have netted $450,000. You gave up on a trade that was going to deliver 4,000%.

So what was your problem? Simply that you had allowed yourself unconsciously to define your "normal" range of profit and loss. You looked at a job requiring the services of a Paul Bunyan and decided that you were just a Wee Willie Winkie. Who were you to shoot for such huge gains? Why should you deserve more than your best trade of the year? You then abandoned both method and discipline. In other words, it comes down to a question of self-esteem and personal limits. But perhaps more often, it is simply that you have substituted an unconscious, undisciplined observation — that the market had some kind of permanent "normal range" of fluctuation — and then superseded your method with that false idea. This is requirement #1 again, but again, it is such a common method of failing that I included it explicitly.

Some people, probably even a lot of people, are simply unable to accept the fact that they can earn a windfall just sitting around watching a monitor and guessing that a line on the screen is headed up instead of down.

But it's *not* a windfall. That's my point. There's no easy money on Wall Street. You earned it. By taking all those losses correctly and with the required discipline, you earned it.

Doesn't the IRS categorize capital gains as "unearned income"?

Yes, but that's baloney. It's *hard* to make money in the market. You deserve your losses, don't you? Well, you richly deserve every dime you can make, too. Don't ever forget that.

What is the biggest mistake experienced futures traders make?

They're either too scared or not scared enough.

* * * * * * * * * * * * * *

The Elliott Wave Theorist
December 9, 1979

"Trading consists of long hours of boredom punctuated by moments of sheer panic." — Richard A. Trader.

* * * * * * * * * * * * * *

What percentage of success in the markets is a direct result of a good forecasting method as opposed to money management?

In one sense, it's 50/50. That is to say, you need each to be successful, in equal measure. However, a good system is far easier to come by. It is the conquest of human nature that separates the winners from the losers. Psychologically speaking, then, money management skills are 100% responsible for an investor's success.

Do you feel that close contact with the markets is necessary for success?

If you're not close to the markets, you'll lose money. If you're too close to the markets, you'll lose money twice as fast. You should be just as close to the markets as you need to be in order to monitor and protect your investments.

How often do you personally trade?

It all depends. When it comes to proving a point, like what I wanted do with the U.S. Trading Championship, I was trading pretty fiendishly. I made almost 200 trades in four months.

What was the point you were trying to prove?

I did it to advance the publicity on Elliott. But winning actually served a better purpose. If anyone declares Elliott's theories worthless, the burden of proof will be on him, not me.

What percentage of time is the theory right for you?

The theory, I think, is right all the time. But I'm not right all the time. I've made plenty of mistakes. As a matter of fact, one of the reasons, I think, I did well in the contest is that I took a lot of losses. That may sound counterproductive, but it's the people who emotionally can't bring themselves to take losses that always lose money. So I took losses all the time. As a matter of fact, about 50% of the trades that I made were losers. I've heard some of the best traders in the world make profits on only 10% or 15% of their trades. I think that's a good key, being able psychologically to call your broker and say, "I was a dummy, I was wrong, I blew it, get me out of my position."

Do you get out right away when you find something going wrong? I mean, the minute?

The minute I decide I'm on the wrong side of a market, for real technical, objective reasons, I get out. Sometimes it's at a profit. If you're really good at your entry, sometimes the market can go your way for a couple of days, turn around, and do something that you didn't expect. You immediately call and you find out, "Hey, I wasn't hurt after all." Other times you take a bath. With lye soap and pumice.

* * * * * * * * * * * * * *

The Elliott Wave Theorist
December 1983

If you do not take action when the opportunity presents itself, your next decision will always be an agonizing one.

* * * * * * * * * * * * * *

How did you generate your trading signals in the trading championship?

Most of the decisions were made watching the fluctuations in the hourly chart of the Dow Jones Industrial Average and buying or selling puts and calls on index options. A secondary consideration was where some short-term momentum oscillators were on a short-term basis. A third consideration was where the time cycles were, though that always deferred to the condition of the momentum oscillators.

So you looked for situations where these factors indicated opportunities?

Mostly, I was looking for points at which the wave structure said that a change in trend was imminent. Most of that period, February through May of 1984, was a choppy market with a downside bias, not a one-way trend, so it was tough. But it serves the purpose of precluding anyone saying it was just a lucky guess on the trend. The market overall lost ground during that period, so when I saw five waves down, which I did from time to time, I would expect a three wave rally. I would play for that, selling the top of the C wave and looking for a decline, and so forth.

Did you find ways to leverage your Elliott Wave insights?

I'd say 90% of the trades I made were in OEX options. So I was trading the indexes, which is really the best basis on which to make money using Elliott.

Did you nail a couple big moves or catch a lot of smaller ones?

A lot of short-term trades. No big hit or a lucky move. I think that's the way to trade options. If you go for the big hit, you usually get hit.

And were you mostly just buying and selling calls?

I was mostly buying and selling puts, because wave ② was in force, and I knew it.

What type of options were you trading — at-the-money, out-of-the-money or in-the-money?

Mostly in-the-money.

No liquidity problems?

I had to manage my money very strenuously because I started with a small amount of money, a little over $5000. The whole point was to show that you could start with a small amount of money and turn it into something. So the lack of liquidity was very important factor, yes. It added to the pressure. I quadrupled my money from February 1 through May 31. Of course, with all the trades I paid the broker an equal additional amount in commissions.

It must have been fun for both of you.

Frankly, it was awful. I didn't find the experience pleasant at all. It was very time consuming and emotionally draining. I had other difficulties to contend with. One of the oldest adages that traders will tell you is, don't trade when you have personal problems or when you're dealing with something important in your personal life, and I thought, "I'm stronger than this, I can handle it." Which I did, but I couldn't have continued.

Did the personal problems affect your trading?

After the first month of the contest I was up 380% in options. I thought, "This is great, if I can just keep this going, I'll reach 1000%." Right after the first month, there were extreme complications. My wife was ordered to lie flat on her back with our second child, or she would deliver prematurely. She was not allowed to get up even to eat. So I was taking care of her and our two-year-old daughter at the same time as trading. They're both in the house, I'm trying to run a business, and I'm trying to trade this account all at the same time. I'm running up and down the stairs taking care of our young daughter who regressed at the time because she thought her mother was dying. The account fell to a gain of 190% as I lost money for two months.

Talk about contractions. Then what?

One night, the phone rang. It was the doctor. He was speaking to my wife. He said, "You know you could stay on medication for another couple of weeks, but the baby is big enough now, you can come off it whenever you want." I hollered from the other end of the room because I could tell what my wife was saying on the phone. I said, "You just took the last pill." And

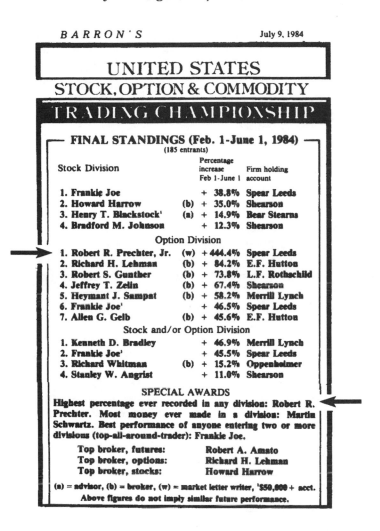

BARRON'S   July 9, 1984

UNITED STATES
STOCK, OPTION & COMMODITY
TRADING CHAMPIONSHIP

FINAL STANDINGS (Feb. 1-June 1, 1984)

(185 entrants)

Stock Division		Percentage increase Feb 1-June 1	Firm holding account
1. Frankie Joe		+ 38.8%	Spear Leeds
2. Howard Harrow	(b)	+ 35.0%	Shearson
3. Henry T. Blackstock'	(a)	+ 14.9%	Bear Stearns
4. Bradford M. Johnson		+ 12.3%	Shearson

Option Division

1. Robert R. Prechter, Jr.	(w)	+444.4%	Spear Leeds
2. Richard H. Lehman	(b)	+ 84.2%	E.F. Hutton
3. Robert S. Gunther	(b)	+ 73.8%	L.F. Rothschild
4. Jeffrey T. Zelin	(b)	+ 67.4%	Shearson
5. Heymant J. Sampat	(b)	+ 58.2%	Merrill Lynch
6. Frankie Joe'		+ 46.5%	Spear Leeds
7. Allen G. Gelb	(b)	+ 45.6%	E.F. Hutton

Stock and/or Option Division

1. Kenneth D. Bradley		+ 46.9%	Merrill Lynch
2. Frankie Joe'		+ 45.5%	Spear Leeds
3. Richard Whitman	(b)	+ 15.2%	Oppenheimer
4. Stanley W. Angrist		+ 11.0%	Shearson

SPECIAL AWARDS

Highest percentage ever recorded in any division: Robert R. Prechter. Most money ever made in a division: Martin Schwartz. Best performance of anyone entering two or more divisions (top-all-around-trader): Frankie Joe.

Top broker, futures:	Robert A. Amato
Top broker, options:	Richard H. Lehman
Top broker, stocks:	Howard Harrow

(a) = advisor, (b) = broker, (w) = market letter writer, '$50,000+ acct. Above figures do not imply similar future performance.

sure enough, 48 hours later, our son was born, and the last month of the contest, I traded great, and finished up 444%.

Would you want to do that again?

It's something I wouldn't want to do for a living. But I think that I could do it for a living if I had to. As long as I scheduled time off every quarter!

What did dealing with those kinds of pressures teach you about trading?

That the essence of trading is to be disciplined enough to fight your emotional human nature. Of course, the stock market movement and the Wave Principle are a direct reflection of natural human behavior. In other words, to be on the correct side of the trend, you must act in a way opposite to what your emotions usually tell you to do in the market. You have to be a decoding machine interpreting your indicators. To fight your emotions is very tough. I recall one afternoon when I had to go upstairs and lie down to avoid making the wrong move. My indicators were bearish and the market was rallying hour after hour. I was about to cave, and probably would have if I had stayed in front of the TV. I was in the fetal position for an hour, then came down to look at how they'd closed. Turns out, I got away from the market within about thirty minutes from the high. The really successful traders of the world have learned how to stay there in front of the screen and not flinch.

What type of investor do you feel stock-index options or futures are suitable for?

If you're a hot-shot speculator and you know what you're doing, then I think stock-index futures and options are ideal vehicles to be using with the Wave Principle. However, there are pitfalls outside Elliott that make these instruments difficult to use, such as the extreme leverage involved and the desperate need for a disciplined money management approach.

So you recommend trading index options?

I would never recommend options to anybody. Sometimes people will write or call and say, "What options do you recommend?" We say we don't recommend them at all. We'd be happy to give you a short-term market opinion, but what you do with that is entirely up to you.

Would you advise a typical investor to stay away from highly leveraged investments?

If there is such a thing as a typical investor, he should unquestionably stay away from those vehicles, because they can separate him from his money in a flash. However, they provide great opportunities for true professionals, people who wish to make a living trading. If you learn how the market operates, you can have a good record of success in calling even the shortest term bottoms and tops. With reasonable stops to contain errors, you can make money with futures and options. But you must dedicate yourself to it and do it full-time as you would any other business where you expect to be successful.

Don't options sometimes fail to move with the market?

Yes. Out-of-the-money options do not necessarily move when the market goes your way. So you're betting on a whole bunch of additional factors when you play out-of-the-money options.

Don't most little guys buy out-of-the-money options?

Joe Granville used to say that he could tell the option traders because their hands would shake when they asked him what the market was going to do tomorrow. In that regard, I was willing to bet that the subscriber who called up and chewed out one of my secretaries because the Telephone Update message was twenty minutes late was an owner of out-of-the-money options. Out-of-the-money options make you angry. They make you angry because if you're wrong on the market's trend, you lose money, and 9 times out of 10, if you were *right*, you lose money. And what's worse, you usually lose 100% of it! Like gambling, these vehicles offer the prospect of a huge return, but only at tremendous odds. I've heard all sorts of excuses, but the bottom line is that if your option expires worthless, you weren't right, even if the stock or index upon which you bought your call is 5% higher. If the underlying stock or index doesn't cross the strike price by a sufficient margin by the expiration date, your decision to buy was wrong.

So you would never touch them?

Not precisely. Out-of-the-money options can be huge money-makers about once a year. If you can buy them just before the onset of a powerful third wave — not four weeks early — and then sell them right at the top of that third wave at maximum momentum — not four weeks late — you reap huge rewards. But playing them as a matter of continuing preference is a one-way road to disaster.

What about at-the-moneys?

For the short term trader, the only options to play are at-the-money because that's where the liquidity is. For the position trader, the worst options to play are at-the-money. You're paying complete premium for something that isn't worth anything.

So the best way for a position trader is...?

The safest and the most productive way to play options is to trade deep in-the-money options. They are worth what you're paying for them. They are forced to move if the market goes in the direction you expect. If you speculate with deep in-the-money options, which carry almost no premium, you will win every time you're right, lose much less when you're wrong, and lose almost nothing when you're right but early. If you're caught in the out-of-the-money option rut, just think about the mathematics, and you'll see why you keep watching them expire worthless. The time to change your tactics is now.

Can you limit your losses on options, say, to 10%?

Impossible. If you can't accommodate big percentage losses, you can't trade options. Sometimes an option can make or lose 50% in an hour. That's why you need defensive money management techniques other than stop-loss.

Do you weight your trades?

Yes. If I have three or four technical analytical indicators all calling for the same direction, I'll make a heavier commitment.

Which atmosphere do you like to trade in more, a bull or a bear?

I prefer bear markets, for reasons I mentioned in *At the Crest of the Tidal Wave*. Bear markets are faster, so you get more action to trade around. Bull markets can be excruciatingly boring at times. Being on the right side of a bear market also brings satisfaction in knowing that only a small minority is capable of handling a downtrend successfully. It's professionally fulfilling to make money while the majority makes excuses and wonders when the trend will reverse to its "natural" direction.

Aren't bear markets also more dangerous?

The January 1987 issue of *Futures* magazine made a reference to turnstiles at the CBOT:

> Aisles in the CBOT Treasury bond pit were becoming jammed by two-way traffic, so the CBOT copied a CBOE idea by putting in turnstiles — two to enter the pit and one to get out.

So the physical reality at the pit represents the market reality. It's always easy to get in. As for getting out, you can exit early, like a gentleman, but if you wait until everybody wants out...well, that's why bear markets move faster. But that really doesn't mean they are more dangerous. Being on the wrong side of a bull market can be worse. The losses are potentially bigger, and they move slower, keeping your hopes up until your capital is eaten away.

Let's look closer at your method, which is first of all a technical approach. How do you sort out all the indicators that are out there? How do you decide which ones you should listen to and which ones you should ignore?

I like to use indicators that help me anticipate. I don't like indicators that make me wait until after the turn has occurred, so I've spent all of my time looking at anticipatory indicators. If I get into the common situation where there are two or sometimes three valid interpretations under the Wave Principle, I use the indicators to help me decide which is more likely. But if an indicator fails me in a big way, I throw it away. An indicator that gives a completely false signal should be discarded.

So which ones have you settled on?

I don't like stochastics or other price velocity indicators that have ceilings. Unrestricted momentum indicators — percent rates of change, for instance — are better. Take the current day's price and compute its percentage difference from its price X time units ago, and do that over a broad time spectrum. Moving averages give signals far too late, as far as I'm concerned. Your goal as a trader should be to buy weakness and sell strength. While top and bottom pickers who don't have a method get destroyed, trend followers by design buy strength and sell weakness, which is a big strike against their potential profit and loss. What's more, every computer jock on the planet uses stochastics and a moving average system, so you're often buying and selling with the crowd, at least on a short term basis. You need to use indicators that allow you to buy or sell ahead of the moving average contingent. Volume is occasionally useful, but only in conjunction with wave patterns. The winningest formula is: (1) The Wave Principle, applied thoroughly and with discipline to price and volume activity; (2) percent rate-of-change indicators of varying lengths, from hours to years, to help confirm the wave status of the market and confirm trend change indications by divergence; (3) a few tried and true sentiment indicators.

Do your indicators as a whole affect the way you view any given indicator? Or does a certain ratio of bulls to bears or a certain divergence from a moving average always mean the same thing?

Many indicators have suffered tremendously because people treat them as absolutes instead of relating them to the rest of the market environment. It is never their *levels* that matter; it is their *relationships* to recent behavior. A momentum divergence, for instance, i.e., a lower high in a momentum indicator against a higher high in the market, is more important than the level of the oscillators.

When the markets are moving against you, what changes your mind?

I don't change my opinions based on how much the market goes up or down. If it goes up, it doesn't turn me bullish. If it goes down, it doesn't turn me bearish. Usually it's the other way around. The higher the market goes, the more negative your indicators get.

In late 1986, gold stocks started up; we had a terrific run-up, more than I thought. But at the beginning I said, "There's going to be a nice rally, but it'll be a bear market rally." Gold got up to something like $390 an ounce, and I said it looked bearish. Well, gold pushed quite a bit further than that, reaching $500 months later. But the technical figures just continued to deteriorate to the point that they were signaling a top of major significance. So it's rare that if it had gone another ten bucks, I would say, well, now I have to turn bullish. Still, there are Elliott Wave patterns that require the market to stop before reaching a certain level, which, if breached, means you have to abandon your previous opinion. Sometimes that means reversing it.

* * * * * * * * * * * * * *

MTA Journal

Summer-Fall 1994

Fundamental analysts rarely appreciate the fact that they must incorporate technical thinking at some point for their analysis to have any validity. Sadly, many technicians don't know it, either. You must always, always think technically.

Let me give you some examples of what I mean.

Suppose you make a good call on the market, a sector, a group or a stock, and your clients tell you they are too afraid to follow it. The market goes your way and seven or eight weeks later you get a call congratulating you on your work. You might just say thanks and hang up the phone and be very self satisfied. Or, you might understand that the phone call has a technical meaning. If you get three more calls that day, you may want to take a good look at your indicators.

Similarly, if you are ever so fortunate and simultaneously unfortunate as to be granted a certain measure of fame...or infame...you will find that publicly distributed attacks against you for all sorts of real and imagined sins are excellent market indicators, and the more vicious and inaccurate they are, the better they are as indicators. The same is true of widespread praise. In other words, instead of taking such things at face value, see if they are a comment on the prevailing psychology.

* * * * * * * * * * * * * *

What do you think of other methods of analysis that come out from time to time?

I look at them all when they come out. Almost every one is some variation, usually very minor, on a momentum indicator. You only need two or three types, and you only need the simplest construction. Advance-decline oscillators and rates of change on the broad market are all I feel I need.

If you want to use an exponential moving average, that's O.K. If you want to have a fancy combination of volume and advance-decline numbers and 60 other things, that's O.K., too. But when you plot them on a chart, they behave in exactly the same way as the simple ones. They give you signals for the same reason — either divergence or extreme readings. So the fact that people can formulate a few new twists on the same old theme and sell them on a disk for $3000 apiece has always been a source of amazement to me.

From a practical standpoint, if you're going to chart stocks, you've got to chart stocks. What method do you use for the indexes as well as individual stocks and index options?

I don't chart individual stocks, and I don't chart any indexes except the New York Composite hourly and the Dow Industrials, and I prefer line charts to bar charts. I mark the Dow Jones with points, that is dots, because the space between them can be very instructive as well, as they show how fast the market moved in the hour.

Do hourly, daily and weekly charts work differently in different markets?

No. The market is fractal, so they all behave the same way. Of course, one degree of trend can be sideways while the other is trending. One of the most interesting comments in *R.N. Elliott's Market Letters* is his comment that "In fast markets, the daily range is essential, and the hourly useful...On the contrary, when the daily range becomes obscure due to slow speed and long duration of waves, condensation into weekly range clarifies." In other words, keep them all and trade with the clear one.

If hourly charts are sometimes useful in ways that daily or monthly charts are not, wouldn't intra-hour, say 10-minute pricing charts on the DJI, sometimes give you an advantage in short-term trading?

Sometimes. But more important, you should use what fits your style. Even when I'm trading extremely short-term, I stick to the hourly chart because I've been using it for years. I'm used to it, and the figures are easily available if you need back data. Besides, personally, my entries are better if I decide that sometime in the next forty-five minutes or hour-and-a-half, we're going to complete a five-wave sequence, and then use any further trend intra-hour to take positions. If I put my bids under the market at that time, I usually come out much better than waiting to count every last tiny little tick. This is particularly true with options. Usually by the fifth of the fifth of the fifth, the professional traders can smell the turn. They can feel momentum waning already. It's too late. The option you wanted to buy at 2⅛ is already 2⅜, 2½. You want to be there at the bid, saying, "I'll buy some at 2¼, I'll buy some at 2⅛, and I'll buy some at 2." I prefer to be there anticipating the low, buying what is coming in for sale. Once the market turns, it's too late.

What are the characteristics of a good technician?

One of the best that I know is Arthur Merrill. Arthur's most intriguing characteristic is his combination of open-mindedness and close-mindedness. He is open-minded in being willing to explore any idea that could be construed as reasonable, yet close-minded with regard to the fact that he requires statistical proof before relying on anyone's assumptions about the effectiveness of an indicator. Through the years, he validated numerous indicators while rejecting, for instance, the utility for stock market timing of the occurrence of full moons — a darling of the astro-forecasters — and also the value of earnings — a darling of fundamentalists. He also wrote an excellent concise exposition of the Wave Principle as an appendix to his *Behavior of Prices On Wall Street* book.

What did Robert Farrell, who hired you at Merrill Lynch when you were first starting, teach you?

Patience, among other things. It wasn't just market-oriented patience, but professional patience in general. Letting things have time to take their course. And, really, this goes back to the philosophy of the Wave Principle itself: You've got to let trends develop to their fullest extent in their own time. What you can do is recognize the pace and adapt to it, and that brings a lot of peace of mind.

Putting Elliott Wave to Work in the Markets

What about the Wave Principle and the way in which you apply it to making money? Is it truly accessible to the average individual investor?

I believe that Elliott is accessible to the average investor. Two evenings with the book, and it's clear to most anyone.

Is applying it an art or a science?

The study of the market must be, and is, a science, albeit one in its early stages of development, as most social sciences are. Therefore, as Charles Collins often said, application of the Wave Principle is an objective discipline. For this reason, only rigorously honest interpretations can be accepted as valid. If you want your hopes or whims fulfilled regardless of the evidence, the market will punish you for that weakness. Take it from someone who had to figure that out the hard way. The worst interpreters of the theory are those who view it as art, to be "painted" with their own impulsive or imprecise "interpretations."

Until the probabilities of the various patterns and ratios can be quantified, applying the Wave Principle will retain many of the characteristics of a craft to be mastered not only by thinking but by doing. *Webster's* defines a craft as a "skill acquired by experience or study;" a "systematic use of knowledge."

That being said, it probably takes an artistic mind to do it well, because the market draws pictures, and you must decide if they are proportioned correctly enough to call them completed. There are types of minds that are rational, yet unsuited for this task.

What do the people who "grasp" Elliott Wave share?

A certain visual sense — an ability to recognize an overall pattern at a glance. This can prove difficult for a person limited to a step-by-step, building block way of thinking.

What else?

What the analyst does is observe the market in real time and compare current conditions with all of Elliott's various patterns to decide which pattern is most likely in force. There are certain junctures that are extremely reliable in terms of identifying where the market is and where it's likely to go next, and other junctures that are not as reliable. So it requires a good deal of patience. It also requires the ability to be decisive, because sometimes a pattern will clear up on a particular day and you must act then or forfeit the opportunity the market has given you. And it requires objectivity and a little bit of humility. If you form an opinion that a week later turns out not to fit the objective evidence of the market, you have to change your mind.

At times, the art must outweigh the science, because Elliott Wave practitioners seem to reach exactly opposite conclusions about a given market. Or is it possible that the odds are just evenly split between an up outcome and down outcome?

Neither. One shouldn't confuse the fact that the practical application of the Wave Principle is an exercise in ranking probabilities with the idea that different opinions are equally valid. Two possible paths for the market are almost *never* equally likely. So, two opinions are almost never equally valid. If two possible paths *are* equally valid, then the analyst who pushes only one of them is in error anyway.

When two wave counts have opposite implications, other evidence monitored by EWT is usually so one-sided that a clear preference can be discerned. Occasionally, the less probable scenario works out, of course; that is what the word "probable" means. However, this occasional outcome does not mean, even in retrospect, that the person who champions a less probable count is or was correct. He was wrong in doing so. A system that is right 70% of the time cannot work if you try to pick the times when you can outsmart it. If you really can outsmart it, then you should be able to alter the rules and guidelines accordingly and follow the revised system.

Are some analysts making things up as they go along?

Not necessarily. They are usually just focusing on a count that by the guidelines should be given a lower probability than another one. From experience, I know that jammed counts rarely work. Twisted "interpretations" that sacrifice some crucial rule or guideline tend to crop up mostly during difficult market periods. Even Elliott did it once or twice, for that very reason. But they are always incorrect and are harmful to the reputation of the Wave Principle.

* * * * * * * * * * * * * *

Elliott Wave Principle

In *Nature's Law*, Elliott twice referred to a structure he call an "A-B base," in which after a decline had ended on a satisfactory count, the market advanced in three waves and then declined in three waves prior to the commencement of the true five wave bull market. The fact is that Elliott invented this pattern during a period in which he was trying to force his Principle into the 13-year triangle concept, which no interpreter today accepts as valid under the rules of the Wave Principle. Indeed, it is clear that such a pattern, if it existed, would have the effect of flatly invalidating the Wave Principle. The authors have never seen an "A-B base," and have every reason to believe that it cannot exist. Its invention by Elliott merely goes to show that for all his meticulous study and profound discovery, he displayed a typical investor's weakness in (at least once) allowing a prior opinion adversely to affect his objectivity in analyzing the market.

* * * * * * * * * * * * * * *

There are exceptions to the rules. Elliott allowed for "extensions," "irregular" patterns, and "failures," which seem, to the untrained mind at least, to allow practitioners to count the waves in ways that fit into preconceived notions of where a market is headed.

These are *not* fudge words. They are words that relate to specific phenomena. Elliott may have chosen some unfortunate terms for naming those phenomena, but then perhaps he was not as sensitive to chronic critics and naysayers as we are forced to be today. In fact, *Elliott Wave Principle* has substituted better words for these, and we use them in our shop. An "irregular" flat, for instance, is better labeled an "expanded" flat, a "failure" as a "truncated fifth."

You've said the Wave Principle is relatively easy to understand. How about application?

The basic idea is easy to understand. The intricacies can take a fair amount of time to learn. But once you've learned them, it becomes an easy step to recognize forms in the market. When you can recognize five wave moves, A-B-C corrections and Elliott triangles, a glance through your commodity charts will show definite buys and sells with no additional work whatsoever. It offers the best reward-for-the-effort-expended ratio I know.

On the other hand, however, you've also said that it is mastered by a relative few. Out of all investors, how many do you think the Elliott Wave method is geared for?

Only people who want to put in the extra effort. That's frankly a very small group. I think everybody will find the idea of the Wave Principle fascinating. People who aren't even in the market find it an interesting concept. But the people who should actually apply it are only the people who want to make the market a very large part of their lives. You can't make money at something without working at it. The Elliott Wave Principle demands that much because the market demands that much. They are one and the same.

It's deceptive — a construct that is simple and easy to understand, but because of the inherent uncertainty, it demands rigorous and disciplined application.

Well, the rules of chess are simple, but winning the game is not so easy.

The essence of the task is to order the probabilities correctly. How is this accomplished on an ongoing basis?

The first thing you have to do is eliminate the impossible by applying the rules of wave analysis. At any market juncture, there are certain events that are impossible. For instance, for reasons specifically spelled out, a small five wave rally following a large five wave decline cannot possibly constitute the entire advance from the low. While a small pullback may occur, further advance is required. Therefore, calling for new lows to occur immediately must be rejected as one of the possible paths for the market. Remaining may be a formidable list of possible interpretations. However, each possible interpretation must then be judged according to its adherence to the guidelines of the Wave Principle, including alternation, channeling, Fibonacci relationships, relative sizes of waves, typical targeting methods based on wave form, and volume and breadth, if appropriate.

The interpretation that (1) satisfies the most guidelines and (2) does so the most satisfactorily is the one that must be considered as indicating the most likely path of the market. The next most satisfactory interpretation indicates the next most probable path, and so on. These are sometimes referred to as preferred and alternate interpretations.

The analyst must then monitor the market closely to determine if and when any one of the less probable interpretations becomes the most probable due to the elimination or decline in probability of other interpretations.

This sounds complicated.

Not really. Often, the best interpretation is so clearly superior that an investment decision is easy. Similarly, sometimes, the top two or three interpretations have the same implications regarding market behavior, also making an investment decision easy. At other times, interpretations with different implications carry nearly equal weight, dictating a "stand aside" posture. In the latter case, sooner or later the scales always tip in favor of one particular conclusion.

* * * * * * * * * * * * * * * *

The Elliott Wave Theorist
January 7, 1985

If you're an amateur, do your own work every day. Use source material as a guide, not the commentary of an untested analyst, no matter how strongly phrased. Much of what is written today is false or lacks thoroughness.

Make sure that the internal subdivisions of your wave count fit the larger interpretation. Make sure that all degrees of trend fit all the rules and as many guidelines of the Wave Principle as possible.

You will know you have arrived when you begin experiencing time after time the deep thrill of discovery and fulfillment as the market follows the Wave Principle and your expectations.

* * * * * * * * * * * * * * * *

Once you're over the fact that you're going to be just plain wrong sometimes, what contingencies do you establish to preserve your investment capital?

The key, in terms of making money, is having a plan for managing losses, which means cutting them short. Trend followers must use arbitrary rules for placing stops. The Wave Principle, on the other hand, is one of the best possible approaches for doing that because it relies entirely on price patterns, which provide a reason for placing stops at certain levels. Let's say that a forecasted weak economy is expected to hurt the stock market. The economy stays weak, but the market keeps going up. If you follow this traditional fundamental line of thinking, what is the basis for deciding you're wrong? If interest rates are high, and the market keeps going up, when are you going to bail out? But the Wave Principle has a built-in method for keeping losses small. When a price pattern that you think is unfolding isn't doing what it should for your opinion to be correct, you must change your mind — you are forced to change it, unless you evade the implications. The Wave Principle is unbeatable for determining where to place a stop-loss order. You're given an objective place to put a stop. It forces you to be disciplined, and in the long run, that is the only way you can have a good track record.

Even a technical indicator, like a put-call ratio, might give a sell signal, and if the market keeps going up, what are you going to do? A market sentiment indicator will tell you there are many bulls around and may give you, based on historical figures, a sell signal at Dow 1000 — so you sell. But then the Dow moves to 1100 and it still says sell, and then 1200, and then 1300. What is your recourse? Nothing, except bankruptcy. You would lose money and lose money and lose money. The Wave Principle won't allow you to justify riding a losing position like that. Of course, you can fight or rationalize the message of the market. I've done it. But that's a personal problem, not an Elliott problem. As Elliott once said in a letter to Collins, "The application of rules requires considerable practice and a tranquil mind."

Do you use stops?

I've used stops in almost every issue of *The Elliott Wave Theorist* I've ever put out. Very few have been triggered. Those that have been triggered have been worthwhile, because they meant I was dead wrong, and they usually stopped us out very close to where the market recommendation was made. There's rarely been any loss as a result. And that's a big plus, because if you can make a lot of money when you're right and keep yourself from losing a bunch when you're wrong, you've got a good system.

I have also gone a few times without a stop because I was so certain. That has worked every time but one, when I shorted stocks and they kept on going up. Live and learn.

When you were in the trading championship, what kind of a percentage did you establish as the limit for how much you were going to allow yourself to lose?

I didn't. You can't successfully use a fixed percentage to take a loss. All stop-loss decisions must be objective, that is, based on a reason to say "I'm wrong." Let's suppose I'm bearish on the market, and we get an up day, and I buy a put, and then the next day is up. That means one of two things. It either means I'm wrong, or it's an opportunity to buy another put cheaper. If all the evidence is still saying I'm right, I'll buy another put. That way, I'm using the Wave Principle properly. The decision is not arbitrary. Let's suppose the market continues in the direction I did not expect. It may still be well within the bounds of a corrective process, in which case I would use the opportunity to buy another put. But if something happens in the wave structure to say I'm wrong, that's when I get out, right then and there. So I use the market itself to tell me when I'm wrong. That's my stop. Any other type of stop is arbitrary.

What's wrong with saying before you get in, if this loses 10%, I'm out of there?

You will take a lot of losses that are unnecessary. What happens after you take the loss and the market goes the way your method said? Do you then re-enter the trade at a worse price? With another arbitrary stop that can be hit again? That is a formula for disaster. A 10% stop is arbitrary. You cannot base a system on the arbitrary.

Arbitrary if you say, "I'm not going to lose more than 10%, that's it?"

Why not 9%? Why not 11%?

You have the choice...

To decide on what grounds? Look, your intellectual goal is to be right on your analysis. Your practical goal is to trade according to it. Ideally you should know before taking the trade at what point in your market analysis you will come to the conclusion that your prior conclusion was incorrect.

Is trading with options the same in that regard?

Well, you can't put stops on an options trade; you have to pick up the phone and call in a sale. So you have to approach options from a little different frame of mind than you would a futures contract. If your option is down 50%, by the time your phone call hits the floor, it might be down 80%, in which case you're probably selling the low. In fact, at that point, it may be a screaming buy. You might want to add to your position so that a bounce back to 50% of the original price will get you even. The whole point is, what does the wave structure say? If it says you're still right — the trend is going to turn in this particular direction — then you may want to add to your position.

Let's switch to your thoughts about the profession of investing. Why is it that most mutual fund managers are not able to consistently beat the S&P?

There is only a small percentage of independent thinkers in the money management field. The statistics on how well the funds have done proves that. You find that 80% underperform the S&P 500, and except in big bull markets, a large percent underperform passbook savings accounts. Obviously, the number of independent thinkers is very small in relationship to the total. You can see it in the excellent records of some managers over long periods of time. They think independently, they do their own research, they are contrarians, and they look for value and all the things that you hear people say over and over but hardly ever do. But someone has to pay the costs of having a market — in other words, paying brokers and market makers to do their job. All those transaction costs come out of people's accounts. They're paying to keep the machine oiled, which means that everybody can't beat the averages.

You're saying that trading long-term trends makes the most economic sense, but you made a fantastic return trading 200 times in three months.

I paid my broker as much as I made in profits. I spent as much on trades as I profited. You have to be really right to do that.

Much of what you've said so far speaks to traders and investors alike, but it seems like your overall focus is more like that of a trader. For those that don't want to speculate, are all the guidelines the same?

All investment is speculation, and there is no speculation more dangerous than one that is confidently viewed by the majority as an investment. Take long term bonds in 1946, for instance. Or gold in 1980. Or stocks here in 1995.

Let's say you're in charge of writing the regs for money managers. You're now at the head of the new national agency involved in making certain retirement funds are properly managed. What would be your first step?

First of all, I think the whole concept is immoral. I don't think any government agency should tell people how to invest or who to invest with. Second, the average regulator is a fundamentalist. He thinks that in order to buy the stock of a company that sells textbooks, you have to go out and make a case that the schools will have a greater need for textbooks next year. That just isn't the case. So, you really can't set rules. The only way to judge the efficacy of a method in the long run is by whether the guy makes money consistently or not.

You've stated that the waves are there to the smallest possible degree. But can a short term trader use Elliott to manage the micro-waves profitably?

One of the great things about the Wave Principle is that you can chose which of the trends you want to trade with. If you bought stocks in 1982 and said "I'm just going to hold these until this giant cycle is over," I'd say that's a perfectly good investment strategy. It is also perfectly all right to have attempted to exit for the intermediate corrections. Some people are day traders, and the Wave Principle is applicable to that, too. R.N. Elliott discovered the basic pattern of market movements, and he found this pattern over and over, even on the smallest degree charts. If you chart tick by tick, you can see it recurring, and I know some super short-term floor traders who try to trade off of that. Of course, they don't pay commissions.

This ability to reflect both microscopic *and* telescopic price trends is one of the things that makes the Wave Principle a unique instrument of stock market observation. But what about when the microscope is telling you one thing, and the telescope is telling you the other, do you play favorites?

Very rarely during the bull trend of the 1980s did I recommend shorting stocks. Selling yes, but not shorting. Obviously there were periods of time when shorting would have been lucrative. However, my philosophy of recommended action is to use the underlying trend to the best advantage. It's very difficult, for instance, to make money on the long side in bear market rallies. If you've seen the start of a bull market, you know the difference. Then people are eager to sell because the profits have come so easily they can't believe their luck. Thus when I perceive that the major trend is up, I will suggest buying, selling and re-buying. When the major trend appears to be down, I will suggest shorting, covering and re-shorting. This way errors in timing will have a better chance of being redeemed by the overall trend. When you assess the underlying trend incorrectly, you lose money, of course, but even then, because you are trading the moves at one smaller degree, you don't get hurt too badly. Unless you're wrong on both, which has happened. But the odds of that occurring are low enough to survive it happening from time to time.

For you, the difference between investing and trading is more a matter of reasoning down from the Grand Supercycle degree. That's more subtle than what most market observers would argue. Most say that trading is buying and selling and investing is buying and holding. You've always made your views on the buy and hold approach quite clear — whether we acknowledge it or not, we're all market timers.

The difference between investing and trading is simply a matter of the degree of trend. Speculating on the minor trends is called "trading," while speculating on the major trends is called "investing." There is no other difference. That's why I use the words interchangeably when I discuss strategies. Everyone must have a market opinion at some degree of trend, even if he denies that he does. A buy-and-holder is bullish because of recent history, so he is bullish at Primary, Cycle or perhaps Supercycle degree. Or all three. If he sells later because he's worried, he has made a market timing decision. If he doesn't sell, he has retained his opinion. But he still has one. Investors' actions require a timing of entry, whether the timing is approached emotionally or rationally. Sometimes people's timing is unrelated to a market timing decision. For instance, someone might sell a stock because there is a family medical emergency. But it is preferable to have good timing reasons behind your decision.In your approach to investing, you also make some other important distinctions that are left out or contradicted by the financial planning manuals. What's the difference between being an investor and a trader?

Diversification and Other Myths

The other concept that the consensus in recent years has made almost synonymous with investing is the idea of diversification. It is very nearly universally held that risk is reduced through acquisition of a broad based portfolio of any imaginable investment category. Where do you stand on diversification?

Diversification for its own sake means you don't know what you're doing. If that is true, you might as well hold Treasury bills or a savings account. My opinion on this question is black and white, because the whole purpose of being a market speculator is to identify trends and make money with them. The proper approach is to take everything you can out of anticipated trends, using indicators that will help you do that. Those few times you make a mistake will be made up many times over by the successful investments you make. Some people say that is the purpose of diversification, that the winners will overcome the losers. But that stance requires the opinion that most investment vehicles ultimately go up from any entry point. That is not true, and is an opinion typically held late in a period when it *has been* true. So ironically, timing is often the thing that kills people who ignore timing.

Sometimes the correct approach will lead to a very diversified portfolio. There are times I have been long U.S. stocks, short bonds, short the Nikkei, and long something else. At other times, however, a very concentrated market position is indicated. My advice from mid-1984 to October 2, 1987, for instance, was to remain 100% invested in the U.S. stock market. I wasn't interested in the long side of the debt markets, and I wasn't interested in the precious metals. So I said to stay with stocks. During the bull market, I raised the stop-loss at each point along the wave structure where I could identify definite points of support. If I was wrong, investors would have been out of their positions. The potential was five times greater on the upside than the risk was on the downside, and five times greater in the stock market than any other area. Twice recently, in 1993 and 1995, I have had big positions in precious metals mining stocks when they appeared to me to be the only game in town. In 1993, it worked great, and they gained 100% in ten months. Diversification would have eliminated the profit. In 1995, I'm still waiting, but the point remains. And every so often, an across-the-board deflation smashes *all* investments at once, and the person who has all his eggs in one basket, in this case *cash*, stays whole while everyone else gets killed.

* * * * * * * * * * * * * * *

The Elliott Wave Theorist
April 29, 1994

It is repeated daily that "global diversification" is self evidently an intelligent approach to investing. In brief, goes the line, an investor should not restrict himself to domestic stocks and bonds, but also buy stocks and bonds of as many other countries as possible to "spread the risk" and ensure *safety*. Diversification is a tactic always touted at the end of global bull markets. Without years of a bull market to provide psychological comfort, this apparently self evident truth would not even be considered. No one was making this case at the 1974 low. During the craze for collectible coins, were you helped in owning rare coins of England, Spain, Japan and Malaysia? Or were you that much more hopelessly stuck when the bear market hit?

EWT's position has been that successful investing requires one thing: anticipating successful investments, which requires that one must have a method of choosing them. Sometimes that means holding many investments, sometimes few. Recommending diversification so that novices can reduce risk is like recommending that novice skydivers strap a pillow to their backsides to "reduce risk." Wouldn't it be more helpful to advise them to avoid skydiving until they have learned all about it? Novices should not be investing; they should be saving, which means acting to protect their principal, not to generate a return when they don't know how. For the knowledgeable investor, diversification for its own sake merely *reduces profits.* Therefore, anyone championing investment diversification for the sake of safety and no other reason has no method for choosing investments, no method of forming a market opinion, and should not be in the money management business. Ironically yet necessarily given today's conviction about diversification, the deflationary trend that will soon become monolithic will devastate nearly all financial assets except cash. If you want to diversify, buy some 6-month Treasury bills along with your 3-month ones.

* * * * * * * * * * * * * *

Do you have to forecast the trends with a lot of specificity to make money?

Forecasting the stock market in detail is infinitely more difficult than merely deciding whether to be long or short. The decision to be long or short gives the analyst a 50/50 chance of being right over any chosen time period, and even if he's wrong, in some circumstances he can wait for the trend he expected to emerge. *Forecasting* the shape, extent and time element of the market, however, is an exercise that must always produce some degree of failure, since no forecast could ever be perfect. The market has an infinite number of options in terms of the path it chooses to take in making either the "longs" or the "shorts" profitable. So forecasting, which is what I try to do in *The Elliott Wave Theorist,* is much harder.

If forecasting is harder than trading, why aren't more market forecasters good traders?

Forecasting and trading are two different skills. Forecasting may come after some study, whereas if you add the serious and heavy emotional trauma of trading real money, an individual may not be able to think so clearly. It is a different skill. Conquering your emotions and being able to act with discipline are two things that successful traders can do that the successful forecaster doesn't necessarily need to perform successfully. Good forecasting is required for good trading, but it alone cannot guarantee profits. If you are wrong on market direction only two times in five, you have an amazing forecasting record. But if one of the wrong times wipes you out, you are a lousy trader.

Do you invest in the markets you tell other people to invest in?

I always follow my own advice. Who else's would I follow?

Do you trade the way you did in the contest much?

Not any more. I'm lousy at it when I'm only paying part-time attention. I just can't write my newsletter, run a business, and be a professional short term options trader at the same time. But I do invest in the long term trends according to the Elliott Wave outlook.

Do you believe predicting the market can be learned?

Yes. Competent market forecasting is not based upon revelation, instinct or gut feel, but upon knowledge. The field is not embodied in a single course or textbook, however. So the information is more difficult to attain than that for many fields. Nevertheless, as in the field of physics, some people are just not cut out for it.

How can I become an expert forecaster?

The first key is what doesn't matter. Only then are you ready to learn what does. But in the meantime, here are two axioms to live by: (1) Put 100% of your effort into dealing with the markets, but don't expect to get 100% of your fulfillment from it. Make sure other parts of your life matter to you. (2) Don't get married in October. You'll find out that during half your anniversaries, the market is collapsing.

Over the years, one of the striking aspects of your letter is the way it has pieced together the big picture in the financial markets, one wave count at a time. Most other services take the opposite approach. They deduce the direction of the markets by extrapolating down from an elaborate world view or one key market that is said to sway all the others. The influence of the bond markets and interest rates is probably the best example. Everything boils down to the Fed or whatever. By doing just the opposite, you have consistently confounded your colleagues and anticipated sweeping global trends, like the shift away from inflation in 1980. In your own mind, however, do you have any way of reconciling all your forecasts with each other?

I learned my lesson early to treat each market separately, to analyze stocks, bonds and gold on the basis of their own wave structures, without regard to whether they "fit" the other markets. The reason is that markets very often don't fit together, according to conventional concepts. By the time the consensus recognizes the obvious "fact" that when market A moves, market B moves in apparent response, the markets change their behavior. When I did try to "make the markets fit," I found that I made more mistakes. And six months after the fact, there was always a fundamentalist around to explain how the forces of x-flation had caused the changed relationship.

If my forecast for stocks or bonds or gold is incorrect, so be it. It's happened before, at which time I just have to adjust for an error in one market. When I insist that they fit together based upon some presumed relationship, I often find myself wrong on more markets.

But we've seen bonds and stocks rise together for more than a decade. Before that they were both in bear markets. Don't you feel like it would be risky to predict that one would rise and the other fall?

Let's answer that with something that R.N. Elliott was big on: historical observation, i.e., empirical research, not ivory-tower theory. Let's look at one forty-two year period. In 1942, interest rates were less than 3% and the Dow stood at 95. By 1984, after a steady and nearly unrelenting climb in nominal interest rates to the 10-12% area, with real interest rates near their highest level in United States history, the Dow was not at 20, it was at 1200, up over 1163%. Does that fit the theory?

Now let's look at a shorter period. In 1976, with the Dow at 1000, short term interest rates were 4%; by 1984, with short term rates at 10%, the Dow was not at 300, but at 1200, and the Dow has been the worst performing index! Had you shorted stocks in 1976 based on a certain knowledge of where interest rates would be eight years later, you would not only not have become incredibly rich, you would have lost money. Doesn't it strike you as odd that no one was running around that year screaming that "rising rates are bullish for stock prices?"

* * * * * * * * * * * * * * *

The Elliott Wave Theorist
June 2, 1986

> Wait a minute. Stocks hit a new high on Friday, and bonds hit a new correction low on the same day? Isn't that supposed to be impossible? Aren't bonds and stocks always in "lock step?" Yep, like gold and silver and platinum and oil and the Tierra del Fuegan army.

* * * * * * * * * * * * * *

Well, what about over short term periods?

Well, in 1976, when rates were 4%, the Dow stood at 1000; in February 1980 after an unrelenting climb in short term interest rates to above 16%, the Dow stood at 870, only 130 points lower. In the final collapsing wave of bond prices during that period, from December 1979 through February 1980, the Dow actually rose a net 50 points. The ensuing 130-point drop in the Dow accompanied a sharp *drop* in rates. So percentage-wise, the Dow lost more when rates finally fell than when they quadrupled. Notice I'm not using a minor example. This was a time of the most dramatic moves in interest rates ever. The theory that interest rates "kill" stocks would have had the DJIA at 100.

Let's take some even shorter periods. In 1980-1981, bond prices dropped from 87 to 55, a whopping 32 points in a defla-tionary environment. The net drop in the Dow during that period of interest rate agony was a mere 52 points. A decline, yes, but hardly a disaster. A bit later, cash T-bonds registered an inter-mediate term top on November 4, 1982, and declined until May 30, 1984. The net decline in the Dow?...Whoops! It was a net advance of 50 points!

What about short term rates during that period?

Well, yields on 3-month cash T-bills bottomed on August 13, 1982 at just below 7.5%. Not only was that not bearish for stocks, but the Dow ended its great bear market on August 12th, almost the very same day! As short rates rose steadily to above 11% by August 28, 1984, the Dow rose 444 points, a full 56%.

Move ahead ten years and take a look at 1994. The bond market had its biggest 13-month decline in U.S. history, and stocks were unchanged.

O.K., maybe rising rates aren't always bearish. But we know from the experience of the last 15 years that *falling* rates are *bullish* long term.

If you had lived in the 1930s, you might conclude, as the consensus did, that falling interest rates are *bearish* for stock prices. As stock market historians know, the biggest crash in our history, 1929-1932, was accompanied by falling short term interest rates. The recovery was accompanied by rising rates. At the time, the theory was that stocks and bonds compete for investment capital. So as bond prices rise, money is being pulled out of stocks; as bond prices fall, more money is shifting to stocks. Sounds perfectly sensible, doesn't it?

Yes. In fact, I can't refute it. On the other hand, I don't see anything wrong with the idea that high interest rates, which means *falling* bond prices, compete with stocks. You hear it every time bond prices fall with stocks, people must be putting more money into short term bills, so there is less money for stocks. It makes perfect sense, but it is the opposite point.

Whatever. You should know that even if the evidence had revealed a strong correlation between the stock and bond markets, I wouldn't have changed my mind on the idea of keeping the analysis of each market separate. Market relationships change, as we've seen many times in recent years, and wave analysis is the most reliable forecasting tool available. So use your tools for the job they were designed for.

More important, don't believe everything the so-called experts tell you. Check the charts yourself; you'll be light-years closer to an intelligent decision. There's nothing like a few facts to confound a myth.

But there are times when interest rates at least seem to affect stock prices.

That's true. And it's also the basis of the trap. If a correlation works *sometimes*, how do you know when it will change? And what do you do about it? Let's consider a real-world example, the 1986-1988 period. Bonds made a multi-year high in April 1986. The Dow rose 40% during the next sixteen months as interest rates rose. They rose so far that stocks succumbed to the 1987 crash. But that's easy to say only in retrospect. Besides, the stock market indicators gave a "sell" near the high of the stock move. If they hadn't, and bonds had stopped falling earlier, then the market would never have succumbed. If there is a lagging relationship at times, which many people claim, then one must discern the lag with some method. And market analysis remains the best method. At most, I keep an eye on other markets as an indication of the economic background for the market I'm following. They can help direct your gaze at the right indicators sometimes, but they are not a substitute for market analysis.

What about the trend of the dollar? Doesn't that affect the bond market, which sometimes affects the stock market?

The Wall Street Journal recently repeated the conventional wisdom that a weak dollar is bearish for stocks. And here the dollar has fallen relentlessly from 1985 to 1995, during which time the DJIA has more than tripled. The desire to cling to a false causality is stronger than reason in the investment marketplace. It will ever be thus. But *you* can be diligent. Study the trends side by side. If you find a useful correlation, I'd love to see it.

Well, maybe the rising stocks are just adjusting for the weak dollar. I mean, if a currency is devaluing, then maybe stocks can rise to reflect that fact.

You should write for *The Wall Street Journal*. Question: Then why didn't stocks collapse in 1984-1985, when the dollar soared? And why is everyone desperately hoping for a rising dollar now to make stocks go up? And why is it one way one time and another way another time? These are either difficult questions, or impossible ones if there is no consistent correlation. So considering them either complicates your work or ruins it, take your choice.

I've always heard that interest rates and gold trend together, as both reflect the pressure of inflation. Is that wrong, too?

Very wrong. Sometimes when deflation reigns, rates soar and precious metals collapse. Just look at 1980-1982.

Well, what about gold and other commodities?

Aargh!

* * * * * * * * * * * * * *

Investment Vision

July/August 1990

Before he became editor of *The Elliott Wave Theorist*, Prechter began investing in the early 1970s by buying South African gold stocks. He believed that gold was about to experience a major price rise, and he guessed right. The price quadrupled, and his stocks fared even better.

In 1974, after gold had dropped back to $130 an ounce, Prechter foresaw another big price rise, and bought another round of gold stocks. Here, too, he was right: gold rose to $200. But this time, to his surprise, his stocks languished. The metal moved up, but the companies that mined it did not.

In early 1975, Prechter had a similar experience, when he was convinced that the Dow was about to soar. To prepare for the upsurge, he bought half a dozen low-priced stocks. He was right about the Dow, which swelled by an astounding 25%. But the stocks lagged far behind, rising only 5% — just about enough to cover commissions.

From these two experiences, Prechter learned that even markets that appear to be intimately related don't always move in tandem. Gold stocks generally follow price changes in gold, but not always. And if you're betting on a rise in the Dow, don't assume that smaller stocks will necessarily follow.

* * * * * * * * * * * * * *

O.K., so the relationships among markets, if any, can change. Can market behavior itself change?

Almost every time I meet a group of people at a seminar, I hear a passionately argued case that the market is acting completely differently today from the way it did in years gone by. Some argue that options have increased volatility by encouraging manipulation; others argue that options have decreased volatility because of the ability to hedge. Some argue that technology has speeded up the markets because of instant access to information. Others argue that technology has slowed down the markets because it makes them more efficient. Some say that futures serve to decrease the volume on the NYSE because they have attracted trading money. Others say that futures have caused an increase in volume on the NYSE because they allow market makers to accept huge blocks of stock, covered with options, which they then redistribute. Last but not least is the old favorite: the market "doesn't make sense any more" — as if it was crystal clear in real time in the past.

As I see it, markets are people, and people never change. The specific tools of the trade are irrelevant to the dynamics of the process. This isn't just a theory. You can prove it to yourself by studying the price action of past markets. It is unlikely that there is a soul on Wall Street who could recognize a difference in either price or volume behavior between a chart of today's stock market and one of a comparable period 40 years ago. And from my standpoint, the wave patterns are still there. The ebb and flow of volume is the same. Prices still channel, and they still meet standard mathematical targets.

You mentioned that forecasting is harder than choosing to be long or short. Why do you bother to forecast — to guess in detail about what's going to happen — when it would be so much easier to just tell people to get in or out?

For one thing, the advice would have to be different depending upon what class of investors an analyst is addressing. If he expects the market to be "up" next week, he might say "buy," with option traders in mind. However, if that rise is to be the final "up" week in an eight-month advance, the better advice for institutional portfolios might be "sell aggressively." If he has no expectations regarding the future, to many investors his advice is useless. In other words, investment conclusions imply a forecast anyway. So you should give your followers your entire perspective, which is the most valuable service you can provide to them. It allows each individual to tailor his own actions to his own situation.

Another aspect is that forecasting gives you a framework for decision making. You still have to be right on the 50/50 question often enough to be net profitable. So you need a method to do that, and projecting trends is part of my method. If the market doesn't follow my forecast, I need to rethink my position.

In general, is there any way for a person to tell a good forecast from a bad one?

There is a subtle way to tell a potentially useful forecast from a useless one. Most published forecasts are at best descriptions of what already has happened. I never give any forecast a second thought unless it addresses the question of the point at which a change in trend may occur. As an example outside the markets, a sportswriter for the *Atlanta Journal* published his ratings (scale 1 5) for each of the players on the Braves baseball team as a forecast of how they would perform in 1984. At the start of the season, he rated 1983's Most Valuable Player a "5," Atlanta's slugger a "4," and the right fielder a lowly "2" due to bad performance in 1983 following two excellent years. Later in 1984, the MVP was batting only .215, and the slugger was batting a dismal .179, while the lowest-rated player, the right fielder, had hit 8 home runs and led the team in batting average and RBIs. The point is not that the sportswriter was wrong in his predictions. The point is that *he didn't make any predictions*, even though he thought he did and said he did. He was merely rating the 1983 Braves in retrospect. He ignored possible bases upon which to *forecast* the 1984 season, things like motivation, new developments or events in a player's life, cyclic changes in playing success, etc. As with most forecasts, these things weren't even considered. Read forecasts carefully. If they are mild-mannered extrapolations of a recent trend, it's probably the best policy to toss the paper aside and go search for something potentially useful.

Obviously the same holds true in finance.

All the time. When economists say, as they so often do, that they see "no reason to expect anything different" from the recent past, they mean it from the bottom of their knowledge. The linear projections they typically employ result in logic such as that expressed by an economist in a national newspaper, who said, "This rising consumer confidence is good news for the economy. Rising confidence spurs the economy, and the pickup in the economy then serves to heighten confidence." By this line of reasoning, no change of direction could ever occur. That's why absent other knowledge, the only forecasts even worth your time considering are those that predict a *change*. Not because the forecaster is certain to be right, but because it shows that he is thinking and perhaps employing a tool that can anticipate trends.

* * * * * * * * * * * * * * *

The Elliott Wave Theorist
May 11, 1981

By early February, it was common to hear that "the market will generally be heading lower, probably testing the 900 level, or even 850." By late February, forecasts were for the Dow to "remain in a narrow range between 930 and 960." By early April, predictions of "a slowly rising market will probably attain 1050 by summer; stock groups will rotate." By late April, the general forecast was for the Dow to "remain in a narrow range between 980 and 1015-1020, tracing out no clear-cut course. Now the talk is that "a declining market will probably persist into the summer, with the Dow testing the 900 area." If you read over those "forecasts," you'll see that every one of them is merely a description of what had already been happening.

* * * * * * * * * * * * * * *

So the word "prediction" doesn't necessarily apply to the future!

Right. And it's those predictions about the future that are the tough ones. That's why economists stick to predicting the past, which is a crafty solution. It leads to misery among the public, but doesn't seem to affect economists' jobs, so it certainly keeps *them* happy!

Do you think that predicting the economy is possible?

It is not only possible, it is downright easy compared to predicting the stock market. Some economists have gotten a lot of chuckles by saying that the stock market has predicted 20 of the last 13 recessions. However, that is only a reasonable statement if you believe that the government's definition of a recession is the only one that is viable. In fact, if you look at the ebb and flow of economic activity and generally realize that it has a lag to stock market activity of between zero and twelve months, you will find that there is no better single indicator of what the economy is going to do than the stock market.

* * * * * * * * * * * * * *

The Elliott Wave Theorist
September 28, 1990

THE ECONOMY

The latest report from Blue Chip Economic Indicators made headlines on September 11 by revealing that "half of economists surveyed say the economy is in *recession or will be by the end of the year*." For the record, this formulation means *that the majority of economists still do not believe that the U.S. is in a recession*, although, as the article in *USA Today* put it, "business executives and other people have been saying for some time that a recession is already underway." Despite the fact that national magazines know there's trouble, the Administration (like the average economist) still sees no serious problem. Here's the latest, from the September 26, *Wall Street Journal*:

Economic growth slowed to a meager 0.4% in the second quarter, revised data show, well below the 1.2% the government estimated earlier. The White House continued to insist that the economy isn't in a recession, even though the revised figures don't reflect recent soaring oil prices.

What's wrong with such pronouncements from economists and government is that they *hurt* people in the real world. Just ask the homeowners in L.A., where real estate prices were "never going to fall:"

"It's gotten to the point where we can't even sleep at night," said Darryl Jackson, who has been trying to sell his house for nearly six months.

Jackson and his wife, Debbie, are suffering from what some realtors have dubbed the "home sellers' blues" — a sad litany of frustration, anxiety, desperation and even anger.

It's a tune that's being sung by hapless would-be sellers in many parts of Southern California, with backup vocals provided by millions of home-owners in depressed housing markets across the nation.

Sleeplessness. Headaches. Upset stomachs and — as one would-be seller puts it — "a general state of disorientation. I think about it when I'm at work. I think about it when I'm cooking dinner. I think about it when I go to sleep at night.

"It's all just sort of hovering there. I feel like I'm in the twilight zone."

"Frustrated sellers are angry at the world, and they want to place blame on somebody for their problems," said Irene Goldenberg, a family psychologist and professor at UCLA.

As you may see by the last paragraph, denials of financial danger at a peak ultimately lead to serious and dangerous social problems.

When the preceding entry appeared in The Elliott Wave Theorist, *the economy was in the middle of a recession that the economics profession did not officially acknowledge until the spring of 1991. The November 1990 issue of The Theorist added that "a broad poll of 'economic forecasters' by* The Economist *magazine in October showed a clear consensus among international economists that "there is no recession in sight anywhere." All the economies of Europe and Japan were soon experiencing what was by many measures the worst recession since the Great Depression. The Bureau of Economic Research, the profession's official recession sanctioning body, reported in April 1991, that the economy did in fact go into a recession in September 1990. In December 1992, the bureau reported that the recession ended in March 1991. In other words, economists were not able to officially state that the seminal business downturn of the 1990s was on until one month after it had ended.*

* * * * * * * * * * * * * * *

Do *Elliott Wave Theorist* subscribers make money?

Lots of them do. My favorite letter ever was from a couple who made a million dollars in the 1980s following EWT. They moved to Hawaii, bought their dream house, and left the market behind. It has also been a joy to see what a large percentage of the winners in the U.S. Trading Championship have been *Elliott Wave Theorist* subscribers and consultation clients. Obviously, the winners have benefited from knowing the Wave Principle.

Of course, just finding someone who can forecast successfully doesn't remove us from our own clutches. You've said that many of your subscribers have not benefited fully from your predictions. How does this happen?

As a class, my subscribers are by far a higher caliber than most. It takes some market experience to understand what I'm saying, as I do assume a certain base of knowledge. But I do think it is kind of a sad thing that people — because they are people — are more likely to lose money than to make it. Many subscribe to six market letters and they want all of them to agree at the same time. Whenever it happens, their collective advice is probably the wrong thing to do. And each one of them could be successful, i.e., right 65% of the time, and there would nevertheless always be disagreement.

There are always reasons for people either to refrain from following my good recommendations or to follow only those recommendations that they're comfortable with, which are often the bad ones. Or they wait until I've been right five times and then go with the sixth one. Or they bet each time and bet more the more often I'm right. Once I'm wrong, they'll be the most heavily invested, and then they'll get shy again. There are an untold number of ways for a subscriber to follow a very successful forecaster and still end up at the end of the year without any money.

What's the best way to follow a forecaster successfully?

The only way is to do absolutely everything that the forecaster suggests and do it with an equal amount of capital every single time. If the forecaster has a winning record at the end of the year, so will you. But most people try to bring their own judgment in. When they're the least comfortable, they'll read something in the newspaper or another newsletter which changes their mind at the wrong moment, and they'll get out of the position because they never made the disciplined commitment to follow the newsletter in the first place.

You've been up-front about the mistakes you've made over the years. Do they ever make you want to chuck the whole theory?

Suppose you asked a baseball player if he had to change his entire philosophy of hitting because he struck out three times in last night's game. Would it not be legitimate for him to answer, "No, my batting average is still .360, and that's about the best that can be done?"

To provide at least some kind of perspective, I've always said that a correct application of the Wave Principle should generally produce correct calls two out of three times. In many environments, it does better, and in some it does worse. The only thing that application of the Wave Principle has ever promised is that you will have a hell of an edge over other approaches, which will make you right more than almost anyone else. And that's quite a lot.

Still, you will not find the next 20 years of stock market prices plotted before your eyes. Don't forget that A.J. Frost and I were Cycle degree bullish during most of 1975 through 1982. Low priced stocks rose almost nonstop throughout the period, but there were times when the Dow fell for as long as 12 months.

Was that a failure of the theory? If you think it was, then don't use it. If overall you believe it provided a perspective that no other approach could or did, then retain it as something of value. I think the current period is analogous, because a top of Grand Supercycle degree is forming, and the aftermath will make abundantly clear what I've been talking about.

* * * * * * * * * * * * * *

The Elliott Wave Theorist

(from the publisher's note, included in every issue)

Be advised that the market timer that never makes mistakes does not exist. Long term success in the market demands a recognition of this fact.

* * * * * * * * * * * * * *

After the crash of 1987, you expected the market to stay down, but it has continued to new highs. Has that been a difficult time emotionally?

Being wrong on a market is an excruciating experience personally because I work so hard to be right. It happened once before in bonds for six months and another time in gold for about a year. No one who hasn't had his every word scrutinized on an international stage can possibly understand the experience. But as another prominent analyst likes to say, "It comes with the territory." Each of those times, the market ultimately moved in the way I was expecting it to and resolved its technical conflicts. I expect the stock market to do the same. The problem this time is that the degree of trend change is so large that to most people's perception, I have been wrong for a long, long time.

When people fail to become "professional" in their approach to the markets, they frequently exit the way frustrated gamblers leave Las Vegas: absolutely convinced that the deck is stacked in favor of the house. Usually, there is a feeling that the game used to be fair, but it somehow became rigged against them. Is this accurate?

Yes and no. The game is not rigged, but it is *stacked* against them, because their opponent is their own unconscious emotional mind. Can *your* cerebral cortex beat your very determined unconscious mind?

But you have to have some sympathy. Looking back on paper, October 1987 is just a line on a chart, but as they lived through the crash, many found it very hard to understand how values could legitimately go from where they were on August 25, 1987 to where they were on the morning of October 20.

Well, of course I sympathize, both with the pain and the lack of understanding. All I am saying is that the latter must be fixed before success is possible.

How?

Most investors believe that they are dealing with a law of cause and effect with the market's action on the "effect" side of the equation. The market, if it does operate in a cause and effect world, is a reading of what is on the "cause" side. The market's behavior itself just IS. It is a manifestation of naturally rhythmic mass mood change. A student of the market, as opposed to a theorizing model-builder, will have to find himself coming ultimately to that conclusion. George Lindsay, in his very last market letter, published in February 1985, said this: "Is it a 'crazy' market? Most professional market men call this a 'crazy,' 'outlandish,' or 'weird' market. I can see nothing about it that differs materially from other strong advances...." That is from a man who wrote market commentary for 34 years, and saw all types of markets. A fox only appears to be crazy if you expect it to behave like a chicken. Similarly, the market only appears "crazy" if you expect it to behave according to the laws of physics rather than those of sociology.

* * * * * * * * * * * * * *

The Elliott Wave Theorist
September 30, 1985

THOSE EVIL INSTITUTIONS!

Lately a number of dire warnings have been issued regarding some institutions buying index futures and selling stock when they believe that futures premiums are too low. Some have gone as far as to say that this simple arbitrage game "threatens the integrity and stability of America's stock markets." Every imaginable new structural event in the history of stock trading has produced such pronouncements. They usually appear during downtrends when people are losing money. In the 1910s, "the big money boys" were supposedly "rigging" the markets. In 1929, the "shorts" had "engineered" the crash. In the later 1930s, the Dow Theory's popularity was blamed for the occurrence of several "confirmed" tops and bottoms in the market. In the late 1970s, options were supposed to be the tail that "wagged the dog." Now it's futures contracts! The danger in believing these theories is that market losers will place the blame for their losses on someone else, and thus fail to learn anything about trading. (I hate making mistakes, but I don't blame someone else for them.) Such an "out" is almost irresistible, like a conspiracy theory. Here are some observations on the latest concern:

1) The wave structures on the hourly chart look no different from those of the past, so no effect of this nefarious practice is evident. The times when these structural selloffs and rallies are supposed to be occurring just happen to fit right into the "third wave" position of the smaller waves, a natural place to expect volatility.

2) I was told at a meeting of the San Francisco Society of Technical Analysts that computer studies of volatility showed no support for the widely held belief that the market is more volatile today than at all other times in the past.

3) I haven't yet spoken to an institution that has gleefully explained its wildly profitable "program selling" schemes. Could the extent of this practice be a fantasy? Suppose the occurrence of low premiums is largely a natural event when tuned-in floor traders determine that there are large blocks of stock for imminent sale? Then the low premiums would reflect what the value of the market is to those closest to it. After the selling occurs, the premium returns. Ultimately, the extent of this practice will be revealed in the extent to which the institutions outdo their prior-year performances relative to the market and to the public, which can't afford to conduct program selling.

4) The idea that arbitrage tactics will "snowball" the market into a bottomless pit or unstoppable rally is ridiculous. It's the same case we hear every time the market makes a major bottom. Remember? It goes like this: "The margin accounts' equity is so low that it will force more liquidation, which will force the market lower, which will force more liquidation," etc. There's always an article to that effect on the week of a bottom.

5) At some point, the arbitrage game becomes only marginally profitable. When a large enough number of institutions catches on to the profits available, they will act to keep a very tight rein on futures premiums. The arbitrage will then be just another service, like shoe-shining, and will be paid accordingly.

6) Arbitrage is actually a good thing. It provides, without intention, a service for less accomplished traders, particularly the public. If futures premiums were not arbitraged, their values relative to the cash markets would fluctuate even more wildly than they do now, precisely as they did on Value Line futures in 1981, before arbitrage. Then it would be even harder for the "average investor" to profit. The professional traders, who can smell panic and greed, would do even better. If I were a professional

trader, I would be all in favor of outlawing the practice of futures premium arbitrage.

I recently received a letter from a subscriber who quit investing in the market, saying, "the odds of figuring out the direction of the market have changed drastically since these institutional programs have begun to dominate the market. The *Business Week* issue of September 16 finally convinced me I have no chance." I think *that's* the poor guy who was done a disservice, by those who blame their difficulties on manipulation and conspiracies. Once the market turns up again, you probably won't hear any more about it.

* * * * * * * * * * * * * * *

Will you at least admit that professional traders have an unfair advantage because they have instantaneous access to resources that part timers and amateurs do not?

Think a minute. Isn't that the case with every business? Why would anyone expect a professional commodity trader to trade as poorly as does the general public? So they have an advantage, but it is not an "unfair" advantage.

Even then, there are several points to make. First, if anyone would like to become a professional, he can choose to give up his life and crawl into the pits with the professional traders, thereby gaining all the latest "information." Secondly, the "information" he gets late is, nine times out of ten, erroneous or misleading or irrelevant to the trend of the market. Finally, even a cursory examination of commodity charts shows a remarkable propensity to trend, and split-second timing is really unnecessary. If you call the trend right, you'll make money. If you make a lot of casual assumptions about hot, up-to-the-minute "information" without studying the way markets act, you'll deserve to lose every penny you put at risk. In fact, it's long been shown that the in-and-out trader who relies on the latest news flash has the worst results. Many so-called "insiders" blow themselves out in just that way.

What about the manipulation of computer programs? We've seen the markets do some pretty crazy things when program trading was in force. Traders on the floor know those programs are there, too. Is it not logical to assume that there are times when insiders know the trend is artificial and short-lived, but the computers don't? At such times, can't we conclude that they are going to push prices to a certain point and create an exaggerated response?

I'd like to meet these insiders who *know* that a trend will be short-lived or long-lived! Even the idea that traders can "muscle" prices into triggering computer trading systems is probably untrue. In the first place, they can only buy or sell enough to do it if the other side of the market allows them to, in which case prices would probably have gotten there anyway. If someone could actually conspire to "trip" a rush of computer-generated buy or sell signals, then there is a problem in the computers' trading systems. Anyone who designs a trading system that purposely buys strength and sells weakness is going to be whip-sawed. There is just no wishing away that fact, and griping about conspiracy is the way most program designers and salesmen cover up for an ill-conceived system. And if such activity is part of the trading game, then the computers had better factor that into their programs, right? Is it really a legitimate gripe that a simple-minded trend following system, which most technicians can construct after their first week of training, won't make you rich beyond your wildest dreams?

So conspiracy theories are an easy scapegoat.

Conspiracy theories have an appeal, not only because the money loser can rationalize his failures, but also because it keeps him from having to admit he's too lazy to do the exhaustive work required to figure out how to make money at trading. They are a substitute for taking responsibility.

You've said that such theories do have one merit. When an analyst finds that one such theory is believed by most people, he or she can be sure that they are close to a market turn, usually a bottom. What are some other characteristics of a major market bottom?

General despair. Investors completely give up. Sometimes you even begin to hear arguments as to why that market really has no reason to exist. For instance, in 1932, people said capitalism was dead, stocks were dead, and they'd never go up again. We had that situation in gold in 1971, when the government decontrolled it. Several economists came out and said that as soon as they took off the price controls at $35 an ounce, gold would drop to $6 an ounce because it had no industrial utility.

The market is an amazing beast. It even manages to do damage on the way up. Richard Russell has said that the "diabolical objective of bull markets is to advance as far as possible without any people getting in." The opposite is apparently true in bear markets.

Exactly. It's the old story. Bull markets climb a Wall of Worry. I made up a parallel maxim: bear markets slide down a Slope of Hope.

You applied this idea to the great bull market when it was just getting underway. You said, "Somehow the Dow has to get to 3600+ with almost nobody aboard."

All I really meant was that for the mechanism of the market to be satisfied, there must be reasons for people to disregard really important advice at the time it is most important that they actually take it. The psychology of 1984-1985 was exquisitely instructive in this regard. There is a section in *At the Crest* about that phenomenon. Advisors, newspapers and brokers *hated* the market. They were amazingly bearish. So the market went up with the fewest possible people participating. In fact, they were shorting and losing money as it rose. The history of markets shows that over 90% of investors cannot make money in the market. The few successful ones you occasionally hear about usually took the approach of long-term, buy-and-hold, without regard to trend, and they were lucky enough to be in a multi-year bull market.

But so-called typical investors just don't make money for long. They get interested in the markets at the top of every bull trend, and they get scared out at bottoms. The short term traders lose even faster. They're sending 2 or 3% of their accounts to the brokerage industry in commissions every week or so. How long can you survive that without a good rate of market success? Since people's hopes and fears are the engine of the market — their hopes make it go up and their fears make it go down — the result is that most people must lose money. It is their fears that make them sell near bottoms and their hopes that make them buy near tops.

Let's say you could dissect the average investor's stock portfolio over the course of a full cycle. What would it reveal?

More than 75 years ago, Don Guyon, the pseudonymous author of *One Way Pockets*, wanted to discover why his clients always lost money in a complete bull-bear cycle. It might be argued, he reasoned, that at worst, they should have broken even, since at the end, prices were back to where they were at the start. He found that the answer lay in the clients' temporal orientation to the market's future. At the beginning of a bull market, he found all his clients were traders. At the top, they were all "investors." This is not only precisely the opposite of the correct orientation for making money, but also entirely natural for human beings and a key reason why the market repeatedly behaves as it does.

* * * * * * * * * * * * * * *

Don Guyon

One Way Pockets

When the bull market was in its infancy, each of the accounts showed purchases of industrial stocks at prices which a few months later appeared ridiculously cheap, yet advances of from one to three points brought these stocks back to the market. When Steel was in the 60s and Baldwin was nearly 100 points below the figure it finally reached, the accounts showed scores of completed transactions yielding profits of less than two points, liberally interspersed with losses. Then as a gradually higher level was established, these stocks were repurchased, usually at prices considerably higher than those at which they had previously been sold. At this stage, larger profits were the rule; three, five, seven and even 10 points were taken. [Later,] as one after another soared to unheard of heights, stocks were bought freely, and they were not for sale even when the purchaser had ten or fifteen points profit. What was fifteen points? Hadn't Bethlehem advanced over 500? The customer who three months ago had been eager to take a point profit on 100 shares of stock would not take ten points on 1000 shares of the same stock now that it had doubled in price. Just why the public should almost invariably do the wrong thing on Wall Street can be explained only on psychological grounds.

* * * * * * * * * * * * * * *

Your contention is that we're heading into a long term top of historic proportion. Is there evidence that the long term orientation is the predominant orientation today?

The Elliott Wave Theorist has gone to great lengths to communicate that the entrenched "focus on the long term" buzzphrase of recent years is of paramount importance in judging the psychological condition of today's market. Such exhortations are always made comfortably at market tops. "Buy and hold stocks regardless of anything you see, hear or read," the wisdom now goes. "Focus on the long term and hold your stocks" is what people said in 1930, 1946, 1969 and 1973, too. If a long term bull market ever "rings a bell" as it forms its top, this is it. Back in 1974, 1978, 1979 and 1982, you almost never heard that kind of commentary. The public certainly had no truck with it. Today, it's everywhere. People are writing books about how if you just buy stocks and hold them, you'll ultimately get rich. I think that's an excellent description of the past, but I don't think it's going to describe the next 10 years *at all.*

If the most popular investment gurus of the day, John Templeton, Peter Lynch and Warren Buffett could hear our discussion, they would say, "It's nice to talk about declines, but nailing down when they are going to occur is almost impossible. So, individual investors should just buy the best stocks they can. If they diversify internationally, they can't get killed because they will have to spread the risk out all over the world. Forget about trying to forecast everything." What would your response be to that?

I have a lot of respect for those people because they have risen to the top of their field. However, their field is stock picking. They have been professionals during one of the most wonderful periods in history to be a stock picker. The trend, for the most part, during the past 40 or 50 years has been up. When that situation changes, so will the fortunes of the stock pickers.

But they have a point. Buying and holding works.

It *worked.* That's different from saying it works or will work. It is also easy to say now. It was not easy to say in 1949, when almost no one followed that advice. So this supposed intellectual point is simply a description of the past. Has it "worked" for bonds since the mid-1940s? Has it "worked" for gold for the past fifteen years? Buying always pays off as long as the relevant trend degree is up. When the trend is down, you could just as easily say that one should sell short and hold. If buy and hold is in, then market timing should be out, which it is today. It's more or less routine to hear about some new study that shows all the gains over the last 100 years came in less

than 100 specific days, and investors should therefore be in
the market every single day. In the second half of the 1970s,
after the market had cycled for a decade, market timing was all
the rage.

**Does this buy and hold attitude, in and of itself, mean that the top of
the stock bull market is in?**

These studies do not pinpoint the day of the top. However,
they do provide critically, if not decisively, important information about the market's psychological environment. The evidence
EWT has been presenting is not merely of anecdotal interest. It
is crucial to understanding that the state of the market is typical of the distributive phase that unfolds at the end of a long
bull market. When investors are standing stock still (pun in-
tended) mentally, they are in for trouble.

**You've said technical analysis is up against "something of a brick wall"
when it comes to gaining acceptance among fundamentalists, but added
that technical analysis has had its moments — like the 1970s and the
1930s, and the 1940s, when it was widely in vogue. Did the bull market
of the 1980s help or hurt the cause?**

In long-term bull markets, no one really needs market timing because the market is always going up. This was true during
the 1950s and 1960s, a period of market strength. And it has
been mostly true since 1982. From 1966 to 1982, though, the
market was very cyclic, so investors couldn't sleep like a babe
with a buy-and-hold blanket like they do today.

But timing is still the most important thing?

R.N. Elliott said quite properly in 1946, "In the matter of
investment, timing is the most essential element. *What* to buy
is important...but *when* to buy is more important." Regardless
of today's bull market rhetoric, that is still true. Once you are
satisfied that the trend is safe, you can then concentrate on
stock selection. In fact, just to demonstrate that this is not new
with *The Elliott Wave Theorist*, I will read this quote from over
12 years ago, in April 1983: "Large institutions will probably do
best by avoiding a market timing strategy and concentrating on
stock selection, remaining heavily invested until a full five Pri-

mary degree waves can be counted." That statement was possible only because of the luxury of having a perspective on the market from a timing standpoint. The gist was, "Now you can forget about timing for awhile." Now that timing is wholly forgotten, it is again absolutely crucial to success. Needless to say, the last eight years have brought back into fashion the recurring belief that market timing is passé and useless, if not counterproductive: "All one needs is good stock selection. Just stay in good stocks, and you will make money and be safe." Well, we'll see.

So, who's right? Or is it just another timing play — a relative thing in which technicians are right at tops and fundamental buy and hold strategies are right at bottoms?

Technical analysis is the correct way to approach markets because it accommodates both bullish and bearish positions. "Buy and hold" is not ever right philosophically, it only appears so by definition when the trend is up. The top technicians were bullish at the 1982 low. There are magazine articles to prove it. But they will be about the only people bearish at the top. The craft will only expand in influence as the years go by.

Technical vs. Conventional Approaches

But where's the advantage over a buy and hold view? The timer and the buy-and-holder are both in favor at exactly the wrong time.

When thinking technically, one continually notices this kind of irony. It is precisely the position of the market in its overall trend that induces people to say that the position of the market in its overall trend is either irrelevant or crucial. But to your question: It is irrelevant to the validity of each approach which camp is *in favor* at a particular time. That just means that it is embraced by more novices, and says nothing about its utility. The only useful message results from the very fact that one is popular, which is technical in nature. Technicians can observe and profit from such irony in the marketplace every day, while conventional analysts produce irony every day without knowing it.

* * * * * * * * * * * * * * *

The Elliott Wave Theorist
June 6, 1988 and February 25, 1994

OF BAIT AND HOOKS

The stock market loves hooks. Hooks are conditions at important turning points that command investors' focus and force them to conclude that a turn is impossible. This major top, if that's what it is, has hooks for every type of investor: professional and novice, fundamentalist and technician.

Remember when every stock market watcher waited in fear for the weekly money supply report? It was widely and firmly believed that that figure would determine the course of stock prices. When that fixation died, the bond market became the key. Every tick in bonds was scrutinized for foreknowledge of the next short term move in stocks. Later came the insistence that the near term trend of the U.S. Dollar held the answer to where stocks would go. The most recent craze is for monthly trade balance figures.

The key to understanding these points of focus begins with an observation. Each one of these "key figures" was in fact counterproductive to a correct assessment of the trend of the stock market. The popular argument concerning the money supply was that a "high" figure would be bearish because it might result in higher interest rates, which are bad for stocks. The only thing contradicting this conventional wisdom is the fact that the money supply roared throughout the life of the bull market, and when the increases finally slowed in 1987, the market crashed. In other words, the correlation was the opposite of that which popular wisdom supposed. The "bond market indicator" became very popular by 1986, on the theory that since interest bearing instruments compete with stocks for investment dollars, and since everyone knows this, then every blip on the U.S. T-bond futures chart would translate into a blip on the stock market chart. (There was no mention of why this shouldn't happen the other way around!) The daily and weekly trends between stocks and bonds began to diverge at that point, and became entirely disconnected by April 1987, when the biggest money was being bet on their prior lock-step relationship. The dollar's value was the next point of focus. Its decline from 1985 was initially welcomed because its high value had supposedly hurt exports. However, the drop created full-blown worry by early 1987 because it had gone "too far," with little change in exports. Nevertheless, the unruly DJIA continued to soar, enjoying its most dynamic phase of advance as the dollar fell.

What do these fixations have in common? First is that they reveal a desire among investors to have one simple indicator of the future course of stock prices. Secondly, not one of them is an indicator derived from market activity itself; all are outside the market and simply presumed to have an impact upon it. Thirdly, all have apparently logical "explanations." Finally, all served to keep investors' eyes off the ball, which from 1982 to 1987 was the fact that stocks were acting in a manner consistent with a long term bull market.

Now let's look at the recent fascination with the trade figures, upon which investors are "fixated" and "riveted," according to *The Wall Street Journal*. Again, it acts as a simple indicator of stock prices. It is derived from outside the market. It has an apparently logical explanation: trade deficits are bad for our country's balance of payments, so it's bad for our country, so it's bad for stocks. There's only one problem. It doesn't fit the facts. In the most ironic hook since the worry over the money supply, the facts are once again in direct opposition to the assumption. A cursory perusal of [Figure 2-1] will reveal that the monthly trade deficit figures worsened persistently throughout the 1982-1987 bull market. Had the devil himself approached you in 1982 and offered to give you five years of trade balance figures in advance, you would have sold short right then and gone bankrupt six times over as a result. Ironically, yet predictably, when the market peaked in 1987, the figures began improving. Was that bullish, as everyone said? Based strictly on the chart, people should be rooting for perpetually soaring deficits!

Each new "key relationship" claim always appears at first blush to sound reasonable, but it is never seriously connected to history or reality. There is justice in the world, though. The multitude who stay up nights trying to guess these various figures haven't done any correlative research, and they keep paying the price for being lazy. The least you should do when the next "key indicator" is discovered and touted is ask politely, "Oh? Please show me your historical evidence."

* * * * * * * * * * * * * *

As a matter of fact, some of the hooks since 1993 have been so convincing they have hooked some of your colleagues. At a gathering of the Market Technicians Association, you said the reputation of technicians had gone below the normal level of disrepute it suffers at tops "when paper profits appear to have validated all kinds of incorrect decision making processes." How so?

"Technical analysis" is in low repute with technicians themselves. A former president of the MTA, who for years had the word "technical" on the masthead of his institutional publication, recently took it off. Why? Part of the reason is that technicians themselves have not defended the term to the extent that it deserves. We compromise like Neville Chamberlain and say, "Technical analysis is useful *in conjunction with fundamentals*," "It can help the money manager decide when to buy the stocks he has *already chosen* using fundamentals,"

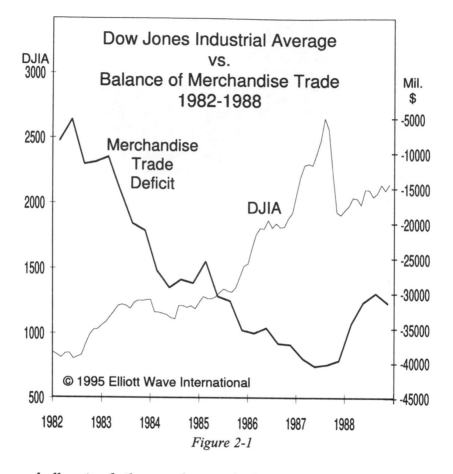

Figure 2-1

and all sorts of other mealy-mouthed non-defenses of our craft. Even worse, technicians, who are supposed to be looking at charts, which means studying history to see if their statements are valid, have turned into fundamentalist assumers. Recently I heard on television a long discussion about the stock market that focused on interest rates, the economy, corporate earnings and the Fed. This is, of course, quite common on financial television. However, the discussion was provided by a technician. When I encounter such presentations, I become disturbed beyond measure. This kind of talk undermines our profession, our case, our cause and our principles.

To the average person, the idea that stocks go up when companies make money makes perfect sense. Stocks are near all-time highs and a lot of companies are more profitable than they've ever been.

Well, since 1932, corporate profits have been down in 19 years. The Dow *rose* in 14 of those years. In 1973-74, the Dow *fell* 46% while earnings *rose* 47%. Twelve-month earnings peaked at the bear market low. Earnings do *not* drive stocks. As Arthur Merrill showed years ago, earnings *lag* stocks. As many practitioners have pointed out, the economy lags stocks. It is therefore impossible for earnings or the economy to drive stocks. Even most economists know this, since they use the stock market as a leading indicator. So today's high earnings are a confirmation that yes, stock prices have risen over the past five years. But it doesn't say where they are going *next*, and that is always the task at hand.

* * * * * * * * * * * * * *

Speech to the Market Technicians Association
May 1994

Rising earnings are the fruits of a bull market. When the fruit is ripe, the tree is already in its declining season. If you wait for the fruit to ripen in order to turn bullish on the trend of the tree, it is too late.

* * * * * * * * * * * * * *

The old saying is that the market is a discounting mechanism — earnings lag stock prices because smart investors anticipate future events correctly. Is that it?

While this position is a time honored and valiant attempt to explain why events lag stock prices, I believe it is false. In fact, because markets are patterned, it *must* be false. The truth is that rising earnings are *caused* by the action of human beings spurred on by an increasingly ebullient social mood, and the presence of such a mood is reflected by a bull market in stocks. This direction of causality explains why aggregate earnings can almost always be predicted by the movement of aggregate stock prices.

When you put it that way, it sounds like something a believer could get downright radical about. You are undermining Wall Street's entire fundamentally driven research establishment. Why don't we see and hear more insurrectionary statements from technicians?

In general, advocates of technical analysis have been content to defend it meekly as having an ancillary value, as providing a little extra that might help some investors make some decisions. However, the truth is *far* more profound than that. Technical analysis is not just one approach to determine value or a trend. It is based upon a fundamental overriding *fact*, the fact that collective human behavior is patterned. Conventional analysis is not a hallowed sensible approach; it is nonsense. It is founded upon a false premise, which is that there are no patterns, only unpredictable, random causes of behavior to which men respond like puppets. Conventional analysts can't see their own contradiction, that it is men who cause the causes. It is men who raise interest rates and create earnings and all the rest. But to the conventional analyst, each is as detached a cause as a meteorite striking the earth. Because many technicians have not made this distinction and contemplated and validated its meaning, they have been afraid to defend technical analysis as one would defend any dearly held truth of human existence. They are afraid to say that the real fundamentals of market analysis are human beings and their patterns of behavior. The result is that today, university professors, who have recently validated the spread between futures and cash prices, relative IPO volume, and even trend following as being predictive of stock prices, are getting the credit for work we did decades ago. Why? Because today too many technicians are talking about the economy, the Fed, interest rates and the health care bill instead of breadth, volume, point & figure, on-balance volume, rates of change, non-confirmation, divergence, trendlines, relative strength, institutional cash levels, allocation percentages, derivative premiums, short selling ratios, public participation ratios, fear, hope, greed, and the cycles and patterns of human behavior.

Can you suggest any changes that will move the burden from the shoulders of technical analysis?

My recommendation years ago was that we drop the term "technical," which is used as if it is some subspecies in a universe of various acceptable types of market analysis. The only craft *is* market analysis. At a larger scale, it is social analysis. And the approaches technicians take are the *only* valid approaches to performing it. Conventional analysis is something else entirely, and technicians can leave it up to its practitioners to define and defend it.

But what about when there are extreme extra-market events like interest rate spikes or world war? In 1974, for instance, one may have been misled by earnings, but an insightful political or oil analyst could have been able to extrapolate Watergate or an energy crisis into trouble for the stock market. Can a big enough event change the psychology?

I become a little more radical every year with my opinions on that. I believe that *all* external social events *follow* changes in the market. They are not events that affect the market. Changes in mood show up later as fundamentals. If people become more optimistic after a period of extreme pessimism, it is only natural that a few months later the economy picks up, because those changes toward optimism result in decisions that expand economic activity, and that change shows up in the economic indicators a few months later.

What about something like the North American Free Trade Agreement? Isn't that almost certainly going to have a positive effect on business — if not here, then certainly in Mexico?

This may be difficult to accept if you have been steeped in financial "analysis" from newspapers, magazines and TV, but the passage or non-passage of NAFTA or any other political resolution has no causal forecasting value whatsoever. NAFTA or a peace treaty or whatever might *coincide* with a market turn, but not because the decision per se went pro or con. Even if the future of that treaty were known to you before it went into effect, you wouldn't know what to do about it. It's mind boggling to see how much energy goes into discussing such supposed indicators of market behavior. Yet no one has done one bit of study to see if there really is a correlation between trade treaties and markets. They just barrel ahead confidently on unencumbered assumption.

Markets reflect social mood, and mood trends eventually produce social events. Since mood precedes events, you cannot forecast mood using events. The only forecasting value that some events possess is that certain events can occasionally imply an *extreme* in mood, further implying that that mood is more likely to reverse soon than to continue. However, this is not to say that the event itself is causal. And analysis on this basis is a complex task that requires a good deal of sophistication about the relationship among markets, mood and events.

Why do you say "supposed" in referring to the indicators used by conventional analysts?

They are truly not indicators at all. They are utilized because of a simple *presumption* that they are valid, not because of any rigorous back-testing. Conventional analysts do not bother to study history. They merely assure us, for instance, that the passage of NAFTA will guarantee another decade of rise in stock prices because it *seems* as if it should. Wouldn't it be a delicious shock if a light bulb suddenly lit up in some reporter's head and he or she asked, "Pardon me, but have you by any chance *checked the historical record* to see if trade agreements in fact are typically followed by stock market rallies?" Don't hold your breath. The reason conventional analysts get away with their suppositions is that they sound utterly reasonable to the average man on the street, who, as we all know, is sophisticated in the ways of markets. Technicians, on the other hand, *do* study history. That's what a chart *is*.

So, ultimately the technical evidence will manifest itself in some fundamental form. Does that mean you can forecast what most people call fundamentals?

Absolutely. When gold was $850, we had the knowledge that it was likely to drop to more than half its value, and when stocks were at 900, we had the knowledge that the averages were likely to quintuple. Armed with that information, *The Elliott Wave Theorist* was able to make a lot of forecasts regarding what the "fundamental" environment would be like in ensuing years. I said that disinflation was likely, that there will be an improving economy and social mood, that the president in power would get re-elected, these kinds of things. I think you can apply the same idea right now, which is what I did in *At the Crest*. As long as you are pretty well on top of your forecasting, you get a tremendous advantage over most methods of reading the market because you have something very few people have: perspective. Then you can forecast a lot of fundamental events. Elliott and the markets have always been a greater value in forecasting fundamental events than vice versa.

You look first to the market. And that's as far as you really have to go, because in the market itself, you have everything you need to make money. But as a secondary exercise, you're saying you can actually

extrapolate the kinds of fundamentals that normally accompany the kind of market you're predicting. Then how come anyone who reads the papers or listens to the news or knows the first thing about supply and demand from Economics 101 knows that the game on Wall Street is played by scores of analysts and economists who get paid big money to chase down the factors behind every little squiggle in interest rates and stock prices? They all start with the fundamentals, which is the opposite point of view.

Quite so. One of the great paradoxes of forecasting is that so-called "fundamentals" (i.e., current events and conditions) have no value in prediction, and yet that's where people focus their attention when attempting a peek into the future. On the other hand, forecasting based upon the tenets of social pattern allows one to predict "fundamentals" to some degree. In other words, when an analyst understands some of the truly mean- ingful indicators of coming social trend change, he can then describe some of the types of events and conditions likely to follow. The markets are the best forecasters of economic and social conditions. I think that economists should use markets mainly for that purpose, and of course, they don't.

Another example of this paradox in action was the barrels of ink that were used by the financial media to discuss what effect the "Crisis in the Gulf" in late 1990 would have on the stock market. There is no way whatsoever to guess at such a thing, since its extent could not be predicted at any point using only the knowledge of its current state. On the other hand, not a drop of ink was used in discussing the fact that cycles of market prices, and thus social mood change, are valuable in predicting things such as international conflicts and their ex- tents. The fact that the stock market was at a four-year cycle bottom, and that by one count, it was ending Primary wave ④, increased the probability of armed conflict. *At the Crest of the Tidal Wave* predicts an increase in warring on the heels of the coming great bear market. Thus, understanding how wars have fit into such patterns in the past is valuable in predicting a dramatic increase in the likelihood of war, whereas wars them- selves have no value for predicting the course of stock prices except to indicate that collective emotions are near an extreme.

Could you use a strong trend in stock prices to predict that a seemingly important crisis would have no importance to the trend in prices?

Oh, yes. If the stock market is in a large impulse wave, no crisis will derail it. Here's a chart of nine years of stock market action. A complete surprise to the entire country was the assassination of President Kennedy. Can you point it out? Here's another chart of recent weeks. Can you identify when the U.S. government was forced to shut down in a budget crisis?

* * * * * * * * * * * * * *

Examine Figure 2-2. Try to guess which bar represents November 1963, the month of the Kennedy assassination. Then examine Figure 2-3 and try to guess what week the U.S. government shut down amidst an unprecedented budget confrontation between the President and Congress. Then check your guesses against the actual dates, shown in Figures 2-4 and 2-5 on the next page.

* * * * * * * * * * * * * *

You might ask, what about peace treaties? Or the San Francisco earthquake? Or the assassination of President Lincoln? What about the hurricane that devastated the coast of Florida and South Carolina or the floods that damaged so much of the Midwest? Are there corresponding market moves? No. The patterns of the market go around and through events of that type. It is moving in its own cycles of optimism and pessimism and is not buffeted by such events. If you go back far enough in history, you will find that almost any recurring fundamental event will appear to coincide with a rising market in some periods of time and with a falling market in other periods of time. A severe change in mass psychological mood always results in major events, but such major events do not cause trends.

Are you saying that if you were in the stock market for technical reasons and able to know ahead of time that the President would be assassinated, you wouldn't lighten up on your position?

I would buy some puts and sell them five minutes after the announcement. Otherwise, I would not change my position.

But if you knew ahead of time what the major events were going to be, how can you say that even that would not help you to know what the markets would to do?

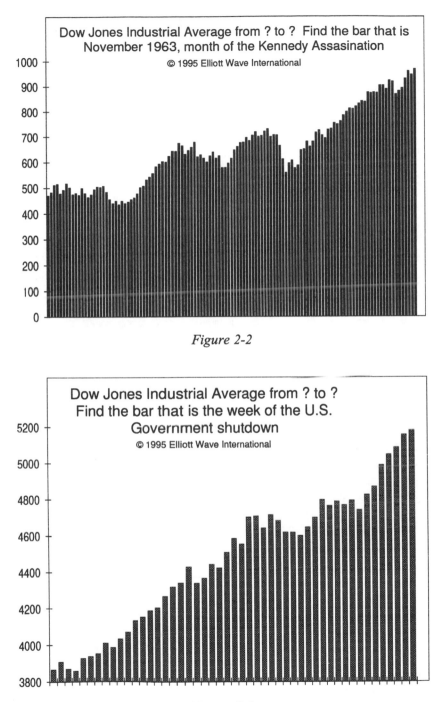

Dow Jones Industrial Average from ? to ? Find the bar that is
November 1963, month of the Kennedy Assasination
© 1995 Elliott Wave International

Figure 2-2

Dow Jones Industrial Average from ? to ?
Find the bar that is the week of the U.S.
Government shutdown
© 1995 Elliott Wave International

Figure 2-3

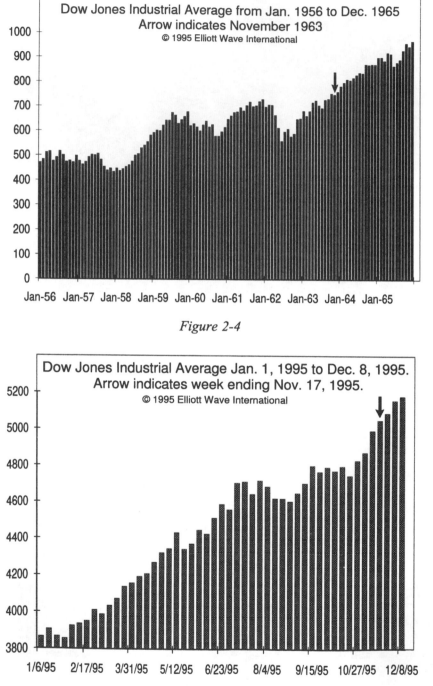

Figure 2-4

Figure 2-5

If the devil had come to you in early 1986 and said, "I've got some inside information. The Democrats will take over the Senate by a wider margin than even they expected. We'll have the biggest financial scandal on Wall Street in 60 years (the Milken/ Boesky insider trading debacle). And Ronald Reagan, the most beloved president in history, will be caught in the midst of a national scandal regarding Iran." If you shorted a bunch of stock, if you assumed the news would have an affect on future trends, you would have lost. Suppose you knew in 1992 after 12 years of Republican reign that a Democrat would get elected, enact the largest tax increase in U.S. history and attempt to socialize the entire medical industry of the U.S. Would you have sold? Fundamentals don't work.

What about something that is known to everyone and has an obvious effect? Suppose you see interest rates begin to rise in February 1994, and despite your earlier case that the effect is not guaranteed, you have reason to believe that we are in a cycle in which rates and stocks will go in opposite directions. Isn't that a good solid fundamental reason for getting out of the market?

How do you know that interest rates didn't stop rising today, in which case stocks are a buy?

Let's suppose the latest economic report showed strength.

How do you know that the economy didn't peak that month?

I'd wait for a change of some kind, a report of a slower economy or a lowering of rates by the Fed.

How do you know that that economic report won't reflect the *only* economic down tick or that the Fed won't lower rates *once* and then start raising them again?

The Fed usually moves in multiple steps.

Aha! By forecasting the behavior of your supposed cause, you are engaging in technical analysis of your "fundamental" data. You're forecasting the behavior of an agency based on the history of its own behavior, in this case using the technical idea of trending. This agency is then considered to affect a market (i.e., interest rates) that will affect the one you actually want to predict, i.e., stocks.

So you're saying....

You cannot avoid employing technical analysis at some point. Since it must be employed, isn't it far easier merely to perform technical analysis directly on the market in question? Instead of saying, "The trend of Fed action is toward higher rates until that trend changes," you could simply have said, "The trend of stocks is down until *that* trend changes" and saved all the trouble and avoided the pitfall of requiring a whole chain of causality to maintain itself, for which history shows numerous exceptions.

So all that interim reasoning is superfluous.

Exactly. I'm saying that the chain of predictions concerning each supposedly causal indicator in such exercises will be endless until the conventional analyst finally provides a prediction based on technical analysis, so why not start with it?

Sometimes all these experts really say is that they see no evidence of a change in trend for their supposed cause. That's a technical statement, too?

Yes, trend following is the crudest form of technical analysis, and it is employed by nearly all conventional analysts and economists. Unfortunately for them, they often make it far *less* useful than it already is by following the trends of *lagging events*. Some such indicators, for instance, earnings, can time themselves exquisitely to produce maximum error in forecasting the stock market. So why doesn't he just start with the trend of the *market* and forget earnings?

Furthermore, a conventional analyst cannot adjust for error. If interest rates fall and stocks fall with them, or if earnings fall and stocks are going up, he has no basis upon which to modify his stance. Technical analysis provides a built-in method of changing one's mind.

All effective forecasting *requires* technical analysis. While technical analysis can be utilized perfectly well on its own, there is no such thing as valid analysis apart from technical analysis.

I think we've uncovered the basic flaw in the conventional approach to markets. But I'm not sure exactly what that is.

Conventional analysts have to predict their own indicators. If the comment is made that the economy is going into a recession, and thus stocks are going to go lower, an assumption has been made about what this fundamental indicator itself is going to do in the future. For example, an analyst once said he was bearish on the stock market because long-term rates were high and rising. That implied that rates were still rising. But in fact they had already peaked. He had to forecast a continued rise in order to explain why he was bearish.

A technician is not reduced to predicting his own indicators. He can look at the evidence at hand without forecasting the indicators and say the indicators right now are bullish or bearish. This is not to say that such indicators are always right, but at least the chain of argument is direct and finite. The indicator speaks to the future, and that's that.

Ultimately, however, isn't it reasonable to say that the driving force behind long-term appreciation is always the same fundamental force: earnings? No matter what 20th century success story you're talking about, Coca Cola or IBM or Microsoft, the common element was an ability to deliver on the bottom line. So if you can forecast profits, can't you be expected to forecast rising stock prices?

How many people forecasting profits predicted the stock market one year ahead in mid-1929, mid-1930, mid-1931, and mid-1932? The best forecaster of *earnings* is the *stock price*. Now, once you have established that a bull market is in force, which is a task requiring technical analysis, then you can perform one type of useful fundamental analysis: you can set out to learn more about a company than the otherwise best-informed people in the marketplace. A really dedicated fundamental analyst who gets inside a new company and believes it has a huge advantage over the competition and believes that its stock price does not reflect that potential can make an intelligent choice. He is, in effect, predicting profits and therefore the relative price of one stock.

In the area of individual stocks, can fundamental approaches be effective in ways that even the Wave Principle is not?

Sure. In fact, I think stock selection is the only place fundamental analysis is valid. A guy doing fundamental analysis has to do his homework, he has to be on top of the company, he's got to know the key people, and he has got to really know what is going on. He has to have a good feel for the future and the competition in that area. So I think it's a valid approach in picking undervalued and/or emerging companies. This approach takes immense work. You're not just talking about investigating Microsoft. You're talking about investigating 100 or more companies just to *find* the next Microsoft. This approach only works on the micro level, and *only after* the macro level is judged to be acceptable for the exercise. Otherwise, a bear market will kill the stock price of your presumed new Microsoft.

Are there classes or methods of fundamental analysis with which you agree?

There is a hybrid form of "value analysis" that involves both technical and fundamental ideas. This is the Graham and Dodd approach of searching for stock value by comparing stock prices of seasoned companies to company performance. This is not the same as the fundamental analysis I discussed above because it is not an attempt to find emerging companies or assess the management, etc. In fact, it requires a company that has been around awhile so that it has a history of figures. Nor is it as pure a fundamental analysis as the former approach, since this one is based heavily upon relative stock price, which is a measure of investor psychology, and thus crosses decisively into the domain of the technical. I have no quarrel with this approach as an *adjunct* to technical analysis. I do, however, have a quarrel with those practitioners who say it is the *only* valid approach, as many of them do. Ironically, many who employ this approach do not realize, or admit, that they are using technical principles.

Still, at least 50% of Graham and Dodd is earnings statements and balance sheets. You're willing to allow that into the analysis of individual firms?

Actually, the reliance on corporate performance statistics, which is the "fundamental" factor, weakens the reliability of the message, because profits, earnings and dividends can all change after an investment decision has been made. An apparently cheap stock by such formulas can fall 50%, after which the company reports poor performance and dividend cuts and so on, so that it is no longer cheap by the *same* measures. One often hears of such people who become frustrated with this approach and become technicians. Rarely does a conversion take place the other way around.

Is there any common ground or point in a market cycle at which technicians and fundamentalists will tend to agree?

There is a stretch in the *middle* of a bull market when technicians and fundamentalists tend to agree. That's when momentum is strong and earnings have started to grow.

Technicians have not out-predicted these hybrid analysts over time, have they? Mark Hulbert of the *Hulbert Financial Digest*, a newsletter rating service, has compared the performance of two groups and said that this type of fundamentalists had "about an equal showing" with technicians.

Yes, so far. But this equal showing has been achieved during a period of consistently rising prices. It would be dangerous for someone to assume that these two camps would also perform equally if the market entered a bear market. It has been rather widely recognized that fundamental analysts get killed in bear markets because they are virtually always "long." Undoubtedly, many technicians would get killed as well, but the top performers will be technicians. To make assumptions about long-term value, performance, and risk using only data from bull market years will prove to be a dangerous thing when market behavior changes. The mere possibility that technical analysis can serve to help an investor avoid a bear market of historic proportion or duration gives it the edge.

James Cloonan, president of the American Association of Individual Investors, has reported that the likelihood of loss in buying and holding a diversified stock portfolio falls to 4.3% once the holding period reaches five years. That's with stock portfolios begun in each of the past 50 years. The odds are even better when considering a diversified portfolio of small stocks.

Merely claiming that being fully invested all the time has been superior to being sensitive to market trends doesn't hold water. Such an approach may have provided good returns over the past 50 years, but the fact that most of the past 50 years has seen rising markets says little about the future. To rely on that record in justifying a fully invested position is no different from relying on a mechanical technical trading program fitted to back data.

* * * * * * * * * * * * * *

The Elliott Wave Theorist
July 6, 1979

Those of you who have heard A.J. Frost speak have heard him refer to technicians as *falcons*. Falcons, you may have heard, fly in a widening spiral to confuse their prey, and then begin descending in a contracting spiral until they zero in on their prey and strike at speeds of up to 200 miles per hour. You might ponder the following headline from a *Wall Street Journal* front page article: "Rare Falcons Adapt to a New Habitat Teeming With Prey — Stately Birds Soar and Hunt Amid Heights and Canyons of a Modern Wilderness." Are the daily, weekly and hourly charts of the Dow Jones Industrial Average the "Heights and Canyons of a Modern Wilderness?"

* * * * * * * * * * * * * *

What about the academics? Whose side are they on?

Most academicians' models of stock market behavior are based upon the premise that all investment is based on rational decision-making processes in an environment of random price movement. Does that make sense to you?

When you put it that way....

No, *they* put it that way. And in fact, each idea is as patently false as putting them together is illogical. Most investments are made for emotional reasons and because everyone else is doing it. Such are not rational decisions. And as far as randomness is concerned, the Wave Principle disputes that. Study the charts. The major events do not show, as we discussed earlier, but the wave patterns do. In fact, we're making headway in *proving* that the market is not random. More on that in a coming publication.

Most "ivory tower" types still argue that prices are a random walk. In other words, neither technical nor fundamental systems are any better than a thrown dart.

This theory has held academia captive for decades. The researchers had already formed the opinion that they were smarter than most other people. But then they discovered that *they* couldn't make money in the market. So they were ripe to conclude that therefore it must be a random walk, because otherwise, they could figure it out.

But when people demonstrate they can do better than chance with a method over a long period of time in a speculative market, they have essentially refuted the random walk hypothesis. I know traders who make a seven-figure income every year trading stock index futures, using the market's emotional patterns to guide them. The Wave Principle can even make a precise forecast every so often, and the total record is better than chance. Examples of some predictions using the Wave Principle are Charles Collins' prediction in 1957 that the top of Primary Wave Ⓥ would be 1000 and Hamilton Bolton's prediction in 1960 of the top at 999. On February 9, 1966, the 3 p.m. hourly reading reached a high of 995.82, less than ⅓ of 1% error. A.J. Frost in 1970 forecasted a bear market low of 572. In December 1974, the DJIA hourly reading low was 572.20. In the summer of 1976, I predicted the expected low for the fourth wave expanding triangle in progress would be Dow 922. The low occurred at 11 a.m. on November 11th at Dow 920.63. In 1980, I forecasted a drop in gold to $477. It fell to $474. Then I forecasted a rally to $710. It topped at $720 in September. While we cannot do such precise forecasting all the time, we can do it *sometimes*, and that means the market is not random.

In 1995, academics suddenly began advocating a "buy-and-hold" approach to stocks, saying that while the fluctuations in stocks were random, the long term uptrend was reliable. So they said, "buy stocks for the long term."

Yeah. They weren't saying that twenty years ago. *Now* they tell us. What's really going on is that they are predicting the past. I can do that, too. So can you. But these irresponsible people have taken the step of advising average people that because stocks have gone up so persistently for years, they should buy *now* and hold for the long term. They say *you* should buy stocks in 1995 because *they* can't time the market. I guess we'll see how *that* advice, and that's what it is — advice — works out.

But you seem to be an advocate of long term orientation.

Most definitely! But a *proper* long term orientation. *Elliott Wave Principle* did in 1978 and *At the Crest of the Tidal Wave*, I hope has done exactly that this year.

To give them their due, in recent years, some academicians have uncovered cracks in the efficient market theory, the idea that markets are a random walk. How do these signs of acceptance in scientific circles make you feel?

It is very heartening. Not only is the technical analysis profession roaring toward the realm of science, but science itself is roaring toward technical analysis. In fact, it will change our profession over the next decade in a most shocking way. The latest scientific frontier, that of chaos science, will eventually make conventional analysis, involving the idea of causality from events to markets, obsolete, just as those same studies are swiftly making obsolete the idea of random walk. Chaos science recognizes nature's processes of self-organization. Now that that principle is understood, it is only a short step to realize, as some have already done, that society operates the same way. That's why free societies are more successful and productive than controlled ones. They self-organize far more efficiently than any human directors could make them do. Nature's processes of self-organization, furthermore, are patterned. This applies to human self-organization as well, which is exactly what R.N. Elliott said and exactly the phenomenon that technical analysis studies. The market has the same paradoxical order in its wildness that nature does. Its order comes from its wildness, i.e., its interactive organizational mechanisms, not from imposition, such as one finds in a garden.

Is that true for the economy, as well?

Yes. Just like the communists who could never figure out who was directing the industrial success of the United States, conventional analysts keep trying to find the unidentified "directors" that make everything in the market happen. Guess what? There aren't any. The only director is the behavioral dynamic that human interaction produces. Chaos science is beginning to establish this fact, albeit in a foggy way with respect to markets. Academics are years behind, presenting studies that admit to a slight psychological component to stock price activity by investigating whether the stock market occasionally "overreacts," when in fact it does not "react" in the first place. I maintain that analytical study should be focused upon the patterns of human behavior in the area of self-organization, and at least increasingly, if haltingly, that is exactly where it is being focused. Technicians will benefit immensely from this trend, if we have the sense to know that it is providing a ringing validation of our approaches.

Basically, the long-held academic point of view is that market predictions are impossible. Your view has always been that they are difficult, which philosophically is a world of difference.

True, but I'll give them one thing: they probably sleep better — at least in bull markets — if they pay no attention to market forecasting. On the other hand, I have a lot more fun.

3. IMPLICATIONS

Society and
the Grand Supercycle

Now that we've covered the money-making aspects of the Elliott Wave Principle, we can move on to the some of the larger questions that it implies about society. Over the years, you've extended your stock market studies to the economy, popular culture and social trends. This extension has pushed the debate over the direction of the markets into its largest possible context. On Wall Street, it is common for observers to consider the market's performance a by-product of politics in Washington or the latest global crisis, with such phenomena cited as causal explanations for market behavior. According to you, the correct relationship is the other way around. The market explains social change because the market is a "coincident register of mass emotion." Thanks to its long history and the diligent record-keeping of market pioneers, it is clear that the market is a precise recording of mass mood in finance. In your 1985 report, *Popular Culture and the Stock Market*, and issues of *The Elliott Wave Theorist*, you've focused on the connection between the market and everything from the popularity of exercise to the cancellation of TV shows. The first question is: Is there really a foundation for making such sweeping observations?

Let's start by taking a look at Figure 3-1. Observe that the pattern of prices since 1932 has reflected R.N. Elliott's stock market model exquisitely. Look at the beautifully constructed parallel trend channel. The odds of the outcome depicted on this chart being random is infinitesimal. If the stock market were simply a record of people's reaction to randomly occurring political and social events, then such precision would not occur.

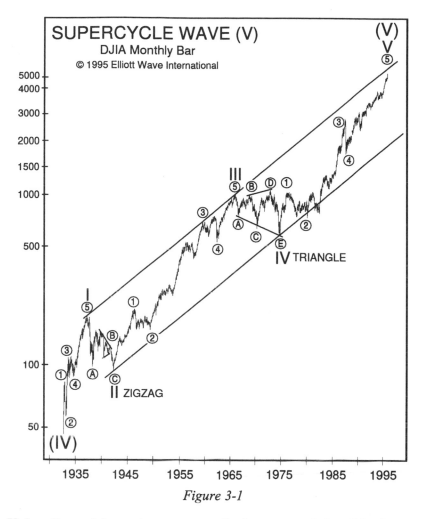

Figure 3-1

Unless the social events were so perfectly patterned that this picture resulted.

Exactly. Almost everyone believes that *events cause psychology.* Think about it. If that is true, then events must be so perfectly determined that they create patterns such as this. Given the market's precision in creating Elliott Wave forms, for people to claim that the latest idea from the White House or the latest law passed by Congress or the latest statistic on the trade deficit or earnings or war or natural disaster such as flood, earthquake or hurricane has any *effect* on the market's pattern, that such things are *determinants* of stock prices in any way, is suggesting a far more radical view of the harmony of the universe than I am. In other words, to argue that events cause the state of social psychology is to argue that *events* are patterned, which is determinism. In that case, free will is invalid, in which case no one could make money from the Wave Principle, which we have already shown can be done.

On the other hand, if *social psychology guides the tenor of events*, then it is only mass psychology, which is apparently a process governed by the unconscious mind, that need be patterned to produce structure in markets. Its patterns underlie social behavior, and behavior ultimately produces results in the form of social action that are viewed as important events.

So given moods, or wave counts as you call them, always produce the same events at similar junctures in the count?

No. Social events are manifestations of a patterned social mood, but the moods may be manifest in countless ways. Social actions are an outlet for the patterns of mass psychology, expressing it in diverse ways that give rise to the myriad events of human history.

You don't consider fundamentals?

On the contrary, Elliott Wave analysts are the only ones who do. The patterns of social psychology that occur naturally *are* the fundamentals of the market.

On Wall Street, analysts contemplate the ramifications of events in Washington, Tokyo and all points in between as much as the people who make their livings there. Then they proceed to build a market opinion from an initial observation about a political or social event that they see happening. They say, "The Democrats are going to win, and the President is going to do such-and-such, and that's going to cause stock prices to..."

Right. And they have about as much success in predicting markets as economists have predicting the economy.

Isn't it possible that there is no pattern — that the five wave subdivisions in the market since 1932 and the formation of that long-term channel are an accident?

That's the typical response from Wall Street observers: "Another coincidence." When patterns of this tremendous size continue to work out time after time, it becomes a matter of faith to continue to believe that the Wave Principle is *not* reflective of stock market behavior.

It's an elegant idea, but in the workaday world of Wall Street, the average broker or economist or reporter is going to say, "Fibo-huh? The Fed just raised interest rates."

And what do they say when the market goes up despite a rise in rates?

They evade the contradiction! But as they see it, it's not a matter of maybe a wave pattern is meaningful and maybe it's not. A rise in rates is a matter of fact. That's something a broker can sell, an economist can speculate upon, and a reporter can write about. If everyone believes in the significance of an event, isn't such an event significant?

Many people believe in ghosts, but that does not make them real. Nor have they escaped the question of "maybe it's meaningful and maybe it's not." If it's something to "speculate upon," there is at least as much uncertainty as to implication as there is with a wave count.

A belief in the power of the Fed or earnings equals belief in ghosts. Maybe you don't realize how heretical this sounds.

I actually took my position for granted for a dozen years. Then I began to discuss it with people and realized that they had never thought of the idea and never considered it. But after they hear it, most people *do* see the internal logic of it fairly quickly and right away become quietly thoughtful. Accepting it as depicting reality is a bigger step. I am confident that people will take this step, though. I may present a radical theory of social causality, but it is the only one that makes sense.

The Wave Principle presents a profound truth: sometimes the dynamics of social psychology are impelling the mass mood toward optimism, and sometimes toward pessimism, regardless of all news. At most, events serve as a background for the rationalization of opinion. The key to anticipating markets is recognizing extremes in psychology, which requires knowing the patterns. The natural path of psychological development is described by the Wave Principle. When wave five ends, it's time for a reversal, regardless of all other possible considerations.

This concept elevates the status of technical analysis, certainly to a level well above the more accepted methods on Wall Street. But it also suggests that technicians who grasp the psychological components of the market can do things even they don't routinely attempt: anticipating some of what's in store for society at large.

Right. The implications are enormous, because with this background, we can appreciate the wider applications of market analysis and realize that it is the only basis upon which to do what man has forever wanted to do: predict the future, at least in some areas and to a limited degree. Events do not shape the market; it's the forces behind the market that shape events. Events are *results*, and when you know what they result *from*, i.e., social mood trends, you can often predict the general tenor of such behaviors. If one knows the species of a tree, he can predict what kind of fruit it will bear. Events are the fruits of a bull or bear market.

If that's all true, market technicians should be successfully predicting all kinds of changes in our social experience.

Yes, and I am not alone in this realization. Bob Farrell of Merrill Lynch observed that he is often able to make forecasts about upcoming changes in the market's backdrop based upon the implications of his market analysis. I argue further that such is the *only* logically sensible direction of forecasting between the two sets of data. If we are dealing with a mass psychological condition that pervades our collective life and expresses the direction in everything that we do as a group or society, the predictive possibilities can't stop at stocks.

So people following news for clues to market direction are wasting their time?

Of course, and I am not the first to say that. But I am the first to recognize the depth of the irony and paradox behind the exercise. It is not precisely correct to say that news and other extramarket events and conditions are irrelevant. For one thing, they provide a basis for the *rationalization* of a market opinion formed simply by one's emotional state, the pervasiveness of which is precisely *why* markets are patterned. It is rationalization that allows people to avoid exercising reason and therefore to act on the basis of their emotional states. So the pervasiveness of people's pretending to follow news is why markets are patterned and why following news cannot work.

But we've all seen the stock and bond market bounce or dive on the release of money supply or Consumer Price Index figures.

Sure, for a few minutes. And sometimes it *doesn't* react, does it? It need not do so because after all, what created the money supply figure and the CPI figure in the first place but people acting in concert *before* the number was announced? Their actions are in the fabric of our experience well before the number comes out, and the motivations that produced it come even before that. The release of such figures never changes the market's larger trend. Rather than presume that such brief news reactions support a premise that all market trends are the result of reaction to news, people would do better to focus on what happens *after* the two minutes of reaction. Usually the market returns to where it was before the news. If they focused on that typical behavior, they would have to start asking deeper questions, such as why, on all time horizons longer than two minutes, news *lags* the market.

Although fundamentalists seem to be completely in the dark about the temporal relationship between the market and news on the larger scale, technically-minded analysts have recognized it for decades. They say the market "discounts," or correctly guesses, the outcome of a vote or a war.

This theory is initially enticing because in preceding social and political events, the market appears to sense changes before they occur. However, the idea that investors are clairvoyant regarding social conundrums is somewhat fanciful. Did investors panic in 1929 because they suddenly realized that the worst depression in history was coming and that ten years afterward, Germany and Japan would be bombing their neighbors? The very idea is revealed as absurd if you take the time to contemplate it.

So what *is* happening?

The cause of future events is changes in the mass emotional outlook. That's what comes first. The market is a mirror of those impelling forces, which are affecting humanity both in and out of the market arena. The market doesn't "see into the future," as the discounting concept suggests; it records, like a barometer, the causes of the future. For instance, increasingly optimistic people expand business; increasingly depressed people contract their businesses. The results show up later as a "discounted" future. It's not the politicians who gallantly "save" a bear market by returning to policies of economic sanity. It is the mass emotional environment, as reflected by the market, that forces them at some critical point to do it. People's emotional states cause them to behave in ways that ultimately affect economic statistics and politics. The market *is* the news. In that context, the panic of 1929 marked the initial downturn in the trend of social mood. Its ultimate depths *caused* the psychological environment that produced the events that followed.

If all the conventional news-mongering is just empty talk, isn't it therefore just a harmless activity?

Sure, if you have no stake in the market, social events, or your own time. But truly, this false premise of market compulsion by news leads to a fog of uncertainty in every conceivable area of anticipating the social future, from market forecasting to anticipating cultural trends to predicting elections to planning for the comfort and well-being of one's family or the safety of one's nation.

The Economy

You've already stated that in inflation-adjusted terms, the advance from 1982 is not a fifth wave, but a B wave. What does that imply for the economy?

B waves are an echo of the preceding bull market, but not part of it. Even B waves that manage to achieve a moderate new high are properly identified as being part of the early stages of a new bear market, for reasons consistent with both theory and practicality. From the standpoint of the Wave Principle, the ongoing A-B-C correction dating from 1966 now needs wave C, which always exposes the weaknesses in the market's foundation. B waves and fifth waves reveal the dominance of bullish psychology over reasonable valuation more than first and third waves, as the discrepancy between the two is so large. The advance from 1982 has been a B wave in constant dollars and a fifth wave in current dollars, both fitting the psychological environment. Third waves are healthier in that the rising emotional climate produces excellent tangible results. The economy does better during and for a while after a third wave. When the expansive feeling wanes at the end of a B or fifth wave, the less powerful fundamentals it produced cannot justify holding stock prices up, and they fall precipitously. Compared to wave III from 1942 to 1966, there is not as much economic strength resulting from and thus underpinning the current wave V bull market, which is yet more evidence that it is a fifth wave.

Can you demonstrate that?

Of course. I've examined over 80 charts of economic activity, some of which are displayed in the chapter on the economy in *At the Crest of the Tidal Wave*. Despite the fact that the Dow is at new all-time highs by a huge margin, the recent peaks in the rate of change of economic activity are *lower* than those of the 1960s and 1970s. That difference reflects a fundamental change in the health of the economy and says that what we are experiencing is not just the end of the expansion in force for the past few years. This loss of expansionary momentum reflects a top of much larger degree.

And this is because...

A fifth wave in the stock market always diverges against the third by technical measures. In other words, even though prices are at a new high, the rate of change is less, the overbought condition is less, the breadth isn't as good. The same thing is true in terms of the market's background, which likewise isn't as good. For instance, the economy during Cycle wave V has been productive, but there is a much wider disparity between the stock market's valuation and economic performance today as opposed to those of the early and mid-1960s. The fact that indicators of capital intensive endeavor peaked in the early 1970s fits the Elliott Wave thesis that what occurred in the late 1960s was not the ultimate extreme in psychology, which occurs in the fifth wave, but the extreme in the *ability to render real* the bullish psychology of the time, i.e., to translate ebullience into actual capital production, which is accomplished most effectively in the third wave.

If the 1980s were to their preceding decades what the 1920s were to their preceding decades, i.e., wave V, then the economy should have painted the same picture back then. In fact, that's exactly what it did. In *At the Crest*, I show a chart of business activity from 1919 to 1929 that shows the same phenomenon that has occurred from 1972 to the present. The peak in economic activity at the end of wave V in stocks in 1929 was lower than those within the preceding wave IV and undoubtedly the preceding wave III as well. The same thing is true today, and I think the result will also be the same.

But there are valid reasons to expect excess capacity to be consumed this time. Eastern Europe, for example. There's a market that was not even open to U.S. manufacturers in 1966.

First, it is just such hopes that create the psychological environment for a top. But like all such arguments based on so-called "fundamentals," it has two sides. In your example, Eastern Europeans are not only consumers, they are becoming producers. Very cheap producers, too. Won't that be a negative influence on U.S. wage rates and profit margins, at least temporarily? Look, you can spend all day discussing "fundamentals" like this, but the fact is that economic expansions since 1972 have reflected a slowing long term trend. That fact overrides every "yeah, but" you can come up with.

The majority of pundits are saying that the changes in the worldwide outlook for capitalism and other favorable "fundamentals" are bullish for stocks.

Sure they are. How else could the global stock market make a top? The worldwide outlook for capitalism in 1942 was terrible, so it was a great stock buying opportunity.

What is your economic scenario exactly?

Stock prices should take their biggest fall since at least 1929-1932. If it happens, the late 1990s and early 2000s will be depression years. No Supercycle decline in stock prices on record has failed to produce a depression. The 1840s and 1850s during Supercycle wave (II) saw a depression. The 1930s during Supercycle wave (IV) saw a depression. This time, the correction will be of Grand Supercycle degree, which should usher in a debacle in the areas of finance and the economy followed by a long period of erratic economic behavior within an overall period of stagnation. As opposed to the depressions of the 1840s-1850s and the 1930s, a Grand Supercycle contraction in economic activity will be deeper and may last longer.

You say that the coming stock crash will lead to a depression. If so, wasn't the 1987 crash wrong? The economy has gone on to record activity and new highs.

All crashes don't lead to depressions. The 1962 crash, for instance, which was Primary wave ④ of Cycle wave III. The 1987 crash was in exactly the same position as that one: Primary wave ④ of Cycle wave V, although because of its large price movement, I didn't realize it at the time. The coming crash will be different. It will be much larger, part of a Grand Supercycle bear market. That guarantees a huge depression. As with 1962, the 1987 stock market crash signaled the end of the acceleration period of the corresponding bull market. The rise has slowed greatly since 1982-1987, and that is a long term warning for stocks. The economic expansion has slowed since 1989 as well. In fact, the past four-plus years has seen the weakest among all post-WWII recoveries that have lasted at least this long.

If you apply the guidelines for a typical long term Elliott Wave to the current position of the market, what time does it have the most in common with?

The 1720 peak. That's when the investment manias associated with the South Sea Bubble in England and the Mississippi Scheme in France ended. The expected difference is that while the bear market of the 1700s produced 64 years of a zigzag pattern, a very simple down-up-down shape, this one is likely to a sideways pattern, which will manifest at plummeting major declines punctuated by tremendous rallies back to near or even slightly past the old highs. If you take a look at the Dow Jones Industrial Average chart from 1966 to 1982, you can get an idea of what I'm expecting, but it will occur on a larger scale.

What about the accompanying economic turmoil? How quickly will depression arrive?

Because the economic changes that are occurring are of such a very large degree, they will occur in a fashion different from the slam-bang progression of typical recessions of the past fifty years. I think the weak expansion in force since 1991 is ending, and we will then have another contraction which is deeper than the last. You will undoubtedly hear continual reiterations that this "mild recession," whenever it's finally recognized by the majority of economists, will end in "six months or so, a year at the most." However, this is a big cycle, and over its course might even contain an "up" quarter or so that makes it appear as if a recovery has begun. However, any such bounce will just be a bear market rally against the larger trend. When the bottom is reached, the economic devastation will be front page news, just like it was in 1933.

In 1989, didn't you call for the long term contraction to begin?

Yes, and a worldwide slowdown in business began the following year. The 1990-1991 recessions in Europe and Japan were the worst since the 1930s by many measures, and the U.S. is *still* hemorrhaging jobs like it's 1931, despite over four years of "recovery."

If the trend toward depression actually began then, when will it end?

The current short term rise in the business cycle should end in 1995 or 1996, as I argue in *At the Crest*. The bottom of the depression should occur in the first decade of the new century.

So the depressionary trend will last five to ten years? That's huge. We've never had a period like that except the 1930s.

There have been several, actually. The 1930s is one. The 1840s and '50s were two depressions back to back. There was a pretty bad time in the 1890s. There were two examples in the 1700s. So it's on that magnitude that we are talking about, yes.

Do you see the same thing happening globally?

The United States is topping out economically, but so is the rest of the productive world. Japan is undergoing a raging deflation, which cannot help but have a negative effect upon its economy. Europe is recovering weakly from a wrenching recession that in my opinion is only the first salvo of a developing depression. So all these signs indicate a worldwide bear market and depression, not a local one.

Most economists would dispute that any major change at all occurred in 1990, much less one with the implications you discern.

Most economist don't study the evidence of long term economic trend change. But the reason most people don't think we have begun a process toward depression is simply that it's not at bottom yet, so it's not obvious. Some time late in the process into depression, I think we'll see studies and articles pointing out that early evidence of the major trend change took place in 1990 in many measures but "no one" understood their significance.

And then?

And then they'll repeat the mistake in the other direction. By the time the bear market and depression are ending, the front pages will be fretting that they will never end, and we'll be looking for subtle signals of an upward turn.

* * * * * * * * * * * * * * *

The (New Orleans) *Times-Picayune*
September 23, 1990

Many people would indignantly say,
"Today is not like 1929."
Prechter said they're right. It's worse.

* * * * * * * * * * * * *

You say conditions are worse today than in 1929. Why?

Because they're better. When but at a major top in world-wide social mood would you ever have had the Berlin Wall come down, Communism rejected, sanctions lifted on South Africa, and the idea of "a new world order"? This type of psychologically-induced event on the world stage, including Mideast, IRA-English and Bosnian peace agreements, 20 American free trade agreements in 34 months and, in October 1995, a photograph commemorating the largest gathering of world leaders in world history, has continued right though today, so it's a huge top. At the bottom, international tensions will be high and include active conflict, as always.

What will be the prime indication that the great economic contraction is about to start?

The stock market will be the main indication. When it starts down in a big way, we'll be off the cliff.

How far will stocks fall?

The average stock will fall at least 90%.

* * * * * * * * * * * * * *

From a long term perspective, Prechter's outlook has remained surprisingly static. Here's an excerpt from an interview that was done with Joe Bradley in 1979. On Grand Supercycle issues, it is not materially different from another one with Joe Bradley that was conducted in November 1995.

Investor's Hotline
June 14, 1979

Fasten your seat belts for one of the most dramatic forecasts ever made on *Investor's Hotline*.

A couple of people I spoke to concerning A.J.'s forecast said that he has been calling for these very high stock market figures for two or three years and that a number of these forecasts were actually called incorrectly. Is that true or not?

Well, from one viewpoint it is. I've been doing the same thing. As we approached the low, as matter of fact the first time he and I were interviewed in *Financial World* magazine in October 1977, we said, "We're coming toward a bottom right here. And it's going to be the bottom that's going to lead us up to above 2,000." Well, we got a bottom a few months later. Actually, it was one month later that most stocks bottomed. He and I were both saying, "We've made the bottom that's going to lead the market up to 2,000." But if you'd acted on the advice and expected to be at 2,000 within six months, or even by the next year, you would have been wrong. From that standpoint, we were wrong. [Still,] I think the next important move is going to be up and break the Dow out to new all-time highs. I think if you want to buy stocks cheap, you should buy them here. Right now, I think the safest speculation in the world is that the U.S. stock market is going to go up.

We'll probably have an environment where we'll see stock speculation like we haven't seen since the late 1920s. And actually, if Elliott's right, we're absolutely going to dwarf that particular bull market in terms of speculative frenzy, because we're not just starting a fifth wave of Supercycle degree. We're finishing off a fifth wave of a Grand Supercycle as well.

There's one other minor thing — or maybe it's not so minor. That is that England has just elected a Tory (Margaret Thatcher), the Canadians have just elected a conservative and the trend in the Western world is very obviously away from socialist policies. Now, whether or not that occurs here — we may even end up electing Ted Kennedy; I don't know — but the drift is certainly there. And I would think that merely that perception is something that could stabilize us for a few more years and give that feeling of "Hey, we've got it licked." Whether we do or not.

Once it reaches a bigger high several years down the road, it's going to be set up for an incredibly important crash. You can't name a crash in history that hasn't occurred from a period of euphoria and extremely high expectations. Right now, we are nowhere near that point. But I think we will get there, and at that time, when the gloom and doom seminars only have six or seven people attending instead of 6,000 or 7,000, you will really be set up for a problem crash. [Note: the 1995 NCMR Conference averaged one-tenth as many attendees. – Ed.]

When this bust comes, what do you really think is going to happen? Do you think we are going to lose our freedom?

I woke up one night last week and I wrote a few paragraphs [on that topic] that I'm going to put in an upcoming letter. At the top of my letter I write, "Grand Supercycle. Significance to: U.S. Survival." And under strategy, "No action warranted." I can't fit the word "yet" in that square. I think there are only a couple of possibilities, if you think about the magnitude of the decline that Elliott has predicted from that point, we're to go to somewhere around 41 on the Dow. Back to the 1932 low.

Are you kidding me?

No. This either means to me that we will have a socialist government and it will destroy all the capital in the United States and nationalize all the industries, or we'll have a nuclear war. I don't see any other way out of it. Because we are ending a Grand Supercycle that is 200 years long and started out when the country was formed. It's very clear on the charts, too.

Seriously now, do you really believe it?

Yes, I do. I will be making preparations personally.

Bob, I enjoyed talking to you very much!

* * * * * * * * * * * * * * *

But you've moderated your stance a bit since 1979, I understand.

Yes, Dow 41 is no longer possible. The low should occur between 90 and 380.

And war?

The biggest war of the bear market will probably take place mid-century, i.e., not at the first price bottom, but at the second.

There has to be some fundamental deterioration in the U.S. economy underlying such an extended social decline. What will it be?

Perhaps the most widely held belief with regard to the future course of national financial affairs is that inflation will accelerate, or, at minimum, continue. But as I argue in *Tidal Wave*, the case for an impending deflation is overwhelming. The next monetary trend should be a period of severe deflation, just as occurred in 1835-1842, the 1890s and the 1930s. It's a complex phenomenon on one level, yet simple on another. It takes a whole chapter to make the case clear and explain how the phenomenon works.

But as you say, economists are more worried about inflation. In recent years, they're actually thrilled because inflation is down around 2% so that worry has dissipated. And the economy is growing slowly, so they continually refer to it as "the best of all possible worlds."

Yes. I think it's hilarious. The biggest danger sign in three generations, and they think it is positively the best news that could be imagined. They will change their minds.

So some day, people will *want* inflation?

A few of the people who have already suffered from the early symptoms of the deflationary trend are prescribing "cures." A couple of years ago, *The Wall Street Journal* ran two guest editorials on the desirability of government policies that will regenerate the multi-decade phenomenon of real estate values rising faster than the CPI. The essential message is, "Bring back the real estate bubble," delivered under the illusion that the bubble period was normal life and should last forever. Such is not possible, either mathematically or psychologically. But they certainly *want* it. The same desire will extend to the stock market after it tops, and then the economy.

O.K., so what about real estate? In the 1970s, when the economy and the stock market sputtered, real estate did reasonably well.

As big as the disaster in stocks is likely to be over the next five to ten years, it will almost certainly be matched by the upcoming disaster in real estate related investments, which will actually be the continuation of a declining trend that began in 1989.

Are there manifestations of euphoria there?

Oh, yes. In 1989, people camped outdoors in California in order to be first in line to bid on a house. In 1993, investors' mania for real estate investment trusts was not merely another manifestation of the years of financial boom, but a replay of exactly the same mania that has hit twice since the early 1970s. The difference is that this one was more violent. More money was raised in 1993 via initial public offerings for REITs than in any other year in the industry's 33 year history. So the resolution will be more violent, too. The setup is in place. The trap is set.

The trap you see leads you to contradict more of the most deeply held convictions on Wall Street, like the conventional belief that bonds rise when the economy slows. You have them falling in a weak economy. This flies in the face of what the average bond guy does all day long. Every ounce of his energy goes into deciding whether the next "number" is bullish or bearish for the economy. If it's bearish, he's a buyer.

Well, he's right in most economic environments, but you first have to understand that the prevailing professional view is somewhat myopic. It is plainly not good for bond values if the issuers of bonds, i.e. the borrowers, suffer financially to the point of not being able to pay interest or principal, is it? In fact, billions of dollars worth of bond defaults in recent years clearly reveal the problem. What economists should say is that (1) in an environment of general growth and inflation, (2) when only a recession occurs, and (3) when the recession brings a reduction in inflation, *then* bonds typically rise in price as interest rates fall. Unfortunately, to most economists, the post-World War II period is the only relevant history, so bond investors don't place their view in the larger context of economic possibilities.

At what point might the economy deteriorate so substantially that its condition and trend are no longer bullish for bonds, but bearish?

When it reaches depression, and a depression is exactly what is on the agenda for the late 1990s if the stock market falls to the extent that the Wave Principle suggests. The only way for an investor to survive a depression holding bonds is to hold bonds issued by a strong borrower. Among U.S. issuers, there appear few among corporate borrowers and municipalities who are that strong, and neither does the U.S. government qualify. With this in mind, rising rates in a deteriorating economy, at least for a brief period, will not be a mystery.

Wait, you're talking about a presumed "risk-free" rate of return here. What evidence do you have to suggest that the U.S. government is a credit risk?

Several years ago, Earl Hadady of the *Bullish Consensus* developed a simple measure of the government's fiscal health: its interest expense as a percent of total receipts. I discuss this indicator in *At the Crest*. It implies that Federal government bankruptcy will occur, whether via a moratorium on the payment of interest and/or principal, or via a currency inflation following the period of deflation that is soon to begin.

This doesn't bode well for the dollar.

Not ultimately, no. But during the deflation, its value should rise as debt instruments denominated in dollars are defaulted upon, making dollar-based purchasing power disappear and thus raising the value of the remaining dollars. The same thing has been going on with the Japanese yen.

So the dollar is in trouble, but its fall won't be a straight shot.

Did you know that Roman inflation persisted, in recurring waves, for *over 400 years* before the rot was thorough enough to allow invading armies to successfully sack the city? Can you imagine what another 300 years of persistent dollar inflation would do to the political fabric of the United States?

After the initial deflationary hit, what will turn the dollar back down?

The pressure on governments to create paper money to pay off their debts will serve to destroy the value of many paper currencies. Which ones will depend upon what course each government chooses when faced with bankruptcy. I am not optimistic that most will take the honest course. Whether or not all paper currencies eventually go to zero, it will be wise to own gold after the deflation.

Is there an alternative?

The only way to guarantee that politicians will never again inflate is to introduce private money and ban legal tender laws.

Private money? Do you mean gold coins issued by a private mint?

Not *a* private mint. By anyone who wants to issue it! The marketplace will choose the soundest forms of money, and competition will insure that they are produced.

The Cultural Realm

Besides buying or selling stocks and producing and/or destroying goods, how else do people manifest their moods?

The stock market is literally a drawing of how the scales of mass mood are tipping, but the same social psychology that is reflected in the stock market shows up in other areas. We just don't have charts of their activities. For example, extremes in popular cultural trends coincide with extremes in stock prices, since they peak and trough coincidentally in their reflection of the popular mood. Areas of social behavior that quickly reflect mood and mood change and appear to be in parallel with the movements of the stock market include popular music, movies, television, fashion.

For instance...

Mood affects entertainment trends, the style of the media, social themes, cultural symbols, the styling of consumption items such as clothing and automobiles, social harmony vs. conflict, preference for heroes vs. antiheroes, politics, war, and even such deeply emotional tendencies as the preference for relying on reason vs. relying on emotion to solve both individual and social problems.

Elliott never really commented on the reach of these influences into non-financial parts of our life. Were you the first to extend market analysis into the social realm?

No, an MBA from Harvard, Ralph Rotnem, first publicized the so-called hemline indicator. Although it is usually mentioned with a chuckle, there's no question that the correlation goes back well over 100 years.

Stocks go up and down with skirts? Can you really explain a connection?

If the general mood of the population is becoming more optimistic, spirited, playful and daring, it shows up in shorter skirts and higher stock prices. It is not unreasonable to hypothesize that a rise in both hemlines and stock prices represents a general increase in friskiness among the population, and a decline in both, a decrease. Because skirt lengths have limits, the reaching of a limit would imply that a maximum of positive or negative mood had been achieved. The same is true of fashion colors. Bright colors have been associated with market tops and dull, dark colors with bottoms. It is not coincidence, then, that the smaller the skirt or swimsuit, the brighter the colors. Floor-length fashions are more associated with dull, dark colors such as brown, black and gray. All these fashion elements reflect the same general mood. And women aren't the only ones who change their style of dress to reflect their moods. Tie width, heel height, pants leg style and flamboyance or conservatism in men's fashions also fit the trends in the stock market. Remember when London's Carnaby Street was the center of the fashion world in the late 1960s? It was famous for miniskirts and pouffy, colorful men's fashions. Its influence peaked when the Value Line index reached its all-time high in 1968. Suddenly men stopped dressing like dandies and went grungy. The bear market was on.

That's one example. Anything more recent?

Designers rushed the mini out in late 1986 when the bull market had one year left. But the skirt didn't really catch on until 1987. Designers were pushing it for fall wear. I kept wondering, "Why now? Why not wait until spring?" — which was a more natural time to introduce short skirts. Now we know. Immediately after the crash, miniskirt sales dried up so quickly that it made the papers (see next page).

This is *very* interesting, because when you talk about fashion trends rather than market trends, it's easier to accept that they aren't being driven by events. There's not a button somewhere fashion designers push to make skirts go up.

Late 1987

Skirt hems inching up for fall season

July 26, 1987

NEW YORK — From designer boutiques to department store windows, everything's showing up short. The miniskirt, after a nearly 20-year hiatus, is back

USA TODAY, October 7, 1987

It's safe to buy a miniskirt. Whether you're for or against them, short hemlines are in for a long run. This is one fashion trend that has definitely taken off.

Miniskirts are nothing short of a success

October 15, 1987

Italian Greats Ferre and Versace take minute miniskirts to the limit

Early 1988

NEW YORK TIMES, March 9, 1988

As Women Balk, Fashion Rethinks Mini

Designers now show longer skirts and pants, too.

Barron's, March 14, 1988

Most American women want miniskirts about as much as they want cellulite thighs. John Liscio took note of that in Review & Preview in these pages two weeks ago, which no doubt suggested a front page obit in last Wednesday's New York Times: The miniskirt is dead. Again.

USA TODAY March 8, 1988

Milan lowers the short-hem boom

Down-to-earth clothes are replacing poufs and frills as three weeks of European fall ready-to-wear shows get under way here. Though Milan has a reputation for sober styles, the mood promises to pervade other fashion capitals as well.

Sunday, April 3, 1988

Say, what year is this?

Despite fad and fashion, it isn't the Sixties the miniskirt has been rejected by the body politic.

Of course not. Skirts didn't jump from floor length to above the knee because Lyndon Johnson created ebullience by announcing the formation of the Great Society. Skirt heights had been rising for years, and merely continued along the established trend, as did the trends toward bright colored clothes and bikinis. The announcement of the Great Society programs was a political expression of how far the ebullient mood had carried in the previous 20 years. It had permeated the social fabric so deeply that public representatives wanted it institutionalized. Now if you can take the next step and realize that saying that the moods behind the stock market's ups and downs are the result of social events is similarly silly, you'll feel the way I do. The market's trends are very akin to *fashions* in their own right.

This alternating current of ebullience and conservatism goes back to the most basic Elliott Wave idea: Bull markets give way to bear markets, and vice versa. What are the essential ways in which bear market moods differ from those of bull markets?

In bull markets, people focus on progress and production; in bear markets, they focus on limits and conservation.

What are the consequences of that difference?

Bull markets result in increased *harmony* in every aspect of society, including the moral, religious, racial, national, regional, social, financial, political and otherwise. Bear markets bring *polarization*. With that realization, you can predict increasing *cooperation* in all those areas in bull markets, and increasing *conflict* in bear markets.

What about specific consequences?

Well, for example, religious wars were big in the Dark Ages and for a while afterward, but have been a minor concern in the past eight centuries of rising long term trend. Indeed, Catholic, Jewish and Arab leaders are all shaking hands today at the top of a long bull market for Western civilization. Nationalism was the political theme in the 1940s during a bear market. As this bull market has been peaking out, we have seen plans for a European Community, a New World Order, and for the former Communist countries of Eastern Europe to join NATO. In 1994, the leaders of the U.S. and Russia, enemies for decades, clasped hands over their heads in the spirit of cooperation. These trends reflect classic bull market sentiments of human social harmony.

People consider these to be the events that *shape* their futures, but they only reflect the *past* trend of social mood. Indeed, each time one of these grand events occurs, whether viewed as good or evil, the world sees it as a turning point for mankind. Such observations are true, but because they think conventionally in terms of the direction of causality, it is a turning point in precisely the *opposite* direction that they assume it to be. They are therefore entirely unprepared for the next chain of events. The bear market will bring back nationalism, racial exclusion and perhaps even religious conflict. Thinking *technically* about events, that is, observing what they reveal about social psychology, prepares you for those changes, whereas trying to predict the future from the events themselves leads you to the opposite, and wrong, conclusion. Figure 1-1 on page 57 illustrates this point. It cannot be stressed enough, because life-or-death decisions can depend upon your assessment. Notice what marks the major bear market lows of just the last 200 years — the Revolutionary War, the Civil War and World War II.

It's hard to imagine turning bearish when peace is accepted as permanent or turning bullish on society in the depths of scary times. Let's look at the way this plays out over the course of a specific cycle — let's say a Supercycle where the extremes show how the mood change unfolds a logical but still almost totally unexpected sequence of events. Start at the bottom and work your way up.

O.K., let's take the current Supercycle. The collective mood in Germany in 1933 was so negative that its expression resulted in the assumption of power by Adolf Hitler. Hitler's popularity actually climaxed in July 1932, the very month all major world stock markets bottomed out. Now, was his popularity bullish, as a conventional analyst would be forced to conclude, or was his popularity an expression of the negative social mood?

Clearly, Hitler could not be described as bullish for Germany or the world. You're saying he didn't make stock markets go up five times in value? You're disagreeing with economists who say war invigorates the economy.

And I'm happy to do it!

But if his popularity was an expression of the peak in negative mood, why did things get worse instead of better in Europe from that time forward?

"Things" got worse, but mood and stock prices did not. "Things" are the events that I contend result from the mood. In that case, the consequences of the popular action resulting from the deeply negative mood of 1933 took 12 years to play out. The representatives of the negative mood gained great political power at the low. The collective mood in the U.S. also reached a negative extreme in 1933, the year the depression hit its depths. Enrollment in the Communist Party peaked in the 1930s. However, those forces never achieved as much political control as they did in Germany. So the events here were less dramatic. China had the same misfortune in 1949. The negative mood brought about a Communist takeover that has had consequences to this day.

How was the mood shift of 1929-1932 visible outside politics and the market?

Horror movies descended on the scene in 1930-33. Five classic horror films were all produced in less than three short years. *Frankenstein* and *Dracula* premiered in 1931, in the middle of the great bear market. *Dr. Jekyll and Mr. Hyde* played in 1932, the bear market bottom year, and the first year that a horror film actor was ever granted an Oscar. *The Mummy* and *King Kong* hit the screen in 1933, on the double bottom. Ironically, Hollywood tried to introduce a new monster in 1935 during a bull market, but *Werewolf of London* was a flop. When filmmakers tried again in 1941, in the depths of a bear market, *The Wolf Man* was a smash hit. These are *the* classic horror films of all time, and they all sold big. The milder horror styles of bull market years and the extent of their popularity stand in stark contrast. Then the old boundaries of horror were exceeded again in the bear market of 1968-1982 with *Night of the Living Dead*, *The Texas Chainsaw Massacre*, *Halloween* and *Friday the 13th*. For the genre, these are the modern classics.

There have been no more horror film Oscars since Frederic March won best actor for *Dr. Jekyll*?

Kathy Bates won best actress for *Misery* in 1990, the year of a stock market correction that in terms of the Value Line index ended a three-year bear market, which included the 1987 crash. *Misery* was a mild horror film, too, and by some definitions, not a horror film. In 1991, *Silence of the Lambs* won three Oscars, including Best Picture. That wasn't a horror film in the classical sense, either. When the market falls 90%, we'll have real ones that win Oscars.

In 1943, the bull market came back, and some horror movies were still playing, but they weren't very scary.

When Abbott and Costello met Frankenstein, horror had no power.

What was the opposite of horror movie popularity in 1932?

In the Cycle wave V bull market of the 1980s and 1990s to date, feature length Disney cartoons have been popular again at the theaters, just as they were in prior bull market decades. But from 1966 to 1982, during the 16 years of sideways bear market action, most people thought such films were silly and sentimental. Indeed, the studio hardly made any. In the past thirteen years, they are back, and they have been blockbusters. They will fade away again when the bear market begins.

The late 1960s was a major turning point under wave analysis, right?

And in social mood as revealed by both stock prices and popular culture, particularly pop music, which was the pop cultural focus of attention at the time. During the bull market of the 1950s and into the mid-1960s, most pop music was extremely happy, upbeat, love-oriented, harmonized, and major-keyed. When we got into the late 1960s, a change took place. Melody and harmony diminished in importance. The hard-edged sound came into being as noise replaced music to an increasing degree. Heavy metal music arrived, and by the late 1970s, punk rock emerged, with its nihilistic lyrics and two-note melodies over two chords buried under lots of noise.

These observations are fun, but perhaps not important to most people.

Unless you are in the entertainment business! So you want important? Well, as I said earlier, every major stock market decline of the last 300 years has been associated near its end with a major war. That could be important information.

When exactly did this whole thesis gel in your mind? What prompted it?

Well, the Beatles' *Revolver* album affected me viscerally. Although I have come to appreciate much of it since, I hated it when it came out. *Sergeant Pepper* was even worse. Besides two or three songs, where were the inventive melodies, harmonies, chord changes, innocence and joy that had made them stars? It was in thinking about that change nearly twenty years later that I realized that the melodic, energetic and rather innocent (at least in retrospect) music of 1958 to 1966, which included doo-wop, teen idols, girl groups, and particularly in the final two years the "British Invasion," stopped dominating the charts precisely at the end of Primary wave ⑤ in 1966. Quite abruptly, it nearly disappeared. That change is what triggered the realization that *everything* worked this way, *all the time*. Not just music. Not just in 1966.

What happened to the happy-go-lucky Beatles once the orthodox stock market top was in?

The Rolling Stones suddenly outdid the Beatles in the number of Top 10 hits with themes of drugs, mental breakdown, crying and death. The name of rhythmic popular music changed from rock 'n' roll to just plain rock, which suggested the hardness of the new musical style. In August 1966, two months before that year's bottom in stocks, the Beatles announced their retirement from live performing and released an album cover featuring dismembered toy dolls and bloody joints of meat. The public's mood had changed so dramatically that the Beatles as a group suffered a worldwide hate campaign. As the bull market returned in late 1966, the "butcher album" cover was quickly recalled and replaced with a bland photo. In June 1967, the Beatles' image "committed suicide," putting their own graves on the cover of an album and announcing their reincarnation as a new band with a complex identity.

That change allowed them to hold on for a while longer?

Yes. Their new style, and that of countless new bands, reflected both the "peace/love" sentiments of a peaking mood and the more world-weary style of a downtrend in mood. This mixture precisely reflected the bull market/bear market battle that was raging on Wall Street, with the secondary indexes heading for new highs against the Dow, which made its orthodox top in January 1966 and was already declining, particularly in inflation-adjusted terms.

But ultimately, the bear market took its toll on all these bands.

No question. The new mood killed them off, sometimes literally, by drug overdose. The switch came in 1970, as the first monolithic wave of bear market ended. A whole new crop of bear market music makers came to the fore.

This seems very pat.

Realize that pop cultural heroes are made by the public, so the public mood determines who's popular. The mood can also affect the creative direction of the heroes as well, so there are two effects.

Your background in music has obviously been of some help to you in this study. You have maintained that a song dominated by major keys, harmony, melody and musicality is representative of a bull trend while one dominated by minor keys, starkness and noise characterize a bear market sound. You can literally hear the difference between a bull and a bear market hit in the composition of the music. But you don't even have to be able to carry a tune to analyze the lyrical content of popular music. On *The Beatles*, which was known to most people as "the white album" of 1968, for instance, Lennon sang "She's coming down, yes she is," and on his comeback album, *Double Fantasy*, in 1980 he declared, "Hard times are over, over for a while." Applied to the stock market, those are two pretty good calls. They show that an artist can be plugged into societal mood. And in retrospect, at least, it's not just a subjective observation. Just about anyone can see and would agree that the early Beatles music was upbeat, and the atonal punk rock of the late 1970s was harsh. The coincident registration of a changing mood is an objective reality.

Yes, but let's not isolate a few lyrics to make our point. That's a typical approach to cultural analysis, and it's not scientific. Lennon wrote a lot of lyrics. But as a whole, your point is correct. His bull market lyrics stand in immense contrast to his bear market ones. What we need are objective statistics on pop music style and content and to see if the chart matches the stock market. I think it would demonstrate that mood and its expression through myriad outlets is an objective reality. It is difficult to prove because the social sciences are so primitive and data so scarce. Some day, people will start collecting the proper data. We may do it ourselves to prove the point.

But people shouldn't require data to understand what you're talking about if they experienced the changes first hand. Do you find that they can relate to the message on some basic level?

Sure. Remember U.S. Secretary of the Interior James Watt's embarrassment when he canceled the Beach Boys concert in Washington, D.C. in 1983 to keep out "undesirable elements"? Everyone laughed at him because they knew the Beach Boys don't attract undesirable elements — they're a bull market band. But no one could articulate that point; they just knew it was funny.

* * * * * * * * * * * * * * *

People
May 11, 1987

Ace Analyst Robert Prechter Says When Skirts Rise, So Does the Stock Market — No Bull

Most stock market analysts happening upon a song by the Sex Pistols in the late '70s would have simply changed the station. Analyst Robert Prechter, a former rock drummer, heard the punk group and cried, "Buy!" Such dark anthems to angst, Prechter reasoned, must signal a low point in the general public mood, meaning that both an emotional and a market improvement lay ahead.

The screwiest thing is, he was right.

* * * * * * * * * * * * * * *

It's a well-documented fact that you were convinced in 1979 and 1980 that there was a big bull market coming. What else was going on in the culture around you to convince you that we were headed higher instead of lower as so many pundits were predicting?

Punk rock was a great sign of a low in mood. But by 1980, the trend was subtly changing. It was as if the public had tired of the negative and was determined to pull itself out of the bear market mood. For instance, body building is popular in bull markets. Remember those Joe Weider ads of the 1950s and early 1960s? The modern focus on fitness was kicked off by the 1976 movie *Rocky*, which was a huge hit as the bull market hit its first momentum peak. In 1980, everyday people started getting the message. The jogging fad began in the early 1980s and turned into a full-blown craze for physical self-improvement. The 1980 method for spreading the craze was through video. Guess what was popular in that very analogous year, 1920? Workout *audio*. The newfangled technology of *that* period gave us phonograph records to do exercises by! There was a new energy building in the early 1980s, and humans had to express it by running, lifting and jumping up and down. "No pain, no gain!" This was a coincident indicator of an *emerging* bull market for stocks. Who was into exercise in 1970? Today we have the opposite situation; the market is still rising, but the public has a subtly increasing defeatist attitude. More and more articles are debunking the benefits of heavy exercise. They counsel walking instead of jogging. This emerging defeatism shows up in all kinds of areas. In politics, polls show that the majority believes that the Republicans will fail to bring about the changes they promised. A fascinating poll recently showed that while the public was split about 65/35 on the guilt/innocence of O.J. Simpson, over 70% believed that the *verdict* would be the *opposite* of their opinion. In other words, we were united in expecting injustice to be done. This and many other signs point to a change in the making toward a negative social mood.

A reader once sent a letter to *Barron's* with a hearty "phooey" to your "Popular Culture" article and accused you of implying that investors should have been reading *Women's Wear Daily* instead of *The Wall Street Journal*.

That's exactly what I was saying.

Can we actually predict the market from the fashions?

Well, let's be precise. I maintain that fashions, music, entertainment, etc., change *coincidentally* with the stock market, as both reflect mood. The point is not that cultural fads *precede* changes in psychology, but that they are a direct reflection of it, as is the position and trend of the stock market. So expressions of popular mood are not a leading indicator of stock trends, but a coincident one. In other words, the widespread popularity of miniskirts doesn't forecast a top, it is the top. Grating music and horror movies do not *forecast* a downtrend; they are *of* the downtrend.

What if a president or industry was able to manipulate these coincident indicators? Couldn't we ban punk rock and, therefore, the bear market?

A number of socially-conscious people have attacked negative-sentiment movies, rock music, literature and art as causing a pervasive negative psychology. This is an inversion of the relationship. The only reason the underlying sentiments are manifested is that we have freedom of expression. To remove that would remove the manifestation but not the reality behind it, which would merely be vented via other avenues. A case could be made that musical, artistic, literary and sports-related expressions of negative sentiment are a healthy release, as opposed to some possible alternatives. Think about this: Negative-mood music or art does not exist to make listeners feel bad. If that were so, it wouldn't sell. It makes them feel good because it mirrors their feelings. Hearing a happy song when you feel angry is an annoyance. It can actually make you feel worse. An angry song says, "Go ahead and admit your anger," which probably helps dissipate it. Imagine how you would feel in a rigid society that only allowed elevator music. Would you really walk around all day with a bland smile on your face, or would you eventually want to lash out, screaming?

Let's say you were advising the President. The stock market is way down, the music has become atonal, the art is ugly and his or her popularity is sinking to an all-time low. Can't you tell him how to change the trend?

Of course, he cannot change the trend! The trend is hundreds of millions of people interacting. Ask any President who's tried. The few times there may have appeared to be a success were simply times that the populace was ready for a leader to escort them in the direction they were going anyway.

So you could not advise a leader on how to avoid war, just that it is probable?

Isn't it valuable information for a nation to know that the risk of war is heightened? Or for that matter, insignificant?

The really scary advice to leaders comes from conventional analysts. Who is more sensible, the man who says, "War is the *result* of a negative social psychology, which is why it occurs near the end of bear markets," and therefore counsels a leader to beware of the impending risk of war in such environments, or a conventional economist who tells him, "I can see that stocks and the economy tend to pick up during or after wars, so war must create economic expansion and is therefore *a good thing*"? That's the man who advises going to war to "get the country moving again." The result of war is destruction, of course, so a moment's thought (which is more than most economists give it) proves his thesis absurd. So tell me, who would you rather have advising the President? Or another country's leader?

How have your pop culture studies been received by your colleagues?

Initially, it got a strong reaction from the financial community, either positive or negative. Today, the cultural trends analysis is the most popular section of our publications.

While my method is a complete inversion of the way everyone else approaches the relationship of extramarket events to the market, it is the only valid approach. It is so sensible that all many people need is to be exposed to that viewpoint to become receptive to it.

What about the academic community — has it corroborated your theory to any extent?

In 1990, Harold Zullow, a research fellow in social psychiatry at Columbia University's School of Public Health, got together a research team to study the optimistic vs. pessimistic rumination reflected by popular song lyrics of the past forty years. He concluded that changes in the aggregate sentiment expressed in popular songs precede changes in the economy. I'm glad this study was done. It supports the broader case presented in *Popular Culture and the Stock Market* in 1985, which argued that tempo, melody, harmony, dissonance, lyrics and noise are all important in reflecting the social mood. While Zullow's study was very narrowly focused, it was meticulous, and that's what's needed to attract attention to the idea. Further, because stock price change precedes economic change, this study supports my case that stock market and pop musical changes are coincident.

Let's go back to the fitness craze, which began gathering steam in about 1980. As the bull market roared through the mid-1980s, the craze matured with Jane Fonda's bestselling workout videos and Jazzercise classes in storefronts across America. In 1988, you predicted its demise. Has that happened?

The fitness craze peaked with the "no pain, no gain" slogan in 1987-1989 and began slipping in intensity as the bull market began losing upside momentum. Major articles have pronounced the fitness craze "dead," although that is an overstatement (see below). It's dying, though. Statistics show that the percentage of Americans who exercise regularly increased for years through 1990, but has dropped 4% through 1992. The reverse happened with smoking statistics, in the same year. Overweight adults account for 2% more of the population than they did in 1987. The most popular men's belt size has gone from 34 to 36. The percentages of Americans saying they avoid exercise, ignore cholesterol, eat fat and smoke cigarettes all rose in 1992. Because the bull market in stocks has continued, there is still a fair amount of focus on fitness, but the fever is gone. When the stock market turns down, many health clubs will go under.

* * * * * * * * * * * * * *

April 6, 1993

The rise and fall of fitness

Recent statistics indicate Americans may be reversing health-conscious trends

August 14, 1993

USA TODAY, October 21, 1993

Exercise not status symbol it once was

Jane Fonda, looking good on less

Gone are the days when Jane Fonda worked out for four hours a day, sweating over her body.

Time, January 16, 1995

FAT

Times

What health craze? Thanks to too much food and too little sweat, Americans are heavier than ever

* * * * * * * * * * * * * *

What do you mean, the bull market is losing upside momentum? The Dow seems to be making new highs every month! It sure feels powerful.

It *feels* more powerful now because your psychology is skewed that way. But it isn't. In five years from 1982 to 1987, the Dow rose 252%. In eight years from 1987 to now, it has risen 200%. Forgetting compounding for a minute, 252/5 is 50; 200/8 is 25. So from 1987 to the present, the bull market has advanced at *half the rate* of the 1982-1987 rise. Slowing upside momentum always precedes a bear market, by the way.

If cultural trends have their own ebbs and flows like the market, then you should be able to predict a change in cultural trends. Have you ever done it?

Yes, we've had a number of accurate calls. For instance, *The Elliott Wave Theorist* predicted the feel-good pop music of the 1980s, the defeat of George Bush when he had a record 91% approval rating, the top of the art and collectibles bubble in 1989, and a sharp drop in attendance at baseball games. In 1986, when top tax rates were brought down, we noted the parallel to the 1920s, when the last fifth wave of Cycle degree occurred. On that basis, we said the top tax bracket wouldn't stay down for long. So our readers were not surprised when the Clinton administration pushed through the biggest tax hike in U.S. history.

There have been many others over the years. In 1986, the bull market was on, and we said that President Reagan would almost certainly survive the Iran Contra scandal when many others were saying the scandal would be his Watergate. EWT added that Reagan would go down as one of the most-loved presidents. EWT said Michael Jackson was in trouble in March 1991, right after he signed a $1 billion contract with Sony. Since that time the "King of Pop," the musical hero of Cycle wave V, has been accused of child molestation, and his album sales have been disappointing despite massive promotional efforts.

Such forecasts may seem trivial until you realize that you can predict wars, and even their severity, using the same methods. All of the forecasts I just mentioned were strictly technically based, on the premise that mass psychological trends produce social events.

Even with intimate industry knowledge, show biz insiders would be hard-pressed to accurately forecast something like Jackson's decline in popularity — especially when you consider when it was made. Indeed,

we know insiders were making the opposite bet by the price Sony had to pay to sign Jackson. Is it typical for companies to sign big contracts at the peak in an entertainer's popularity?

Now you know why they call it paying top dollar. Remember when *The Cosby Show* was sold into syndication for the highest amount ever? It was at the top of his popularity. I'll bet it's a long time before the value of that sale is recouped.

Where can I read more about this?

I plan to publish a book in late 1996 that will address the theory in more detail. The history of popular music fads is particularly interesting in how it ties in with the bull and bear markets in stocks.

Let's backtrack a bit. In your 1985 *Pop Culture* report and *The Elliott Wave Theorist*, you said there would be a Beatles of the 1980s, a smash act that would break all the records. But, at that time, it was not apparent who that was. Subsequent record sales and mass veneration have led you to the conclusion that it was Jackson. Is that right?

It's very clear that the musical hero of the Cycle wave V bull market was Michael Jackson, who was receiving all the adulation that was enjoyed by Benny Goodman, Frank Sinatra, Elvis Presley and the Beatles in their respective bull markets (see Figure 3-2 on page 212). His tour that ended in January 1989 was the biggest selling tour in history. Its net revenues dwarfed every other tour of the year combined. The interesting thing was that a lot of the gushing teenage excitement was overseas. Europe and Japan, places like that. There was a special on TV that would blow your mind. It looked like the Beatles' *Hard Day's Night* movie and was equally intense in terms of audience reaction. People were fainting and crying. It was unbelievable. He was the one.

* * * * * * * * * * * * * * *

EDGE

January 1995

An analysis of the sentiment that surrounded THE pop music idols of the 1930s, '40s, '50s, '60s and '80s shows that they all came in on creative, energetic bursts of public enthusiasm that resembled panic buying on Wall Street.

From Goodman, the King of Swing, through Presley, the King of Rock 'n' Roll, to Jackson, the King of Pop, there is the same meteoric rise. Popular accounts consistently refer to all as episodes in which teenagers were gripped by an unexpected and mysterious delirium. As they swooned and fainted, the rest of the population looked on with a mix of curiosity, bafflement and disapproval. Jackson's white gloves were banned from schools. Goodman's swinging fans were called "deeply disturbed" victims of a harmful nervous disorder. In both cases and each case in between, the artists and their handlers could barely explain, let alone recreate, the feverish emotional high they had triggered.

In 1943, as Frank Sinatra's star was lifting off, his manager George Evans put his finger on it. He told the *Chicago Tribune News Service* that Sinatra's talents provided an "initial impetus." His own planting of "organized and regimented moaning" in Sinatra's crowd accounted for some of the panic. But there was something larger at work.

"Frankie is a product of crowd psychology," Evans finally concluded.

This is, of course, Prechter's point.

* * * * * * * * * * * * * *

Once you fingered Michael Jackson, was it simply a matter of expecting the frenzy to expire — just like it did for all the others?

In a bear market, heroic symbols of the old bull market are torn down.

In March 1991, Jackson was described as "a national treasure" and "the planet's top star." When he signed that $1 billion contract with Sony, we wrote that if Michael Jackson were a stock, he would have just spiked to a top. Within a year of that contract, Jackson's image was slipping. Reviews of his records were mixed to critical. His sister ridiculed him on national television. People sued him for stealing lyrics. His albums failed to exceed previous sales. That was the first wave down. Then came a wave two bounce, when Jackson performed for the Super Bowl half time show in 1993. Soon afterward, upon being accused of child molestation and paying off the accuser, his image collapsed. The list of indignities he has suffered in the downhill slide is stunning. Even his own family is ripping at the image.

Maybe he just lost his edge? Or maybe he went over it?

Well, Jackson certainly kept working hard. His behavior, good and bad, has not changed. It is the public's focus that has changed. Whether he committed wrongdoing that warrants the collapse of his image is irrelevant to the dynamic anyway. The main point with respect to the Wave Principle is not whether

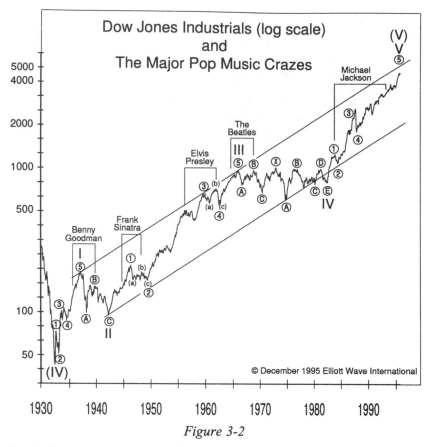

Figure 3-2

the information or revised social image of these various heroes is true, but that it will happen when the time requires. Secretly evil or incompetent heroic figures are protected by bull market psychology regardless of the facts, and truly good or talented heroes are ravaged by bear market psychology regardless of the facts. It is not the *person* that matters. It's the *persona*.

Who else is getting that treatment?

Walt Disney, for one. Who is more of an American symbol than Walt Disney? Few people in the U.S. have been more loved. His image was recently trashed, too, in the book *Walt Disney, Hollywood's Dark Prince*, which alleges that he was secretly an FBI informant, a McCarthyite and several other nasty things. J. Edgar Hoover is another one. He was considered a hero for decades, and now suddenly, after all these years, we are apprised of his secret sex life, that he was blackmailed throughout his professional life into leaving the Mafia free to operate, that he was a blackmailer himself, keeping secret files on the sex lives of presidents in order to control them, and further, that despite being a closet homosexual, he persecuted homosexuals and minorities. This new profile is the polar opposite of the revered symbol of might and justice that held sway in the preceding decades. Want more? Bob Hope was pilloried in a book that alleges that he was a cold, manipulative adulterer who demanded "the best hooker in town" everywhere he traveled. Again, that's quite a change from the image of the beloved guy of the Hope/Crosby road pictures who tirelessly and fearlessly traveled to war-torn lands to entertain U.S. troops for little pay. In England, books, TV and the press paint unflattering portraits of Winston Churchill, Prince Charles and Chairman Mao Tse-tung, all of whom in prior years were sacred cows.

I thought it was very well said by Richard Gere. He was married to Cindy Crawford, who is considered one of the most beautiful women in the country. The rumor allegedly going around was that they're both gay. He said, "You know, some people are really torn up inside. Their lives are all messed up. They think that it's soothing to their own misery if they can tear down somebody else in the process."

I'm glad you quoted that. We've gotten into a topic that is seemingly far from our original topic, markets. But it isn't. As that quote reveals, the public perception is not necessarily based upon an action of Richard Gere or Cindy Crawford or Michael Jackson. Their images are in the collective mind of the public. They can place them in star status, and they can remove their sanction. It is the *same* essential change in the collective mindset that marks the onset of a turn in the markets.

That's a reasonable theory, and granted, you were able to use it to make some predictions that came true. But now to use its fulfillment to say, for instance, that Michael Jackson's sliding off the charts means that stocks are soon going to turn down...a lot of people would say that's absolutely absurd.

Only if you believe that the frenzy over Michael Jackson was due to himself alone. If it expressed a larger culture-wide enthusiasm, then must it not have other avenues of expression? Even in this case, I am not talking only of Michael Jackson. It has been amazing to me to watch in the last 8 years how many popular cultural icons of American identity have been trashed in the media or in books.

It's not just Hollywood people or music people. It involves all types of people who have a public persona that is bigger than an individual's normally is. When you think about it, there is a hero in virtually every field who has been trashed. People recently have even gone back in history to rip George Washington, Thomas Jefferson and even Christopher Columbus, who lived 500 years ago!

We're approaching a Grand Supercycle bear versus a Cycle degree bear market in the late 1960s. From a cultural perspective, how is the higher magnitude of this transition being reflected?

Let me give you a good example. The big musical hero of the '40s was Frank Sinatra. The '50s was Elvis Presley. The '60s was Lennon/McCartney. And the '80s and early '90s was Michael Jackson. *All* survived substantially intact until the recent poisonous social attitude toward heroes emerged, and they were viciously attacked. Widely publicized "unauthorized biographies" trashed the first three, and the press is doing in the fourth (though a book is undoubtedly on the way there, too). So apparently we had to wait until the final top in *all* these degrees of upward trend to see *all* these guys trashed at once. Al Goldman wrote a book on John Lennon and one on Elvis Presley. Kitty Kelly took on Frank Sinatra. To the virtual exclusion of any positive balance, books have selectively created images of Frank Sinatra as a heartless mobster, Elvis Presley as a drug-numbed fat slob, and John Lennon as a cruel, drug-numbed anorexic slug. Michael Jackson has been portrayed as a loon and sexual deviant. The emerging negative mood forces are doing their best to destroy the heroes' images. For a time, it will probably appear that they have won.

Does the building up and tearing down apply even to fictional heroes where the symbolism is consciously constructed?

Absolutely. One of the biggest symbols of America has always been Superman. Superman is the comic book hero most symbolic of American strength, heroism, morality and good will, not just for the 1980s, but for the entire Supercycle uptrend in social mood dating from the 1930s. "Born" in 1934, Superman was an especially popular hero during each of the Cycle degree bull markets within the Supercycle, on a TV series in the 1950s and in four blockbuster movies in the 1980s. He was killed off in the November 1992 issue. DC Comics brought him back, but replaced him with four super-powered characters, a steelworker, a cyborg, a punk teenager and a cold blooded vigilante, which is transparently a fractured and negative view of what the U.S. has become. Today, Superman is so beset by angst he can hardly function. On TV, *Lois and Clark* is bowing to the bull market, but presents a watered-down version of Superman befitting the topping process. Even so, it is easy to contrast his character to that of the superhero of a bear market, 1970s TV hero The Hulk, whose main reason for being was revenge.

Give me another.

O.K. How about another imaginary folk hero, the Marlboro Man? He has single-handedly kept his brand of cigarettes the nation's most popular for years. He's been on the scene since the early 1950s, a heroic image suited to the Supercycle bull market. Of course, cowboys have been the essence of the American image for a long, long time. But in 1992, all that changed. His image began losing its ability to capture consumers' imagination.

* * * * * * * * * * * * * *

The Wall Street Journal
September 14, 1992

Ask anyone on Madison Avenue to name the most successful campaign in advertising history and chances are the Marlboro Man wins hands down.

Yet, after 40 years of riding tall in the saddle, the ubiquitous cowboy is losing his effectiveness. In an effort to try to freshen up the campaign, Phillip Morris cos. executives concede that they have begun moving away from using the classic image of the Marlboro Man on his horse. Many are beginning to wonder whether the cowboy is getting the job done. "The Marlboro Man's problem is old age."

* * * * * * * * * * * * * *

The reason is that the old bull market is losing power. People are looking for different images to reflect the subtle underlying change in social mood. He's probably too classically masculine for the emerging trend. So guess what. He's been redesigned. In many promotions, he's no longer a multicolored man on a horse, he's a black and white half-hidden image. He looks more like a 1950s hood. This change-of-image analysis prompted us to recommend selling Phillip Morris near a high, before it dropped 40% in two months in early 1993.

Even lower tier "nice guy" heroes have been attacked, including kiddy characters Barney the Dinosaur, viciously excoriated and beaten up at malls, and Bert & Ernie, whom rightist groups accuse of subversive homosexuality.

Nothing is sacred.

Not exactly. They are being attacked *because* they are sacred.

I see. Any more examples of an image or icon that was carefully constructed in the bull market years and is now being torn apart?

Well, Barbie is the Mattel doll beauty that has represented preteen girls' ideal since her debut in 1959. In the summer of 1993 came a guerrilla attack on the doll in a book called *Mondo Barbie*. With vicious glee, various authors tore the doll's and her companions' images to shreds. A group called the "Barbie Liberation Front" claimed "credit" for switching recorded voice production boxes between 300 Barbies and G.I. Joes nationwide, surprising parents and children on Christmas day. They were protesting "sexism" in toys. This is a hint of a change in attitude toward the Barbie doll. Whatever your opinion of Barbie, you cannot deny that she is a U.S. cultural icon. My guess is that Barbie's days of high and/or increasing popularity (a Barbie doll is sold every two seconds) are numbered. When the bear market in stocks begins, her image will be seen as hopelessly outmoded.

If Barbie is a sexist stereotype now, she was surely that in the late 1960s. In almost all of these cases, the transgressions for which these heroes are being brought down happened years ago. Why are we just getting around to knocking them off their pedestals?

Because cultural psychology is in a sea change from Grand Supercycle bull to Grand Supercycle bear. Bull markets include a preference for a black-and-white morality. The 1950s' representatives were cowboys and war heroes; the 1960s featured spy heroes; the 1980s gave us military style "action" heroes.

It is now time for more complex role models and antiheroes to emerge. The current peaking period, like that of 1966-1968, is producing a dense combination of cultural symbols. One reflects the nearly exhausted uptrend's extreme, the other reflects the emergence of the new downtrend. The topping phase brings parody, which is the first hint that heroes are being laughed at rather than revered. Prior excesses are lampooned in order to appeal to the newly emerging cynicism.

Who are Winston Churchill, Bob Hope, J. Edgar Hoover and Superman being replaced by?

Emerging cultural heroes in the U.S. include comic book vigilantes, criminal "gangsta rap" artists (one was charged with attempted murder while his debut record sold 800,000 copies in its first week), "shock jock" Howard Stern, who reached #2 on the bestseller list, and mass murderer Charles Manson, whose music is being published and performed for the first time ever. This list is an advance peek at who will be the Andy Warhols and Johnny Rottens of the late '90s. The new trend will get far more extreme before it is exhausted. The dark side of social mood as seen through radio, movies, fashion, literature and even comics is establishing itself with a rapidity rivaling that of 1968-69. Sociopolitical demonstrations, political upset and U.S.-related war activity have slowly begun to increase. All of these are typical of a long-term change in the major trend from "up" to "down." In 1987, the trend fell until it finally affected the stock market. This time should be no different.

Is it only heroes that change?

Oh, no. *Popular Culture and the Stock Market* postulated that symbols of *all* types, for each major social psychological wave, exit the scene when the wave is over. As we talked about before, 1966 provided one of the most dramatic examples, as pop musicians who had specialized in innocent, feel-good music suddenly retired, fell from popularity or changed radically in style. But in addition, a huge number of long running TV shows were canceled in and near the same year, at the top of Cycle wave III.

Similarly since 1992, popular shows and other phenomena associated with the 1980s bull market, and in some cases the Supercycle bull market from 1949 or 1932, have been saying good-bye. This rush to the exits is reflective of the fact that Cycle wave V is ending. The most celebrated, popular and longest running of today's television sitcoms, *Cheers*, has ceased production. This highly beloved symbol of the bull market took to the air in 1982, at the bull market lift-off, and ended in May 1993. Consider star Ted Danson's response to the question of why he decided to call it quits: "*It was just time for me to leave.*" This seemingly innocuous comment struck *TV Guide's* editors as so important that they put it on the cover. Fellow actor George Wendt responded, "I think that Ted's instincts are very well-honed and right on the money. He knew that it was time." The timing of his decision is not without reason, nor is it for a tangible reason. In the world of social phenomena, the deepest reason for change is, "It's time." Recognizing that fact and leaving the scene voluntarily is a rare feat and saves having to endure the downward spiral that is inevitable for any activity that depends upon public favor. *Cheers* is not the kind of show that will spearhead the upcoming bear market. Some other show is waiting in the wings to do that. *Cheers* is hardly alone. Bull market representatives Bill Cosby and Johnny Carson quit their super-popular shows in 1992. The super-popular Roseanne begins her last season in 1995.

It seems as if there must be personality types to which people respond differently in a bull market than they do in a bear market.

Most definitely. Bill Cosby, for instance, is a bull market personality. He hit it big in comedy in the early 1960s, then dropped out of sight until the early 1980s. In 1984, he launched what *TV Guide* called the decade's most important program. Similarly, Johnny Carson took over the *Tonight Show* in October 1962, the month of the Cuban Missile Crisis market low. He made his name in bull market years, and stayed the king of late night for 30 years, exiting gracefully in the final years of an extended bull market. Had he continued for another decade, he probably would have gone out as a has-been. By contrast, Morton Downey had a hugely rated talk show in 1987-1988.

His abrasive style and audience-baiting tactics thrived in that brief period of bear market sentiment.

At major turns in the market, popular entertainment styles end abruptly. So if you can recognize such events, you can make some assumptions about the trend.

There are still upbeat, energetic songs and some love songs being played on the radio today, and plenty of what's getting watched on TV, like the 1994 #1 show *Home Improvement*, is relatively innocuous comedy.

Sure. The bull market is still in force. And in studying it somewhat, I have found that TV is one of the last media to change styles. It's very subtle at first. You have to look in the cracks. *Roseanne* took over from Cosby as the #1 show when the bull market's upside momentum slowed. *Roseanne* is a comedy, but it is not as sugary as Cosby's was, and has a lot of tragedy in it. The first signs of change are never anything absolutely nega- tive. That is saved for the bottom.

Even when you do get a bear market show, it's not total misery. I mean, people must like them or they wouldn't watch. Would they?

Of course they like them. People come out of the theater smiling after seeing *MacBeth* or *Phantom of the Opera*, but they are horror plots. The same thing was true of *All in the Family*, a bear market TV show with endless screaming, insults, stupid- ity, anger and argument. But people liked it. This is not some kind of anomaly; *it is my whole point*. People enjoy such enter- tainment more in bear markets.

In many ways, the avant-garde appears to be way out in front of the bear market, but the average person remains upbeat?

It's normal for the public to be many steps behind the avant- garde, and normal for the avant-garde to anticipate bear markets best. People who have been immersed in an art for a long time often appear to need perversion to be stimulated. This reflects the classic relationship between the public and the stock mar- ket, too. Public optimism comes late in the uptrend, as seasoned veterans begin to get bearish. The public starts buying stocks en masse just before the top, and they remain bullish during the early part of the downtrend, lagging the sentiment of the vets.

* * * * * * * * * * * * *

The Elliott Wave Theorist
February 26, 1993

The longest running #1 pop single of all time, Whitney Houston's "I Will Always Love You," is characterized by *Newsweek* as "an aesthetic of perpetual climax...you go right to ecstasy and stay there...a new model for pop music." This characterization applies equally well to the stock market since 1989. It reached ecstasy and has stayed there, delivering climax after climax of overvaluation in various stock groups.

* * * * * * * * * * * * *

You say we are in a "topping phase," when contesting cultural phenomena are the norm. How does this contest manifest itself?

Newsweek ran a two-page article on the distinct dichotomy between the past few years' biggest selling styles of popular music. On the one hand is a style that they described as "brutal,...exploding with bloodcurdling rage." On the other is a style that is "unrealistically gentle,...cooing about love conquering all." *The Elliott Wave Theorist* first noticed the extreme divergence in trends in February 1989: "The mixed mood of the topping phase can be seen by this juxtaposition between the #1 single and the #1 album of September 1988, which were 'Don't Worry, Be Happy' (Bobby McFerrin) and *Appetite For Destruction* (Guns 'n' Roses), respectively." This dichotomy of forces has been going on since the crash of '87. When the market turns down, the bear market sentiments will assume dominance, and maintain it until the low.

The Beatles are to the Rolling Stones as...

As the last up move in a euphoric bull market is to the first down move of a growling bear. Here in late 1995, the Beatles are enjoying a massive success with their *Anthology* project. I would not be surprised to see the Stones pull off something similar shortly afterward.

What about dress?

Somebody wrote an article in *Barron's* asking, "What happened to the big spenders?" They were talking about *Dallas* and *Dynasty*. Now television has the blue-collar *Roseanne*. In the U.S., the most important development on the fashion scene is the emergence of "grunge." Grunge is a look adopted by many older teenagers. It features T-shirts, old flannel overshirts, beat-up cutoff jeans, long johns and soft caps. The point is to look poor, but in a way that all your peers accept. *Popular Culture and the Stock Market* listed "anti-fashion fashions" as characterizing the "falling transition" phase of social mood. These are the precise words used in articles on the new dress code. (See below.) When was the last time this happened? It was 1967-1970, the years of bell bottom jeans, long unkempt hair, sloppy shirts and boots (and the VW as the car of fashionable choice). Then, as now, the wearers insisted they merely wanted to be comfortable, not fashionable. Not coincidentally, that dramatic shift from the neat look took place as the stock market was making its final run into 1968. That was late in the topping process for Cycle wave III, and today it's late in the topping process for Cycle wave V.

If mood precedes events, as I argued earlier, then isn't it interesting that the grungy fashions of 1967-70 *preceded* the first recession in a decade? The mood behind fashion is father to the outcome. In 1969, people wanted desperately not to look prosperous, and lo and behold, a few years later, they weren't. Fashion signaled a mood change, which had tangible results.

* * * * * * * * * * * * * *

The Atlanta Journal / The Atlanta Constitution
November 22, 1992

The Trickle-up Theory: Grunge, Hip-Hop Looks Going Mainstream

"It seems more like *anti-fashion*," says Derrick McCurdy, wearing a cap he made from old ties over flowing blond hair and long sideburns.

Unlike the political statements for peace or anarchy made by hippies and punks of past decades, grungers aren't trying to say much with their choice of duds.

Most of all, grungers say fashion trends are far from their minds. Cheap threads that protect from the elements (achieved most effectively with haphazard layering) are their priority. Their boutique of choice? The Salvation Army.

Many young fashion designers have been converted. In this month's issue of *Harper's Bazaar*, Christian Francis Roth declares, "I'm sick of fashion. I'm sick of styling."

* * * * * * * * * * * * * *

In a bull market, something that's obviously fashionable is investment. When the mood turns down, what happens to this fashion?

In bull market years, investment and speculation are "in." Investment and speculation are tied to some idea of competence, whether it be the skill of the speculator himself, the success of the company whose stock is being purchased, the favorable prospects for the overall economy or the country, etc. These are bull market sentiments. What's more, investment and speculation serve a positive social purpose in making capital and liquidity available to corporations and investors.

Gambling is the bear market manifestation of the same urge. Gambling was brought to Atlantic City, New Jersey during the 1970s, sparking the greatest run that gambling company stocks have ever had, in 1978. Gambling took a back seat to investment in the 1980s, but continued to spread because the Grand Supercycle bear market as measured in constant dollars is still an underlying influence. As the bear market approaches, real gambling fever is once again emerging. Investment is an activity for people who want to use their brains and effort to earn a million dollars over their lifetimes. Gambling is for those who want Lady Luck to grant them a million dollars NOW. Even gambling that involves some skill, such as poker playing, has no larger social value than rewarding the skillful gambler. However, the type of gambling that is becoming increasingly popular today involves no skill. It is a bet not on competence, but on luck, fate, fortune. Ironically, the largest promoter of this form of gambling is government. Most U.S. states already have lotteries. More are pushing for them. Many restrict casino gambling only to Indian reservations or other area so they can impose a monopoly and collect bigger revenues.

Do you think the critics are right about lotteries being a tax on the poor?

Lotteries are not exactly a tax on the poor. They are a tax on the stupid. First, the odds of winning big are less than those for getting struck directly by lightning. Second, state monopoly lotteries only pay out 70% of the take. Thus, the buyer of a lottery ticket is not betting on average luck, but against virtually impossible odds and with a certainty that 30% of his money will be confiscated. A better term for a government lottery is a lootery.

Ultimately, the grunge look will go well with people's net worth. In the meantime, however, the clash of a runaway riverboat gambling mentality with the wealth that was generated over the last two generations has created a kind of circus atmosphere. From what you've said, I could trace the start of this peak to 1987, 1988 or 1989. Where exactly is the front edge of this big top?

Social events, as EWT has chronicled, say emphatically that something changed after the peak in 1987, when the averages began dramatically slowing their ascent.

You've been talking about this transition phase for eight years. Why is it taking so long?

So far, this transition phase has lasted nearly three times as long as the top in the late 1960s, which apparently is due to the much larger degree of the turn.

I can see how cultural trends could help you confirm market trend changes, but can they help in any other aspect of wave analysis?

In fact, they can. One example of an Elliott Wave guidelines that is useful in social forecasting is that a fifth wave attempts to re-live the technical glory of the third, but manages in the end only an echo. This is true in terms of breadth, underlying fundamentals, and sometimes rate of price change. This observation also applies to social trends. It explains why Disney movies became popular again in Cycle wave V; they were popular during Cycle wave III from 1942 to 1966. That's why we have oldies radio, playing the music of the 1950s and 1960s. That's why in the early 1980s we elected a president, Ronald Reagan, who called for a return to the values of Calvin Coolidge and Dwight Eisenhower, presidents during previous bull markets. Notice that in most of these cases, the extent of innovation in the fifth wave is very low; *innovation* occurs in the third wave, *copying* in the fifth. In attempting to re-live the glory of third waves, fifth waves have a decided bent toward nostalgia.

That explains why people don't really look back at the 1980s with the fondness they have for the 1950s and 1960s. The 1980s were fun, but somehow unable to measure up to the exuberance and spontaneity of the 1960s. Woodstock II drew a big crowd, but by 1960s standards, just the idea of a Woodstock reunion is an oxymoron.

Right. It's not a new idea or event. It's nostalgia.

I see that with the musical heroes you talked about before. Elvis is always rumored to be turning up in some Burger King somewhere.

Yep, they've all been reborn in one form or another. Right in the middle of the bull market, after 50 years, half a page in *USA Today* was dedicated to Benny Goodman. It was a sign of increased interest in the man. And remember, he rose to popularity in 1934. People began going crazy for him in 1936 and 1937. There was a TV special in 1986. Around the same time, there was huge publicity surrounding Frank Sinatra. In fact, record companies are producing multi-CD sets on Sinatra costing over $400. Hundreds of thousands of visitors and annual mourners turn up at Elvis' Graceland, and by many he is considered a deity. There have been active fan clubs and Top 10 record sales for old songs by the Beatles, which have been 1995's biggest money-making musical group. The public has re-lived or rediscovered every pop music icon from the advancing Cycle waves of the entire Supercycle. Why is that? Because the entire Supercycle is peaking and we're nostalgic for all of it.

But it hasn't been a total rehash. We had plenty of new songs in the 1980s, didn't we?

Songs, yes, but not styles. Unless you list rap as a style, which in fact is the ultimate in derivativeness. The artists don't even make their own sounds except the words. They take previously recorded music and then do what's called "sampling," then rap over it.

What seems to be lacking is inspiration and creativity and new horizons. Completely new sounds, new ideas, new approaches. It all relates to stuff that happened 10 to 40 years ago.

Will we get away from this?

Sure! But it will get worse first. The next time of great creativity will be in the next third wave of Supercycle degree, and that is decades away.

So don't look for anything new?

That's not exactly it. Bear markets are not times of great artistic innovation except in the intention to shock. So horror movies will present something new. In art, there will be the new, but little of the artistic, because the point of art in a bear market is to shock. Take punk rock, for example. That was a new approach to popular music, and it was meant to shock. Whether you want to call it imaginative or creative is another matter. There are really two aspects: artistry and newness. Artistry survives the centuries; newness doesn't necessarily. And bear market newness is often derivative, as its purpose is to annihilate something that already exists, not create something truly new.

Politics, Inclusionism and War

Can you apply the rules of Elliott to social trends?

The guideline of Alternation seems to apply. It has a specific technical meaning in wave formation, but also pertains to social trends. For example, you might recall that Richard Nixon won re-election in a landslide in late 1972 at the peak of a bull market. Despite everyone's high hopes, he was hounded as a law-breaker and ultimately driven from office in August 1974 by the social mood reflected by the bear market. Bill Clinton took office with the market at a new all-time high amidst strong popularity, a *Time* "Man of the Year" cover, and high hopes for his performance. Like Nixon, he is being hounded as a law-breaker. Instead of Watergate, it's Whitewater. And Vince Foster, Paula Jones, Gennifer Flowers, you name it. The guideline of alternation points out the *difference* this time around. It was the liberal press that exploited the weaknesses of Richard Nixon. In the current environment, it is the conservative media that are exploiting the weaknesses of Bill Clinton. If the bear market arrives before his term is up, the probability of his drowning in scandal is as high as Nixon's was in 1973. A bear market increases the public's and the media's sensitivity to and desire for scandal, and if a leader is vulnerable to scandal, which in this case he certainly is, a bear market could destroy his popularity, and if it happens soon enough, even drive him from office.

So, you would be surprised to see Clinton re-elected?

What I'm saying is that a big bear market would virtually preclude his re-election. It could even force public attention rather dramatically to his (and maybe his wife's) wrongdoings, as happened to Nixon in the 1974 bear market. Only a three-way race would make his re-election remotely possible, and then it would be a fluke. If the market keeps rising, that's another story.

Back in 1989, when two-party politics appeared assured forever, you predicted a third party and a shake-up of the traditional parties.

Yes, because what normally happens in the kind of period that is approaching is a polarization of opinion in all kinds of areas. It's not just that the left takes over or the right takes over. But during bull markets such as in the 1950s and the 1980s, most people are centrists. In bear markets, you see extreme polarization. You get leftists and rightists on one axis, and authoritarians and champions of individual liberty on the other, battling it out for power.

Is there necessarily a direct relationship? Do the social dynamics that make investors buy or sell stocks also influence the electorate to choose one presidential candidate over the other?

Yes. The single best predictor of Presidential popularity is the trend of the Dow Jones Industrial Average. The precision with which the level of Presidential popularity has tracked the Dow and its rate of change is remarkable. It usually also indicates whether a President will win re-election.

Regardless of who he is?

Of course. When extremes in markets are reached, it merely means that the social mood has swung the pendulum far enough in that direction. For whatever reason, people are ready for a change in the opposite direction, and therefore, they will elect people who will provide the change they want. In other words, the trend of the public's overall attitude is the cause of the style of the president elected, not the other way around. The social psychology that accompanies a bull or bear market is the main determinant not only of how a president is selected, but also how his performance is perceived.

* * * * * * * * * * * * * *

The Elliott Wave Theorist
March 29, 1991

In July 1990, with the Dow at 3000, George Bush was winning praise and high approval ratings. He was "a man for the season," riding "a huge current of political popularity." Just four months later, with the Dow below 2400, as reported in the November 30, 1990 issue of EWT, he was being bombed with derisive headlines. "Bush May Have Lost 1992 Already," "From Sizzle to Fizzle," "a quagmire of indecision and ineptitude which could take him the rest of the Presidency to dig out of" typified the press reports. Here it is, exactly four months later once again, with the Dow back at 3000, and George Bush has a 91% approval rating, the highest in the history of the records, and the media love him again.

* * * * * * * * * * * * * *

I take it this is true not only in the U.S.

The April 1991 issue listed several world political leaders who resigned or reached record low popularity readings in late 1990 when their markets were down. To emphasize how important the stock market is in reflecting the social mood of a country and therefore the popularity of its leader, EWT contrasted their disfavor to the popularity of George Bush and British Prime Minister John Major. In early 1991, Bush and Major governed the only countries in the world in which a stock market average hit new all-time highs. Meanwhile, Australia's Prime Minister Hawke and Finance Minister Keating and German Chancellor Helmut Kohl were way down in the polls, as their stock markets had only an anemic rebound.

West Germany was much better off economically than Britain, but the ratings did not track the economic realities. They tracked the social mood, which is more accurately reflected by the level, speed and direction of stock prices. A downtrend in mood feeds upon itself. Negative mood brings about stock selling, and stock selling brings about negative mood. When people lose 10, 15, 20 or 90% of their money, they tend to get angry in about the same measure. And that's when they tend to vote for more radical candidates. When the next general decline in world stock markets takes place, the popularity of all incumbents will suffer. If the markets fall as far as cycles suggest in the next three years, most incumbents will not win re-election.

So by looking at what markets are doing, you have an objective, mathematical representation of the consciousness of the people at that time, and the consciousness of the people predicts in advance what's going to happen in the political realm.

I would say more precisely that the stock market is a mathematical representation of the *un*consciousness of the people, and the forces behind that unconsciousness drive most social action.

Including the political.

Correct, but you won't really see all the political *results* immediately. For instance, at a market low, you might get a revolution, an election of a military style leader, a coup, or whatever, but the ramifications of *that* come later, as they sometimes take a lot of time to generate.

So a government can effect change based on the old mood trend even if the mood that put it in place is past?

Oh, yes. Governments are almost always acting on the last trend, the one that is already well advanced or over. For example, the stock market ended a 24-year bear market in 1859. So much tension had developed that a few actions ignited the Civil War. The rising market reflected an improving mood, but the wheels in motion didn't stop until the market approached a high.

But aren't there instances in which the government can intervene in ways to throw the Wave Principle off? A lot of people say the Fed stepped in and bought futures after the crash of 1987, for instance. Isn't that an example of enlightened government action? How can the Wave Principle anticipate the actions of a central banker?

You're telling me that the crash would have taken stocks to zero without government action? I don't think so. Their timing was good. I had said in EWT a few days before the low that the 2-week cycle was due to bottom on Monday-Tuesday, and it bottomed Tuesday morning. So if the Fed intervened, it may have gotten an illusion of power by a matter of luck. Or more accurately, because it panicked at the low. But if central banks really did have control over finance, gold's chart pattern of 1970-

1980 wouldn't exist. Gold never would have enjoyed a historic bull market and reached $850 an ounce. If authorities could stop bear markets, then the Japanese market would not have fallen 60%, I can assure you!

No power at all?

Central banks don't even *appear* to run the show unless the environment is right, i.e., unless the trend is behind them to start with. And even then, they control nothing. The market is always running the show. Central banks will try to manipulate things, but when you look back, you find that every hourly, daily, weekly and monthly wave is there. Central banks panic and make decisions the same way the public does. They say, "We've got to control this. We've got to move money here. We've got to move money there." They are racing back and forth in rhythm with the market. Generally late, as a matter of fact.

Politicians are the same way?

Sure. They react to markets, they do not create them. You'll find that a lot of political acts occur at predictable times. Usually at the bottom of C waves and the top of fifth waves. One example was the Great Society program at the top of wave III in stocks. That kind of fundamental event can usually be forecast in advance using a forecast under Elliott.

Since politics is so far behind the curve, why even talk about it?

If you're a trader, there is no reason to do it. If you want to *anticipate political change*, which can be useful, the best way is to understand the forces and trends behind markets. Markets are the premier measure of a society's psychology.

What can we expect in the political arena going forward?

Back in February 1989, when the future was rosy and every Congressman had a bona fide 98% chance of re-election as many studies extrapolating past trends assured us, I wrote several paragraphs about the likelihood of the destruction of one or the other major parties, if not both, between 1992 and 2004. I forecast that parties would get more radical, i.e., socialist, fascist, and/or libertarian, that one or more new parties will be formed, and that at least one new party or independent candidate will win the presidency. Already, with the candidacy of Ross Perot and the wholesale retirement of Democrats by election in 1994 and by choice in 1995, you can see the psychology changing as forecast. Ross Perot came out of left field and shook up the traditional parties. But recall that in 1992 he did not actually begin the campaign. He was pressed by a groundswell of popular support to enter the race. Perot was not part of the establishment, which is, of course, one of the reasons he was so adored. In Japan, voters threw out several career politicians to elect comedians. Anyone as long as he was an amateur! Ultimately, the political change in the U.S. should be at least as dramatic as that of the 1840s and 1850s. Incumbents will be thrown out, because the political leaders get the blame or credit for natural social cycles.

That wouldn't be all bad.

In the modern age, we're very lucky. In ancient times, when bear markets occurred and sovereigns had a lot of power, they went and chopped people up. But in modern days, it's the people that chop up the politicians. Except in war. That's when politicians go back to their roots.

Is there anything on the political scene the waves are unclear about?

Always. What concerns me most is that while I know politics will become radical, I cannot tell which forces will win. Will the U.S. become primarily *fascist*, as it has been leaning with its property seizure laws, anti-free speech laws, RICO, EPA levies, and gestapo-like attacks on private citizens by the FBI, ATF and DEA, or *socialist*, as it has been leaning with its welfarist business laws, demands for socialized medicine, smothering regulation, and taxation of enterprise, or *free*? I don't know.

The combination of authoritarian urges ultimately takes you where the left and the right seem to meet. Either way, the result is the same — a decrease in freedom. Isn't that the basic struggle?

My interpretation of the 1980s up to 1987 was that we had a brief period of increasing freedom. It was, of course, during the best bull market years. Ronald Reagan was president. Even if he didn't increase freedom, I think, for most of that period there was not a marked decrease. During 1988 to 1991, we started losing freedom again under George Bush. He brought in more re-regulation than anyone in the history of the Presidency. The next step was the election of Bill Clinton. Obviously, his programs, particularly in the areas of health care and crime, have been designed to deprive huge numbers of Americans from freedom of choice in very important parts of their lives. The next President is likely to decrease our freedom even more. The final question is this: As the bear market progresses, who will win the battle, the part of the population that will demand a more authoritarian government, or the part that will demand to be free again? All I can predict now is the polarity, not the outcome.

Another major development on the political scene is the number of female candidates. Since the 1992 election, we have seen more and more. Is this a trend?

Well, I made the observation ten years ago that bull markets include a general preference for symbols of distinct sexual identities. Male symbols sport a macho image in bull markets, while female symbols sport an extreme feminine image. At the height of her popularity, Madonna, the queen of Cycle wave V, was an '80s version of Marilyn Monroe, queen of Cycle wave III. In bear markets, by contrast, symbols of sexuality more readily sport mixed or integrated sexual identities, with women becoming more masculine and men more feminine. Even "Wonder Woman" made it to TV in the 1970s. It is of some interest that among the surviving superheroes in DC Comics is a team of women. Japan has just exported a female cartoon superhero. This change in cultural symbols reflects only slightly more concrete developments in other areas, such as politics, where many women are running for office, as opposed to the situation in the 1950s and early 1960s, when a bull market was in force at all degrees. If you recall, the women's movement gained terrific momentum in the bear market of the 1970s. That's when Bella Abzug, Betty Friedan and Gloria Steinem were hot...at least in terms of public image.

In 1995, for the first time, seven of the top ten celebrity product endorsers are women. In 1986, there were none.

That's because we're approaching a bear market. In every field, women gain dominance in bear market periods, and depending upon how the top is formed, the trend can begin a bit before or a bit after the price peak registered on the New York Stock Exchange.

It seems to be something that appears late in the cycle. When Rome went into decline, for instance, there was a similar phenomenon. Some historians have even blamed Rome's fall on the rise of women. These days some use it to say Western civilization's main problem is that it's henpecked.

Well, I'm not saying that such things are causes. My position is different. The position you describe is one that implies it can be fixed. "If men would just change, or women would just change, then civilization would be saved." But sexual roles are not the cause of things. They are a result of, or at least part and parcel of, the social dynamic reflected by Elliott waves. It's not a situation in which men can wake up one morning and say 'Hey, let's stop being henpecked.' At some level, they *want* to be henpecked. Men's role in this is just as important. In fact, one could argue that women rise in relative power because men abdicate it; they become docile and weak, so women fill the void. If men aren't getting the job done, which they do really well in bull markets, women take up the slack by assuming responsibility in areas that men have abandoned. So calling for change is just not going to work.

But is the timing right? It seems like this trend started long before this top. Didn't it start back in the '60s when Donna Reed, June Cleaver and Harriet Nelson went off the air?

Precisely! That's when the Grand Supercycle peaked out as measured in constant dollars and when it was almost entirely a man's world. You have to figure what the mix is in the overall picture, and in real terms, social mood peaked out in 1966 when it was completely a man's world. On a major trend basis, it's becoming increasingly a women's world. We had the feminist movement in the 1970s, more women heading into the work force and so on. I mean, maybe at the bottom we'll see another Joan of Arc or something. Can you imagine how submissive the Frenchmen of the time had to have been to allow England to take them over, then sit by and do nothing, or cooperate like weasels, until a female came along to challenge the English? And the men burned her for her trouble. They just weren't ready to be rescued yet. Later on, they got socially recharged and took up the fight.

You have referred to the Clinton administration's effort to establish a government program to insure health care for all as a very major top signal. Why?

The Black Death occurred in the 1300s at the low of wave TWO in the Millennium degree advance, when ⅓ of the population in Western Civilization died of disease. Historians have credited the plague with inaugurating modern medicine. The Plague obviated the inadequacy of the old "four humours" theory as well as cures based upon religion. So medical science was born at a time when health was considered a rare blessing. Today, personal health in the United States, is considered a *natural condition* that only incompetent doctors could disrupt. The historically unprecedented number and size of malpractice awards bestowed upon customers of doctors by U.S. courts reflects that attitude among the population. In response to it, the leader of the world's most powerful government wants to decree health care a *right* of the entire population. That's quite a change from the situation in the mid-14th century, and it reflects a journey from low to high. Universal health care is such an extreme wish that it can only mean a top. It's not a mid-trend phenomenon. Remember, Medicare and Medicaid were launched at the major top of the mid-1960s.

But universal health care didn't pass.

It nearly did. It had the support of 70% of the population for awhile. Besides, whether any such scheme is adopted or not, it is obvious that such social intentions are *manifestations of an extreme attitude* about human "rights" to comfort and support that may not have existed in history except perhaps in the late Roman Empire and in socialist and Communist countries during the 20th century.

When the time is right, you've said the mood turns down and creates instability. But how exactly does it destabilize the social fabric? Is there a central dynamic to that instability?

There are several: inclusionism vs. exclusionism, hope vs. fear, goodwill vs. anger, hero worship vs. hero destruction, values vs. nihilism, and more.

Let's look deeper at one major axis, this idea of inclusionism and exclusionism. Take some time to expound on that aspect.

The peak of a bull market is marked with the culmination of a trend toward, and a capitulation to, inclusionism, which is a willingness to include more people in one's brotherhood, or an increase in the size of people's unit of allegiance or similarity, the group that they consider to be like themselves. Major bear markets are accompanied by a reduction in the size of people's unit of allegiance. In bull markets, a sense of community prevails. This multi-century top even has people accepting community with aliens, as in the movie *E.T.* The *Star Trek* phenomenon is part of that orientation. At the peak, there is a perceived brotherhood of men, nations, and indeed all living things, which is why there has been an environmental movement, in which trees are embraced as brothers. In bear markets, the trend changes, and the ultimate result is a psychology of "us vs. them." So sociologically, we will see a marked increase in factionalism during the bear market. The larger the bear market, the smaller the factional units. During the reduction process in the size of the social unit of allegiance, one's "in group" becomes smaller and smaller, moving from the universe to the world to the nation to the ethnic, religious, regional or sexual group to the city or feudal estate to the family to the individual. The trend halts at a point along that line dependent upon the extent of the economic and psychological contraction. When the extent is substantial, the unit of allegiance is very small. In the Dark Ages, for instance, the feudal estate was the largest unit of allegiance in Europe. In times of starvation, such as in parts of Africa today, even the family unit can disintegrate, as babies are left to die and individuals fend for themselves.

In other words, at a peak, it's all "we;" everyone is a potential friend. At a bottom, it's all "they;" everyone is a potential enemy. When times are bad, intolerance for differences grows, and people build walls and fences to shut out those perceived to be different. When times are good, tolerance is greater and boundaries weaker.

Inclusionism is a sense of community and goodwill that gathers with a bull market, while exclusionism is the rise of factions and intolerance. Have you made any use of the interplay between these two?

Well, in late 1989, when the U.S.S.R. freed Eastern Europe, EWT commented that such behavior is the opposite of war and is typical of a major social mood peak. A year later, the market was 20% lower, Iraq held American hostages and the

Gulf War began. That was a market bottom. Racially separate living areas had been an official legal policy in South Africa since January 1950, established right at the end of the 20 year bear market pattern from 1929 to 1949 in constant dollars. Despite a U.N. protest against South Africa's racial policies dating from 1948, multiple economic sanctions, and oft-expressed distaste, apartheid remained in place all the way until November 1993, when it was dismantled as a result of the social mood having reached the opposite extreme toward inclusionism. Swiss banks and the U.S. government have lifted economic restrictions that had been in place for years, heralding a new cooperation. Naturally, most observers declare all this good news as a signal of better times ahead. However, it is almost certainly a manifestation of a feel-good mood reflective of a major top in mood. Generally speaking, the time to make long term equity investments is when apartheid is established; the time to liquidate is when the opposite happens.

Is inclusionism the same as collectivism?

Ironically, it appears to be the opposite. Bull markets reflect a trend toward inclusion in that more and more entities are given the nod of acceptance as individuals. Inclusionism is essentially well-wishing one's fellow man, which goes hand in hand with general increases in freedom. Collectivist notions are actually exclusionary in that they divide society into groups and give one group's possessions to another. The most extreme cases in fact occur at major bottoms. Hitler's takeover in Germany in 1933 was at a major bottom. 1949, the year of the communist takeover of China, was the exact year of the end of the constant-dollar corrective pattern that started in 1929. The 1940s also saw collectivism take over Eastern Europe. The disastrous five-year Cultural Revolution in China began in 1966, the year the bear market began. The aftershocks persisted throughout the 1970s. Those are classic bear market phenomena. In the U.S., most of our collectivist legislation came in the 1930s and 1940s during the Supercycle wave IV bear market and again in the late 1960s as the Grand Supercycle bear market began in constant dollars. Here in the early 1990s, look at all of the worldwide examples we have of increasing freedom and inclusionism. Eastern Europe has been freed. Most of Southern China, even though the country is controlled by communists, has been freed up. The Eastern Bloc has been united into NATO.

Sometimes, though, a bear market and its exclusionist forces lead to increased freedom. The 1700s bear market led to the Revolutionary War, which was conducted to exclude the British from America, and the philosophy behind the formation of the government led to men in America being left free.

Is inclusionism good or bad?

It depends upon your perspective. The inclusionism itself is healthy for living things. Unfortunately, an extreme in such feelings and actions, welcome as they are otherwise, are symptoms of a major top, not a buying opportunity. The spectacle of communist governments relinquishing control and territory and admitting freedom is the opposite of the spectacle of Communists taking over countries. So if it was a buying opportunity for stocks when they were taking over countries, what is it when they give them up? The fall of communism reflects a general inclusionist good feeling that recalls, on a grander scale, 1967's Summer of Love and 1987's Harmonic Convergence celebration, both of which occurred at important market tops. This top is of much larger degree, and the nearly unprecedented global social harmony reflects that fact.

Does this inclusionism have any direct economic benefits?

The General Agreement on Tariffs and Trade started to take effect in January 1995. It cuts tariffs worldwide an average of 33%, reduces agricultural subsidies, provides global patent protection, and sets up large cooperating bureaucracies. It was passed with concessions and postponements on some issues because, as was widely trumpeted, "no one wanted it to fail." The key sentiment was *cooperation toward a friendly goal*. That is inclusionism at work.

You might be interested to know that GATT was founded in 1947, near the end of the last great bear market of 1929-1949. Agreements adopted by GATT resulted in trade liberalization *throughout the bull market* until 1969, right at the top. From 1970 forward, protectionist pressures resulted in less free trade through the end of the last meeting in 1979, *right near the end of the bear market*. GATT was reconvened in 1986, well into the new bull market, as the *Financial Times* of London put it, "to re-establish the credibility of GATT." The aim of this new round of talks was to re-establish the old free-trade trend, which they finally did in 1993, well into this bull market. Recall that one of my observations over the years is that fifth waves attempt to re-live the glory of the third wave, but accomplish only a hollow echo. The timing of this GATT accord fits the Elliott Wave interpretation of the long term social psychological pattern. Because it includes a number of restrictive provisions, it accomplishes little more than a hollow echo of the third wave free-trade trend of the 1950s and 1960s, which was in turn a hollow echo of the flat-out laissez-faire environment of the third Supercycle wave in the late 1800s and early 1900s. So the character of the agreement is perfectly compatible with the long term trend. Our next trend will be toward world trade *conflict* and *restriction*.

* * * * * * * * * * * * * *

Welcome to The Elliott Wave Theorist *'s "paradoxical world" of social psychology. Since the fall of the Berlin Wall in November 1989, The Theorist has chronicled a historic string of milestone events that express an unprecedented global social harmony and enunciated the implication: imminent major reversal. But even as The Theorist tracked the blossoming of the inclusionary trend, the exclusionary countertrend has been taking root. "When times are good, tolerance is greater and boundaries weaker. When times are bad, intolerance for differences grows, and people build walls and fences to shut out those perceived to be different. Ultimately, persecution and war result...." (EWT, August 28, 1992). Additional excerpts on the maturing inclusionism of 1990-1995 and comments on the budding exclusionism that will characterize the coming bear market follow:*

Inclusionary High Water Marks

October 1, 1993

The historic peacemaking handshake between the Prime Minister of Israel and the Chairman of the Palestine Liberation Organization, enemies for decades (and arguably for centuries) on September 14 was an expression of the good feelings typical of a *major* stock market peak. As for the "degree" of the event, says *USA Today*, "three presidents and eight secretaries of state witnessed the historic pact."

November 24, 1993

The U.S. House of Representatives passed NAFTA, drawing the entirety of North America into a tariff-free trade agreement, and the South African government ended apartheid after 300 years, inviting blacks to participate fully in the society. Is it merely coincidence that on those two days, the Dow reached hourly, closing and print highs?

December 31, 1993

Last month's issue listed two historic political events that occurred in November at the culmination of the long trend toward global social inclusionism. The events were the passage of NAFTA and the adoption of an interim constitution in South Africa ending apartheid 341 years after the Dutch first arrived on the continent and 45 years after the term was adopted as official government policy. For the record, the final vote on South Africa's new permanent constitution giving all races equal rights came on December 22, in a 237-45 vote in Parliament. Open elections will be held on April 27, 1994 and are expected to lead to black majority rule. This government decision represents a pinnacle of inclusionist good feeling, which is the classic sign of a developing major market top. Remember, apartheid was *adopted* in 1948, at the end of the 20-year *bear* market pattern that unfolded from 1929 to 1949. *This* decision is coming after 44 years of *bull* market, and almost certainly comes near its peak.

Two more such events occurred in December. The first was the December 15 adoption by officials from 117 nations of the latest General Agreement on Tariffs and Trade document after seven years of negotiations in Uruguay. The GATT agreement cuts tariffs worldwide an average of 33%, reduces agricultural subsidies and provides global patent protection.

On the *same day*, the British and Irish Prime Ministers signed what was called "a historic Anglo-Irish declaration, the boldest political initiative in 25 years of violence in Northern Ireland." Violence *began* in Northern Ireland in 1968, two years into the new bear market pattern that began in 1966. Leaders are trying to end it near what should turn out to be the peak of the bull market. The key sentiment once again was *cooperation toward a friendly goal.*

Like NAFTA, all these events are good news. However, in the paradoxical world of social psychological trends, good news is associated with tops, so the technical message is long term bearish. It is the flip side of the bad news of 1933, 1942, 1962, 1970 and 1974, which were long term bullish.

January 28, 1994

In the past four weeks, two more dramatic events have occurred. First, Russia, Ukraine and the U.S., after over forty years of mutual nuclear threat, promised to stop aiming warheads at each other's countries and allies. Ukraine further agreed to *dismantle* the weapons in exchange for

$1b. worth of fuel rods for making nuclear energy. A number of Eastern European countries also asked to join NATO, the western alliance. *These agreements reflect a desire to end over 40 years of cold war antagonism* and are the result of the spreading inclusionist philosophy that accompanies bull markets.

The second event is an attempt to end nearly *two millennia of antagonism* between Christians and Jews, and Christians and Arabs. The Catholic Church on December 30 signed an accord with the Jewish state of Israel in which the Vatican and Israel formally recognized each other. The Vatican is pursuing another accord with the Arab state of Jordan, which has signaled that it is ready to accept diplomatic relations.

February 25, 1994

The U.S. [has] lifted its 19-year-old trade embargo against former enemy in war, Vietnam. The embargo was put on shortly after the end of the last major bear market low and in the midst of the 1975 recession. It was lifted on February 3, 1994.

July 29, 1994

France, in a symbol of post-war reconciliation, invited Germany to parade its soldiers down the Champs-Elysees in Paris on France's biggest national holiday, Bastille Day. The last time German soldiers marched down that avenue was during the last Supercycle bear market, in the 1940s in World War II, when they occupied the country.

This week, after generations of hostility, blood and tears, as President Clinton put it, Reuters reported that Israeli and Jordanian leaders signed a historic declaration ending 46 years of belligerency and agreed on a series of steps to normalize relations. These countries were so hostile to each other that they did not even have direct *telephone* links. What we are committed to, said King Hussein, is the end of the state of war between Jordan and Israel. The five page document declares the peace between them to be permanent. Again, *the bad feelings of the Supercycle bear have been cast aside at the peak of a Supercycle bull.*

September 30, 1994

Bull market sentiments continue to hold sway in the political arena, always the last to express a trend. In August, China and Taiwan held their highest level government meetings since 1949, when China went Communist. China and Russia, enemies for decades, signed a peace pact on September 3, proclaiming an end to any lingering hostility and vowing not to use force against each other. Three days later, following an announcement by the Irish Republican Army of a "complete cessation of military operations" in the province of Northern Ireland, Ireland's Prime Minister and the head of the IRA's political wing pledged themselves to peace. This is the first time in 70 years that the two sides got together, and the end of 25 years of terrorism and fighting.

October 28, 1994

The last arena of social interaction to express a mood trend is politics. How does a peak in social mood feel to the world's two most dangerous longtime belligerents? Late last month, U.S. and Russian Presidents Clinton and Yeltsin sat down for their third comprehensive meeting. Listen to the euphoric mood of hope, cooperation and fun:

Yeltsin leaves U.S. laughing

The third full-scale meeting between President Clinton and Russian President Boris Yeltsin was a rousing success – particularly in comparison with the tension-wracked spectacle of Cold War summitry.

"Relations between our nations are moving forward at full speed," Clinton said.

Yeltsin seemed determined at each public appearance to offer lavish praise.

"I would like to tell you that we've never fought the United States and, I believe...that we will never fight the United States," Yeltsin said at the Library of Congress.

It's become a tradition that Yeltsin dominates the closing joint statement with boisterous glee.

The United States and Russia are like a "humongous, almost half-billion-member family," Yeltsin said.

USA TODAY, SEPTEMBER 29, 1994

January 27, 1995

"Ku Klux Klan Now Lies in Ashes of History," says a headline on January 8, 1995. Upon observing that only 27 people showed up for a national gathering, *The Atlanta Journal* concludes, "The Klan is dead.".... In a related expression of social inclusion, a bronze statue of black tennis pro Arthur Ashe will be erected in March in Richmond, Virginia, home of statues of Jefferson Davis, Stonewall Jackson, Robert E. Lee and J.E.B. Stuart.... North Kórea, for nearly five decades a fierce Communist regime, and now (therefore) bankrupt and starving, has lifted restrictions on trade with the United States and has agreed to allow U.S. merchant ships into its ports for the first time since 1949. The first shipload of oil arrived on January 18, 1995.

June 30, 1995

Is the thick line in [Figure 3-3] some kind of annual average of stock prices, which it resembles so closely? No, it is a chart of the number of nuclear weapons tests annually, inverted. Tests had been rising during the bear market and reached a high in 1982 that coincided with the stock market bottom in inflation-adjusted terms. From there, testing declined persistently as the bull market progressed. It jumped sharply in 1986-87, peaking as the stock market crashed. Then it resumed its decline as stocks resumed their advance. Bomb testing actually reached

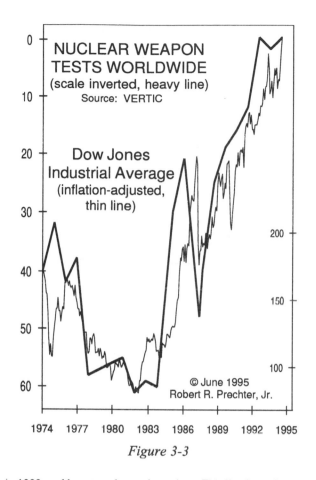

0 — NUCLEAR WEAPON
TESTS WORLDWIDE
(scale inverted, heavy line)
10 — Source: VERTIC

20 — Dow Jones
Industrial Average
(inflation-adjusted,
30 — thin line)

200 —

40 —

150 —

50 —

100 —

60 — © June 1995
Robert R. Prechter, Jr.

1974 1977 1980 1983 1986 1989 1992 1995

Figure 3-3

zero in 1993, and has stayed near there since. This line is ready to reverse direction, though, as France has just announced that it will resume nuclear testing in the Pacific. Social mood doesn't *really* trend with the stock market, does it?

July 28, 1995

In bear markets, anger, fear and the urge to destroy overcome the social conscience. Remorse, on the other hand, is a bull market trait born of the larger trend toward inclusionist impulses. Historic expressions of it would be expected to appear at bull market tops, when the inclusionist mood trend is at its extreme. Today, the climate is that of a Grand Super-cycle top, and regret has reached an extreme in a worldwide drive for forgiveness. The peaking social mood has brought apologies for a host of transgressions that are decades, generations, and even centuries old. Af-ter years of bickering, the Japanese government reached a "compromise" apology for its part in World War II. At a recent press conference, Presi-

dent Clinton resisted considerable public pressure to ask forgiveness for
bombs dropped on Japan eight administrations ago. A group of ethicists
and historians has decided that financial compensation and a formal government apology are due victims of secret human radiation experiments
conducted in the U.S. during the Cold War. The United Church of Canada
has apologized to a host of native tribes for sins of the past. Southern
Baptists, the nation's largest Protestant denomination, have asked forgiveness for defending slavery in the 1800s. (The sect was founded in
1845 in a show of support *for* slavery.) The Catholic Church apologized
to "every woman" in the world for centuries of relegation to "the margins
of society"; then it apologized to the Czech Republic for the Catholic
church's role in the 16th century wars that followed the Protestant Refor-
mation; then it agreed to join Protestants in ceremonies repenting the
Crusades against Muslims and Jews *900 years ago*! According to a Vatican
spokesman, the Pope is "pushing hard toward unity." Though not exactly
apologizing, the U.S. has just normalized relations with Vietnam, its
bitterest enemy, and one of its longest standing, since World War II.

October 27, 1995

The bull market continues to put its dramatic finishing touches on
the cultural landscape. In what may turn out to be the grandest among
historic signs of a long term peak in social mood, New York City has just
hosted "history's greatest gathering of world leaders." It was the political
equivalent of the "Harmonic Convergence" gathering in August 1987. (A
photo of the world leaders standing shoulder to shoulder) is the latest and
most comprehensive in a series of "peak mood" photos of world leaders
embracing or signing peace accords that EWT has reproduced since September 1993. There is every reason to believe that this photograph is a
candidate for being *the* snapshot that represents and marks the ultimate
top in a Grand Supercycle bull market. In past years, the leaders of the
world have not gathered for a photo like this one because tensions between nations would not allow their leaders to stand together in the same
room. In the fall of 1995, however, the U.N.'s media director said the
photo of 185 leaders was a relatively simple matter because "everybody
loves each other." EWT once characterized major mood peaks as involving "amorphous feelings of love," where "everybody's a good guy." That
description certainly fits the mood in most of the world today, this picture
being a concrete expression of it.

The Exclusionary Undertow

July 1, 1994

Separatism is simply a *manifestation* of exclusionism. *The Elliott
Wave Theorist* in 1989 made a reference to the probability of a separatist
movement in the U.S. during the bear market. This comment was no

doubt considered evidence of lunacy. However, it is quite simply a normal result of bear market psychology in C waves of Supercycle degree and higher (as King George found out in 1776-81), and that is what the market faces.

Five years later, this forecasted trend has begun to emerge. According to *Free Market* (Ludwig von Mises Institute, Auburn AL 36849), once a wild dream, secessionism is now a reality of [U.S.] regional politics. Secession goes hand in hand with depression, so it is no coincidence that California, which is more depressed than the country at large, has led the movement. Two years ago, for the first time in more than 130 years, the California state assembly agreed to consider the idea of dividing California into separate states. A similar measure was discussed in the 1850s, and actually *passed* in 1859. Why 1859? *Because that was the exact year of the end of Supercycle wave (II)*, a 24-year bear market. The idea was never consummated by Congress because of a rather dramatic event, the Civil War, another typical expression of a culminating negative mood trend [toward separatism]. Oregon and Texas are also considering state-splitting measures.

At lower levels of government, some suburbs want to secede from Miami, and Staten Island has voted to secede from New York City. Alaska is even discussing secession from the Union. The extreme in secessionary mood lies several years in the future, so while movements on a national scale remain a near certainty, they won't occur until the country is far deeper into depression.

On the global scene, separatist movements and breakups have already occurred all through Europe (in the former unities of the Soviet Union, Yugoslavia and the conceptualized EC).

July 29, 1994

After many years of indifference to the problem throughout the bull market, one of today's hot issues in Washington is how to stop illegal immigration. The emerging bear market has brought this concern suddenly to the fore. Congressmen have introduced more than *150* bills to revise immigration law. One solution proposed is a national identification card. Increased government control is another typical aspect of bear markets, and results from the emotions and fears that accompany them.

During the peaking process of Supercycle wave (III) in 1966-1968, the black American freedom movement became transformed into a militant black power movement, ushering in violent confrontations that carried into the early 1970s bear market. Today, the same forces are operating. Louis Farrakhan and Khallid Muhammad are today's version of Elijah Muhammad and Malcolm X. Both are leaders of the *transition phase* from peaceful tactics to violent ones. The transition phase is marked by the continuation of peaceful physical action but the introduction of angry racist diatribe. Given the certainty of a major bear market in the latter half of the 1990s, violent race-related confrontation that will rival or exceed the level of violence experienced in 1970 is likely.

Trade unions were big during the Supercycle bear market of the 1930s and 1940s. Membership as a percentage of all workers peaked in the U.S. in 1945 at 35.5% and fell to 15.8% in 1992. In 1993, the percentage remained the same, as the total number rose a bit for the first time since 1979, which was near the end of the last bear market. According to one magazine, a growing number of organizers are signing up unaffiliated [workers] with a missionary fervor recalling the crusaders of the 1930s.

In case you haven't heard, Italy's new fascist leader received a lot of votes in the recent election and has praised Mussolini as the greatest statesman of the century. By the end of the bear market, the we vs. they mentality will have permeated every corner of U.S. society and most of the world as well.

September 30, 1994

EWT is on record calling for a major U.S.-Japanese conflict in 1996. That's why this headline from September 23, buried in the newspaper, is of interest: *Clinton Warns Japan*. Of course, this headline has appeared in some variant all year, along with Clinton Warns Russia, Clinton Warns Cuba, Clinton Warns Haiti, Clinton Warns Korea, Clinton Warns China, and Clinton Warns Bosnia. Self-righteous administrations (in this case, Clinton, Kantor, Reno, Reich, and HRC) are a classic bear market phenomenon. It's not "leave us alone or face consequences," but "behave the way we want or face consequences." The latest Japan warning was issued because September 30 is yet another deadline set by U.S. Trade Representative Mickey Kantor for a decision on whether formally to charge Japan with being an unfair trader and then threaten unilateral U.S. trade sanctions. With all the smoke the Administration has been blowing on this subject for a year, trade sanctions appear likely one of these days. Any such thing will be the first big step in a collapse of U.S.-Japanese relations, which have been cooperative for nearly fifty years.

On September 12, Quebec voters gave the separatist party a solid majority in the legislature of the province. A vote on the question of secession will come up within a year. A.J. Frost (see 9/25/92 *Elliott Wave Theorist*) predicted a split of Canada into three nations, and the July 1994 issue reiterated that point. The latest news supports that forecast.

EWT in 1989 also predicted major victories for third parties in the U.S., as well as the dissolution of one or both of the current major parties by 2004. Ross Perot's race was the first manifestation of that forecast. Guess what. Today more people (35%) call themselves Independent as opposed to Republican (29%) or Democrat (33%). In a recent poll, 83% of Americans said we should have a third party.

* * * * * * * * * * * * * *

Where does this unrest and the rising exclusionism eventually take us?

Trends become radicalized. Environmentalism, for instance, will follow an exclusionary path, adopt an "us vs. them" mentality, and become more hell-bent on destroying humans than on hugging trees. At the same time, a severe reactionism to the movement will set in. The same will be true regarding every social question: immigration, welfare, you name it. Exclusion will gain the upper hand. In countless ways, persecution waxes. This is the likely direction of trend for the next dozen years, and on a larger scale for as much as a century.

By 20th century standards at least, it's pretty quiet out there now.

Exactly. The current world scene is remarkably free of war-ring. It is witnessing the warmest relationships between long time archenemies the U.S. and the U.S.S.R. in at least forty years, and the U.S.S.R. and China in thirty years. Periods of peace generally coincide with the latter part of prolonged market uptrends, reflecting the effects of a positive social psychology, which is the engine of bull markets. During the later stages of bull markets, wars are nonexistent, brief, mild or contained. All three fifth waves of Cycle degree in U.S. history, and the years immediately thereafter, have been peaceful.

Did you anticipate this side effect of the bull market?

In the October 1982 issue, a list of expectations for the coming decade included, "No international war for at least ten years."

Those ten years are well up.

So they are. What I am saying now is that the forces of social psychology will soon *no longer preclude war*. In fact, they will be trending toward it into the time of greatest risk: when the market is bottoming and shortly thereafter.

Could Clinton get us into war?

Only if the market collapses, and even then, it is far more likely to occur near a low than a high. The reason is that the peak in negative mood occurs with the extreme low in the thermometer reading of mood, the stock market. I would point out, though, that it has been statist Democrat presidents who have gotten the U.S. involved in every war this century, including World War I, World War II, the Korean War and Vietnam. Also, this President undoubtedly bristles at his "draft dodger" image and would like to dispel it. He is above all a politician, and he saw what the Gulf War did for Bush's approval ratings, and what his own raid on Baghdad did for his, i.e., raised them from 38% to 50% in a matter of days. He can't bring himself to stay out of Bosnia. If his ratings fall again, the risk will be there.

But haven't we had plenty of times when presidential popularity and/ or stocks fell and no war resulted?

Yes. The late 1970s are a good example. We didn't go to war, but Russia did. December 1979 is when they marched into Afghanistan. Still, given all the forces currently at work, if stock prices are to fall to as low as the Wave Principle suggests, then I deem it nearly certain that the U.S. will find itself embroiled in conflict. The global good feelings associated with the bull market will by then have evaporated.

The bull market was not a total love-in. What about the cold war? Isn't that an example of bull market hostilities?

Precisely. Bull market hostilities mean you don't fight. The Cold War is a phenomenon of a bull market. It's the *hot* wars that happen in the bear market trends.

There was a lot of fear, and there were war scares.

Right. And an Elliott Wave analyst would have said, "Don't believe them." Now he says that as the market falls, "If there appear to be *peace* agreements, don't believe them." Remember Neville Chamberlain's peace agreements with Hitler. And Russia's countless broken guarantees in the 1940s. When the Grand Supercycle bear market begins, it will be a technical consideration overriding all others. Then, periods of peace will be temporary. Apparently short wars will prove to be only one battle in a long period of conflict.

What does history say about the possible timing of a major war?

Wars occur during or immediately following "C" waves of bear markets. Going back 200 years, each stock market crash has led to a depression, and each depression has been followed by a war. In fact, the size and severity of each depression and war reflect the *degree* of the associated bear market. Whether that sequence will occur again this time is not certain, but the evidence of history suggests that it is highly likely. I personally will act as if it is certain. The coming drop in the market will reflect dramatic changes in mass psychology from positive to negative, from optimistic, hopeful and cheerful to pessimistic, fearful and angry. That dramatic change will show up first as a depressed economy and later as war. And because the bear market will be of Grand Supercycle degree....

A large degree decline implies a more serious war?

I have observed that the extent and intensity of a war most definitely appears to be a function of the degree or size of the bear market. In the past 200 years, even Cycle degree bear markets have produced significant wars such as the War of 1812, the Spanish-American War, World War I and Vietnam. However, bear markets of Supercycle degree or greater have produced the truly major wars. The bear market of 1720-1782/4 ended with the Revolutionary War. It was followed near the "wave two" low by the French Revolution and Napoleonic Wars. The bear market of 1837-1859 was followed immediately by the Civil War. The bear market of 1929-1932/49 resulted in World War II. The latter two produced far more casualties than any of the wars that occurred in the smaller Cycle degree bear markets. And, true to size, Millennium Cycle bear markets appear to produce prolonged periods of warring, such as occurred in the Dark Ages and into the "wave two" low thereafter.

The market bottomed in 1859, but the Civil War didn't even start until 1860.

As I've said already, the extreme in negative social mood often causes events to be set in motion that play out even as mood is reversing from its extreme. The lesson remains: mood change precedes and creates history. The timing is not precisely the same each time, but the relationship is there.

A lot of people consider the Kondratieff Wave *the* war wave. Does a given war's position within the K-wave affect how serious it is?

No. The Kondratieff cycle low of 1896 produced only the relatively minor Spanish-American war (in 1898), presenting powerful evidence that the Kondratieff cycle itself is *not* the determinant of a war's severity; the degree of the associated bear market, as interpreted under the Wave Principle, *is.*

* * * * * * * * * * * * * *

The Elliott Wave Theorist
December 25, 1989

Various economists in past years have made a case that war is causally "bullish" for the economy (i.e., "let's have a war to get the economy moving"). The result of war is destruction, however, so that thesis is absurd. The process destroys assets; it doesn't create them.

* * * * * * * * * * * * * *

Either way, the implication is that war is likely at or near the bear market bottom. Since the next one will be a major war, shouldn't we have some idea of who it is we are to fight?

The scenario presented in 1989 called for "unrest in the Middle East to accelerate." That was written *before* any hint that the Persian Gulf War was coming. That area of the world will undoubtedly continue to be a hotbed of conflict.

But things have progressed a long way since the Gulf War. Since the September 14, 1993 handshake between the Prime Minister of Israel and the Chairman of the Palestine Liberation Organization, several more historic agreements have been reached between countries and religious factions that have torn the region through centuries of antagonism. Israel, Syria and all of Europe are talking about economic treaties that will bind together the whole region.

Yes, it is quite a different atmosphere from that when Egyptian president Anwar Sadat was gunned down by Muslim militants in 1981, only months before the last major stock market low measured in constant dollars, for signing a similar agreement with Israel two years before. From that bottom in sentiment to the peak you just mentioned took a Fibonacci 13 years. These 1994 treaties terminate, *near the top of Cycle wave V*, a state of belligerence that has been in force since 1948, *near the end of Cycle wave IV* (measured in constant dollars). The feelings expressed by those involved mirror the major peak in social mood. Said Israeli leader Yitzhak Rabin; "The time has now come not merely to dream of a better future, but to *realize* it." When fears are realized, it's a bottom in mood; when hopes are realized, it's a top. "Children born today," said Rabin, "will never know war between us." However, the next major low in mood is due within ten years. The mood *then* will sorely test this promise.

If there is war in the Middle East, the U.S. has already demonstrated that it will be involved. But it's not going to be like the Gulf War, when nearly the whole world was united against one belligerent little nation. Will it be more like the other big wars of this century, with big nations choosing up sides?

Yes. Exclusionism and polarity will be the overriding sentiments. Wars sometimes occur between surprising foes. As one student of wars observed, major wars are usually fought between former trading partners. Our biggest trading partner is Japan. And the U.S. has been belligerent toward Japan ever since Clinton's team got in office.

War with Japan? How is that possible? They have been allies for fifty years.

Iben Browning noted that we have fought most of our main allies twice; we've fought Japan only once. This thought is particularly intriguing when viewed in conjunction with an observation made by R. N. Elliott in a market letter and later reprinted in his book, *Nature's Law* (1946). In 1852, Commodore Perry paid a courtesy visit to Japan and invited the "Son of Heaven" to abandon absolute isolationism. In 1907, 55 years later, tension between Japan and the U.S. came to a head. The Japanese public was incensed with the U.S. over the U.S.-brokered treaty with Russia (1905). They blamed the Americans for a "humiliating peace." The Americans reciprocated with the "yellow peril," a scare in which Japanese laborers up and down the West Coast were singled out for racial discrimination. 1907 was the year Theodore Roosevelt barred the Japanese from immigration to the U.S. In 1941, 34 years later, and 89 years from 1852, Japan attacked Pearl Harbor. If we extend that time sequence and add a Fibonacci 55 years to 1941, we get 1996. In other words, the U.S. and Japan, if they are indeed following Fibonacci sequences in the timing of their conflicts, should clash again, in or very near 1996. The clash, if one occurs, could be economic, which would be more likely if it follows a stock market high akin to the Smoot-Hawley tariffs of 1929, or military, which would be more likely if it follows a stock market low.

But what about the fact that Japan is not even a military power?

But it's an economic power. And the former Soviet Union has lots of weapons and is broke. A simple alliance, or purchase from a starving Russia, could turn Japan into a military power virtually overnight. Since the Fibonacci time sequence in the stock market has indicated 1995 as the most likely turning point year, and since major social events often follow major turns in the stock market, the year 1996 appears to be ideally situated for the conflict suggested by the Fibonacci time sequence noted by Elliott. It may well be that the belligerent, some say racist, politician who penned the Japanese national bestseller, *The Japan That Can Say No [to the U.S.]*, who has been dismissed as an anomaly with less than ⅓ of the country's support, will find himself even more popular as Japanese financial and social fortunes continue to collapse into depression. To many Japanese, the U.S. will make a convenient scapegoat, and the man who said it first, loudest and most angrily will be remembered and rewarded. That is how when the depths of the Great Depression finally arrived in 1933, Hitler found himself placed in power in Germany.

Russia is no longer a superpower. Can we rule it out as a potential adversary?

People have come under the assumption that now that the Cold War is over, things are only going to get better. I think that's wishful thinking. It is certainly linear thinking, which is just as bad. When you use the Wave Principle, you abandon the idea that trends continue forever and begin to learn to look for signs that trends will end. This man Zhironovsky in Russia got 20% of the vote in 1993, a plurality, more than Yeltsin's party. If you have read any of the quotations from him, you realize that this man is a combination of Joseph Stalin and

Adolf Hitler. And he wants nothing more than to cause fear, misery and destruction around the world, whether it be in Japan, Lithuania, his neighbors to the west and the south, or anyone else who would stand up to him.

* * * * * * * * * * * * * * *

TIME

December 19, 1994

Relations between the U.S. and Russia are rapidly turning sour

Presidents Bill Clinton and Boris Yeltsin dropped the big-grin, buddy-buddy act of their previous six face-to-face meetings and traded barbs.

Clinton, Yeltsin exchange only silent treatment

A touch of frost after Cold War thaw

BUDAPEST — President Clinton and Russian President Boris Yeltsin stood apart on the same stage Monday, a day that should have brought smiles as they formalized a nuclear treaty that took nine years to negotiate and three more to nail down.

Neither ventured a word to the other during the treaty-signing ceremony. But their body language spoke volumes — capping a month of public disputes and souring relations.

While Clinton had hearty handshakes and words of thanks for Ukrainian, Kazakh and Belarus leaders, he averted even eye contact with a frowning Yeltsin, who was sitting right next to him.

The silent treatment between Clinton and Yeltsin was only the latest evidence of a recent chill in relations.

* * * * * * * * * * * * * * *

Is he the only obvious successor to Boris Yeltsin?

A popular army general named Alexander Lebed is considering running for President in the next election and has already been proclaimed the probable front-runner by a leading liberal newspaper. While he appears less dangerous than Zhirinovsky, his plan is to emulate his inaccurate version of what Chile's

General Pinochet did, which in his words was "to save the state from collapse, put the army in a place of pride, force people to work, and force the loudmouths, in a brutal manner, to shut their mouths." Says Lebed, "Democracy won't work in Russia. What's wrong with a military dictator?" As the ruble collapses into worthlessness, his vision will become more and more attractive. The U.S. will be a rough place in the latter half of the 1990s, but there will be worse places to live.

Russia will turn authoritarian again?

Historically, when a great power loses it, someone often comes along and says, "I'm going to get it back." And he always tries to do it militarily. He usually doesn't succeed, but he can cause an awful lot of damage trying. I think the Russian people, very much like the German people after World War I, look at the devastation of the Soviet Empire and say, "We didn't deserve this breakup. We're a great people. Let's get it all back." That's why men like Zhironovsky and Lebed have such appeal. Until that sentiment runs its course, and I don't just mean psychologically but through action as well, it's a real potential problem.

Does history allow any way out? Is there an example of a downturn in global fortunes that has not resulted in open warfare?

In fact, there is, and we are probably at a similar juncture. There may be precedent for avoiding a major world war between 1995 and 2005 because the current peak *is* of such large degree. When the last Grand Supercycle bear market began in 1720 with a devastating two year stock market collapse, no correspondingly major war followed. The reason apparently is that that decline was only wave A of the bear market. An important war finally did occur in the late 1700s as wave C of the A-B-C correction was in progress. Similarly, no war occurred after the drop in stock prices in 1835-1842, which was Cycle wave A of Supercycle wave (II), but one did begin immediately following the low for Cycle wave C. World War II did not begin right after the 1932 low, but during the second phase of decline from 1937-1942, which was Cycle wave C of Supercycle wave (IV) in constant dollars. Overall, this evidence indicates that wars are more often the product of C waves in a corrective process, not merely any severe decline in stock prices and social mood.

What happens in the C wave down that results in action?

The wave A drop, no matter how severe, apparently is handled by society. It is the second drop that makes segments of some societies angry enough to attack others militarily. Consider that advance-decline statistics in the stock market during third waves and C waves indicate great breadth of participation. In C wave declines, a broad cross section of the populace is negatively influenced or affected, making the waging of war, which requires great cooperation, more achievable. It might be postulated that major C wave declines are times when *destructive* social goals are achieved with cooperation, just as third waves on the upside are times when *productive* social goals are achieved with cooperation. C waves may also be "the last straw" psychologically for those who suffered once in the A wave. In contrast, A waves find societies unprepared and unwilling to wage war. In the early 1700s, in fact, not only was there no significant war, but a "détente" was arranged among major powers. It was, moreover, encouraged greatly by the heavy weight of debt under which the superpowers suffered, which ironically helped keep a climate of peace among them, at least for a time. That is not unlike the situation today.

So you're hedged on the war question?

No, I took a position in *Tidal Wave*. I said that while conflicts should take place at the next stock market bottom of Supercycle degree, the next major international war, World War III if you will, is not likely to occur until wave (C) of the Grand Supercycle is due to bottom. That is ideally in the 2050s, although the wave label is the determinant, not any projected probable date.

You make a distinction between popular and unpopular wars. What causes a war to be one over the other?

The fact that the Vietnam War was fought (1) during a mild bear market that (2) immediately followed a Supercycle degree high and (3) included two advances back to the level of the prior bull market top may bear upon why it was unpopular. Much of the society was still in a socially positive mood and simply did not feel like fighting. In terms of casualties, it was a minor war.

Totally different from a bear market bottom war.

Right. Such sentiment will not accompany the next war, which will have the support of societies deeply in an antisocial mood. At the outset of the Persian Gulf War, which began at only a Primary degree bottom, 80% of the American people backed the President's call to arms. It is unclear whether they comprehended the implications of their attitude, which itself is reflective of a developing Grand Supercycle bear. They may ultimately wish they had not been so impulsive, but that's how history is made.

As the one remaining super power, shouldn't the U.S. fare well in any war?

Watch out. First, you are projecting linearly. It is well to keep in mind that at the end of the last Grand Supercycle bear market, Great Britain lost the American colonies and accelerated its retrenchment back to the island from its former "sun never sets" position of world power. The peaking of a 200-year Grand Supercycle advance in U.S. progress is probably coinciding with the peak of U.S. influence as a world power. The United States will very likely be forced to remove a great deal of its military and commercial influence from the rest of the globe by the end of the current Grand Supercycle bear market. History shows, though, that complete retrenchment can take a century, or even three. Second, might I point out that the U.S. could be the *dangerous* force this time? If an authoritarian government takes over, look out, world.

A Giant Leap Forward

Quite frankly, your appraisal on the state of affairs in the world is concise and illuminating, but it scares me.

It scared me too initially, when I first began to realize what the charts were saying about the likely course of events over the Grand Supercycle bear. However, putting my thoughts on paper has given me a frame of reference within which to judge events, and that in itself has a reassuring effect. Just think how panicked those people who have no inkling of what lies ahead will be as events unfold. They are the ones most likely to despair. Our forefathers survived crises. Let's live up to their courage.

What would cause you to change your mind on the big picture?

A return of valuations to lower levels, generally bearish market sentiment, and a completed bear market pattern.

There's nothing that could make you say you were wrong, it's time to turn and follow the uptrend?

I have little patience with questions such as "How high does the market have to go, or how long does it have to hold up, for you to turn bullish?" It is as if the sky were filled with clouds, you had concluded that rain was likely, and were asked, "How much darker do the clouds have to get before you'll decide it won't rain?" or "How long will this condition have to remain in effect for you to change your mind?" There is no such darkness level and no such time limit. The same thing was true in reverse in the late 1970s. "If the market breaks what level will you turn long term bearish?" I said then, "I'm not *going* to turn long term bearish. I may look wrong for awhile, but the signs are there and cannot be erased." There is no level at which a rising market can provide an excuse for a bullish opinion in today's historically bearish technical environment, nor is there a time limit on how long this environment can last before the bear comes out of hibernation.

Well, sometimes clouds go away without raining.

Let's not stretch the analogy too far! A comparable event in market analysis would be if companies tripled dividends on average while the public turned bearish on stocks while the pattern resolved into a "third of a third" acceleration while breadth expanded! If that were to happen, then the rain clouds would go away, and the market could keep going. You can bet on it if you want, but betting on it is not just an academic question. We're talking about whether you would agree to leave your priceless stamp collection out on the picnic table for two days despite a sky filled with billowing black clouds.

Let's grant that the market is extended. Can't it get much more extended?

The "greater fool theory" works great until the day it stops working, and then markets can fall straight down, in panic. In today's environment, with each higher tick and every extra month, the risk increases. If the peak price hasn't been seen, it's close, and the downside potential is so great that owning stocks is not an acceptable option, period.

There has to be a bright spot. Can you leave us a glimmer of light for the future? Do you have any reason for optimism?

I am very optimistic that I can help people conserve money. A lot of people say "Hey Bob, you brought us good news for all these years, and now you bring us bad news." I object strenuously to that. Patterns of social behavior merely exist. The bad news is being caught on the wrong side of events. Misery and failure are created by trying to live in the old trend when a new one is in force. If you had stayed pessimistic throughout the 1950s and 1960s, you would have lost terrific opportunities. The same thing was true of the 1980s.

On the other side of the coin, if you had leveraged yourself to the hilt in 1968, you would have suffered tremendously. If you were in tune with the changes that were occurring, you would have come out of the other side financially vigorous. I think we are in a situation similar to that today. The good news is being on the right side of the trend. When the trend is up, it means expanding and producing; and when the trend is down, it means contracting and conserving so that you are fully prepared to benefit when the bottom is at hand. I'm not looking forward to this period, as the bull market has provided wonderful times. But I would rather know it is coming, so I can prepare, and be in position to enjoy the good times when they return.

Declines aren't all bad, either. When I speak of positive and negative trends in the stock market, I'm talking almost in the sense of poles on a magnet. It doesn't necessarily mean all good in one direction and all bad in the other. Some good things come out of the downside.

For instance...

Well, for one thing, sociologists have noted that in tough times, family ties grow stronger. Also, people tend to slow down and appreciate the more basic and, some say, more important things in life.

Another plus is that every big decline provides the building blocks for the next great period of progress. The basic message of the Wave Principle is that the path of human progress, rather than being in a straight line, is a three-steps forward, two-steps back affair. In other words, there is a tendency to take expansion to an extreme and set processes in motion that will result in a setback, and at the bottom of that setback, to have learned something from that experience and thus construct conditions under which a period of expansion can be born again. Mistakes that were made come into consciousness; people realize what they were doing wrong. They set goals to alleviate the problems, and eventually, those actions build a base for the next big boom.

Is mankind learning from this process?

In the long run, it is clear that human beings are learning from their experiences, although at an extremely slow rate. Each setback brings the human experience back to a higher level than did the prior one of the same degree. Each new period of progress and expansion brings the human experience to a higher plain of success and enjoyment.

Will there be a new work ethic when the current house of cards comes crashing down? Or will society increase its demands for handouts?

I don't know. I know it was said in the 1930s that a lot of people seemed rather docile standing in bread lines. But there were also socialist and communist demonstrations. A lot of people postulate that these days are different, that people have come to believe that their neighbors owe them a living. I don't know to what extent that is actually true in the depths of the American psyche. To the extent it is true, there is likely to be more unrest in the next fifteen years than in the 1930s. The degree of the coming bear market is higher, so that supports the case for greater social unrest.

What if preparation could be done on a mass scale? Aren't there things that could be done to soften the downside of the cycle?

There are things that *could* be done, but the real question is — and this question is sociological — *will* they be done? The answer is an unequivocal *no*. Einstein's comment that "God does not play dice with the universe" may have social implications as well. Society undergoes a pendulum-like swing, back and forth between prosperity and recession. It is part of mankind's nature. Therefore, there is nothing that will alter what we call the tidal forces of social change. There appears to be no mechanism to get in the way of that motion — to stop it or reverse it. The alternative would be an absolutely flat-line society that never begins to feel better or worse about itself. And, of course, history shows that there has never been such a thing. I don't think we're going to change.

What if the government changed, cut taxes by 70%, and took us back to a truly free market?

Again, the question is, *will* they? Do you see politicians becoming statesmen today and changing government so that it can avoid disaster? Not even close. They change when a crisis forces them to act, and that will come at the low, not here at the high.

Is there nothing that could get our political leaders to face reality? If they were aware of the Wave Principle and therefore ahead of the curve, they could institute public policies in time to do some good.

Individuals can be induced to face reality. Unfortunately, the fundamental problem with desiring "society" to face reality is that societies go through alternating patterns of facing and denying reality, and that cyclicality appears to be immutable. As far as public policy makers accepting the idea of the Wave Principle for any length of time, recall that *by definition, participants in the markets and the economy must be unbelievers at the turns.* If our opinions were generally believed and respected, they would be wrong. How could it then be a top or bottom? Public people, particularly in quantity, are immersed in the social mood, and act as its puppets. It's that simple.

What about globalization and instantaneous communication — those are modern phenomena — isn't it possible they will help us escape the grasp of history and the Wave Principle?

No. Crowd behavior is rooted in psychology, which has its own pace of development regardless of whether communication speed has increased. Besides, it hasn't increased that much. In 1720, you would have known of a market move within minutes, if you were at the exchange, and maybe an hour later if you were at work. Is it really much different today? Modern communications have simply enlarged the size of what three hundred years ago was a crowd in the town square. Everyone is sitting in his room with his quote machine, reading *The Wall Street Journal*, watching financial television, keeping track of the Dow Jones Industrial Average and the Standard & Poor's 500 stock index — and he's constantly communicating with other members of the crowd. It is a massive soup of psychology, all feeding on itself.

How about New York Stock Exchange circuit breakers and all that high-tech stuff? That's all new. Don't you think that regardless of how bad it gets, we live in a more fluid world, one that can change much more rapidly. This time, can we get back into another bull trend faster?

No. I guess you could answer the question empirically. Did these things speed up the bull market? I mean, the darn thing has lasted a lot longer than I ever thought it would, or anyone else that was bullish in 1982.

Yes, it has seemed interminable.

From a theoretical point of view, it is unlikely that human beings in their nature and essence have changed very much. I think it takes equivalent forces to ingrain a new opinion or a new outlook today as it did 10 years ago or 100 years ago or probably even 1000 years ago. Such changes within a group of people, which result when they cue off each other, are likely to take the same style, follow the same few paths, and last similar durations as they've always done in the past.

Is this true for the entire world?

There is some evidence that isolated societies go through Elliott Wave dynamics that are not necessarily coincident in trend with those in other societies. Cultural interaction, however, clearly plays a role in synchronizing expansions and contractions. Specifically, stock price records for the past 70 years, and to the degree available for the past 300 years, reveal that bull and bear markets have evolved nearly simultaneously around the globe. Their *consequences*, therefore, tend to be felt worldwide.

I suppose the craze for foreign stocks is also a part of the problem rather than any kind of solution.

No crowd buys stocks of other countries intelligently. For decades, heavy foreign buying in the U.S. stock market has served as an excellent indicator of major tops. In the past several years, it is the U.S. investor who is the new "foreigner," and he has been pouring record amounts of money into the stock markets of other countries. To put this buying into perspective, consider that U.S. investors in fact sold Japanese stocks on balance for most of the 1980s, when riches were there to be had. Then as the peak was being approached, they acted as if they had seen the light. The record buying of Japanese stocks by U.S. investors in 1989-1990 marked a major top in that market. Similarly, the more recent pouring of funds into such overpriced markets as those of Mexico and South America are signals of a major long term top in those markets.

* * * * * * * * * * * * * * *

The Elliott Wave Theorist
May 31, 1983

COULDN'T HAVE SAID IT BETTER MYSELF

"If Bob Prechter and I are more bullish than the government-worshippers now, it is because at bottom, deep down inside, we are more bearish than Granville in the long run. This is not a coincidence. It is absolutely of the essence. We are exulting in the wild exuberance of the 1980s because we know that when nature, or destiny, gets behind society, it appears invincible. We also know that the opposite will be the case in the 1990s. Godzilla will be ringing your doorbell, and believe me, he will sell you a gorilla ticket." —P.Q. Wall, *Virgin Method Letter*.

P.Q. is right — enjoy the 1980s! They won't be making 'em again for awhile. Keep your perspective, but don't sit out on the fun. —RP

* * * * * * * * * * * * * * *

The scale of the coming stock market retracement indicates that it is going to have to correct a very serious error in social judgment. What do you think that breach of reason is?

"As this century progresses," says *Elliott Wave Principle*, "it becomes clearer that in order to satisfy the demands of some individuals and groups for the output of others, man through the agency of the state, has begun to leech off that which he has created. He has not only mortgaged his present output, but he has mortgaged the output of future generations by eating the capital that took generations to accumulate." Today, fifteen years after that was written, the U.S. public has virtually no savings and has borrowed to the hilt, trying to make up for the shortfall that has resulted from decades of wealth destruction by government. When the depression hits, the average person's actual poverty will be revealed to him

Are we looking toward a grim century ahead?

The next *decade* or so is likely to be grim, but after that, we should have several very expansive decades. Then we'll have the grimmest decade probably mid century. Overall, it should be somewhat of a roller coaster ride of corrective and expansive forces, if my projections in *At the Crest* are right. Then it will be off to the races for humankind again.

You say in *At the Crest* that the ultimate path of human progress is ever upward; it is merely interrupted by periodic setbacks. That's actually kind of optimistic.

It's not optimism; it's just a description of a net-beneficent reality. The fact that human behavior follows a sequence found in nature indicates that we're a part of nature, progressing in accordance with natural law. Through these sequences, a pattern of progress is evident throughout history, and it is not arithmetic change, but geometric. Mankind is on an upward spiral of progress. Mankind through history is progressing along a natural pattern of growth. It's not willy-nilly. It's not a straight line. It's not cyclical in the sense that we always return to zero. The trend is upward, but always taking the path of three steps forward, two steps back. That is the path of human social progress.

Why does it have to be a look-but-don't-touch situation? Can we influence the wave pattern?

Man cannot change nature's physical laws, but he can understand them and harness their power for his benefit. The same appears to be true of the laws of human behavior. The Wave Principle is the only method you can employ to stay in tune with the dynamics of human history and to be their master, not their pawn.

It gave us the freedom to observe our own nature, but not the means to fix it?

It gave *some* of us the opportunity to observe it, and those few of us can't change it.

It's like a cruel prank. Why does man continuously have to shelter himself from disasters of his own making?

Well, don't forget that he basks in the glories of his own making, too. Just look at the U.S. for the last 200 years. What a great place to live! As for the setbacks, A.J. Frost and I addressed this question in *Elliott Wave Principle*. We said: "Apparently it is one of nature's laws that man at times will refuse to accept the rest of its laws. If this assumption were untrue, the Elliott Wave Principle may never have existed. The Wave Principle exists because man refuses to learn from history. He can be led to believe that the laws of nature do not exist or 'do not apply in this case,' that what is to be consumed need not be first produced, that what is lent need never be paid back, that promises are equal to substance, that paper is gold, that benefits have no costs, that the fears which reason supports will evaporate if they are ignored or derided." I hardly see that today social man has risen above this limitation.

Those that do not remember the past are destined to repeat it. Is that it?

Mistakes are repeated not because people fail to learn from history, as many contend, but precisely because they *do* learn from history, *recent* history, their own experience. People get away with living off their neighbors for a while, so they think they can do it forever. And they think *everybody* can do it. Social patterns result partly from the fact that life span and therefore the depth and breadth of individual knowledge, is limited. There are probably people who know what they are doing is wrong, but they think some future generation will pay, so they get what they can. If the short range is 30 years, they don't care about the long range. Some politicos only care about the time to the next election. Try changing *that*.

* * * * * * * * * * * * * *

The following is a reformulation by Bob Prechter of Edward R. Dewey's comments in the March 1958 issue of Cycles *magazine.*

The Elliott Wave Theorist

October 30, 1981

Did you ever stop to think of the building blocks you would have to make first if you were creating the Universe from nothing? First of all, you would have to create time, since without time there could be no "next." Next, you would have to create space and dimension. Next, you would need matter and energy. And finally, to give direction to these elements, you would have to create law. Time and law together would produce pattern. Once you set the entire machine in motion, you would create progress.

* * * * * * * * * * * * * *

But the Wave Principle increases our knowledge, at least for the individual who possesses it, if not for all society.

Exactly. With the Wave Principle, history is telescoped and the human mind can grasp the impelling socio-emotional pattern. Charts reveal in human social activities a continually repeating pattern that is typical of a progressive life form. That conceptual condensation is a powerful tool whose main practical values are in describing the past scientifically and in anticipating the tenor of the future. This kind of analysis can give you a panoramic view of the past, which by its very nature also implies certain things about the future.

Which is more important, using the Wave Principle to understand history and social change or as a gauge to measure the probabilities in the stock market?

Without question its greatest value is what it tells us about our history and society at large. With knowledge of how the patterns unfold, to the extent of your ability and effort, you will be able to anticipate social trends of all types, including the financial, cultural and political. That is an ability that has deftly eluded man throughout his existence, and indeed has been considered impossible. Nevertheless, we finally have a way to anticipate much about our social future, not with magic or revelation or sorcery, but with science.

You've been describing something that's far bigger than the money part of our lives. If the Wave Principle is as comprehensive as you make it out, isn't it even bigger than social forecasting? It must be deeply personal. We should be able not just to observe, but to take advantage of technical clues in our personal lives?

Without question, Elliott Wave analysis is applicable in your personal and professional life. I've already told you about how it led me to recognize the onset of my professional bear market. But it also told me when the bear market was ending, three months before it did. I wrote a Special Report in December 1992 on the subject, and the low for subscriptions, after a five-year contraction, was in March 1993. Although I was charting my public persona and business, which are *social* phenomena and thus in the realm of the Wave Principle, I have come to believe that every productive person moves through waves of progress and regress through his life. Try to plot yours and see where you are.

To possess history's road map, one need master The Wave Principle. Some people's basic objection to that is it's too simplistic to be true.

Any excuse to avoid the truth.

But if the Wave Principle is *the* answer, why aren't more people trying to nail it down?

The Principle says that the market moves in a way that to most people is counter-intuitive, and a large percentage of people would rather maintain the validity of their intuitions than investigate a challenge to them.

But they don't seem that uncomfortable with their illusions.

While illusions may be comfortable for most people in long bull markets, they provide monstrous stress in bear markets. Many people today are confusing what they consider proper thinking with a bull market. Any approach, valid or not, will make money in such an environment if its end is to buy stocks.

So the bear market will be instructive?

Oh, yes. I am quite certain that the Wave Principle will attract even greater interest, particularly among institutional investors, when asset allocation models and fundamental stock selection techniques appear to stop working. Cyclic and pattern analysis goes in and out of style with major cycles in cultural trends. Some periods seem to be a little more mechanically oriented. Other periods seem to be more humanistically oriented. Some are linear-logic oriented, some gestalt oriented. I think even the development of theories, science and philosophy throughout history coincide with such trends.

You've said there a lot of ways for a disciplined investor to get results. And a lot of really successful investors have done so, even though they ignore these deeper questions of natural law, culture and philosophy. Isn't the Wave Principle a complication?

Any method based on the market's behavior patterns will work if the goal is to make money trading as if it is a business. But I would have quit the business a long time ago if it were not for the Wave Principle's broader implications. Those and the aesthetics of the Wave Principle keep me interested. It is like watching an artist paint, and the appreciation of that process in the actions of collective man are what the Elliott Wave Principle makes possible for the first time. It alone provides a framework within which to observe, reflect upon, and enjoy the beauty of nature in the activity of man. And that is no small blessing.

SOURCES

(American Association of Individual Investors) Journal
Atlanta Business Chronicle
Atlanta Magazine
Barron's
Business Atlanta
Business Week
Cable News Network (CNN)
Chicago Tribune
Commodity Traders Consumer Reports
Discover
Diversified Investor's Forecast
Dow Jones News Service
Financial Planning
Financial Security Alert, Spring 1986
Financial World
Florida Dental Journal
Florida Today
Forbes
Forsyth County News
Fortune
Fulton County Daily Report
Futures
Gentleman's Quarterly
Georgia Trend
Gold and Silver Today
Grant's Interest Rate Observer
Hulbert Financial Digest
Intermarket
Investment Vision
Investors Guide
Investor's Hotline with Joe Bradley
Market Technicians Association Journal
Marketline
Mensa Bulletin
Money Maker
MoneyTalk (TV Show)

New York Post
Newsweek
Physicians Financial News
Power Talk with Anthony Robbins
Prodigy (on-line)
San Francisco Business Times
Successful Investing
Superstars of Investing
Technical Analysis of Stocks and Commodities
Technical Trends
The Acturial Digest
The Aden Interviews
The Atlanta Journal / The Atlanta Constitution
The Business Journal
The (Memphis) *Commercial Appeal*
The (New York) *Daily News*
The Economist
The Elliott Wave Theorist
The Financial Post (Canada)
The International Currency Review
The International Herald Tribune
The Master Indicator
The National OTC Stock Journal
The New York Times
The Sound Money Investor
The Spectator
The (Gainesville, GA) *Times*
The (New Orleans) *Times Picayune*
The Union Leader (Manchester, NH)
The Wall Street Journal
The Washington Post
Tim Hayes Investigative Report
USA Today
Wealth

At the Crest of the

TIDAL WAVE

A Forecast for the
Great Bear Market

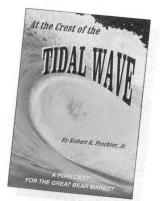

Fifteen years in preparation and a year in the making, *At the Crest of the Tidal Wave: A Forecast for the Great Bear Market* is Robert Prechter's first major book in seventeen years. He and A.J. Frost predicted the great bull market in *Elliott Wave Principle* in 1978. Now, in 1995, Bob makes a persuasive long term case that is even more important to your financial well-being.

Every serious investor must consider the overwhelming evidence presented in this book before forming an opinion about today's financial trends. 475 pages and over 200 charts challenge conventional wisdom like no volume ever before. Those who read this book *early* will benefit the most. Also, check out the companion classic the *Elliott Wave Principle - Key to Market Behavior.*

At the Crest of the Tidal Wave shows you what you can expect when the coming historical turn in the investment markets arrives. Entire chapters are dedicated to these topics:

- ◆ The Economy
- ◆ High Grade Bonds
- ◆ Collectibles
- ◆ Time and Price Considerations
- ◆ Commodities
- ◆ High Yield Bonds
- ◆ Gold
- ◆ Real Estate
- ◆ Investor Psychology
- ◆ Expectations for the Great Bear Market

$49 U.S. & Canada add $5 postage, overseas add $16.

To order, call 800-336-1618 or 770-536-0309 today.

If you prefer send check, money order or credit card information to:
New Classics Library
A division of Elliott Wave International
Post Office Box 1618, Gainesville, Georgia 30503 U.S.A.

Our no-risk guarantee: If you're less than satisfied with the book, you can simply return it to us in good condition within 30 days for a full refund of the purchase price.

Other titles from
New Classics Library
(a division of Elliott Wave International, Inc.)

Elliott Wave Principle — Key to Market Behavior — Eighteen years is long enough to judge whether investors deem a book about an investment method as "classic," and surely the jury is in on this one: ***Elliott Wave Principle*** has been published in **seven** languages, and continues to sell thousands of copies every year. If you don't yet own a copy of this perennial best seller — or if you own an earlier edition — now is the time to read the book that reintroduced the Wave Principle to the world. **$29US**

R.N. Elliott's Masterworks — The Definitive Collection — by Robert R. Prechter, Jr., editor. Gives you the three ground-breaking works, long out of print, in which R. N. Elliott first described his discoveries to the world. You'll also read a detailed biography of Elliott not previously available anywhere, including rare photographs and excerpts from his letters and early writings. **$34US**

The Complete Elliott Wave Writings of A. Hamilton Bolton — Foreword by Robert R. Prechter, Jr., editor. Includes Bolton's book *Elliott Wave Principle — A Critical Appraisal*, all of his annual Elliott Wave articles for *The Bank Credit Analyst*, personal letters, articles and rare photos, plus a memoir of Bolton written by A.J. Frost. **$39US**

R.N. Elliott's Market Letters (1938-1946) — by Robert R. Prechter, Jr., editor. Presents Elliott's real-time analyses and forecasts of market action, along with numerous essays on the application of the Wave Principle. Extensively footnoted and cross-referenced by Bob Prechter. **$55US**

NEW! ***Aerodynamic Trading*** — by Constance Brown, CMT. Reveals the secrets that propel professional traders and world-class athletes to the top of their field. The author has excelled equally in both the intense, high-stakes arenas of international athletics and professional trading. *Aerodynamic Trading* brings you the actual exercises taught by professional and Olympic coaches to world class competitors to defuse the ticking time bomb of self-sabotage found within us. **$35US**

The Spiral Calendar and Its Effect on Financial Markets and Human Events — by Christopher L. Carolan. *The Spiral Calendar*™ is Christopher Carolan's discovery that major turning points in the markets are often related by exact time relationships. This book demonstrates the connection between the lunar cycle and the emotional behavior of investors. **$49US**

For more information and fastest service call
800-336-1618 (U.S.) or 770-536-0309

Preview our
Monthly Publication ──

You can receive one of our monthly financial publications — simply return the attached card or write Elliott Wave International. Choose the publication you want, described below, and we'll rush you the current issue, FREE. (We'll even include our complete Product Catalogue with your free issue!)

The Elliott Wave Theorist ────

The world renowned market letter and vehicle for the monthly forecasts that earned Robert Prechter the title of "Guru of the Decade." Includes stocks, bonds, precious metals, plus social and cultural trends. (10-12 pp.)

World Commodity Perspective ────

Comprehensive coverage includes the CRB, Grains, Meats, Soft and Industrials. Lots of charts, forecasts and Elliott Wave analysis, plus the insights of an editor dedicated to these specialty markets. (8-10 pp.)

Currency Market Perspective ────

All major cash & futures markets, and cross rates, receive in-depth analysis each month, complete with detailed Elliott Wave charts. The editor also covers the political and economic trends that are important to the currency markets. (8-10 pp.)

Global Market Perspective ────

The combined effort of 14 experienced wave analysts (including Robert Prechter) who forecast the price movement of all the major global financial markets — equities, interest rates, currencies, precious metals and energy, as well as social and cultural trends. (100+ pp.)

PRECHTER'S
ELLIOTT WAVE INTERNATIONAL

Post Office Box 1618, Gainesville, Georgia 30503, USA